FIXIN' TO EAT

SOUTHERN COOKING FOR THE SOUTHERN AT HEART

KATIE MOSEMAN

Fixin' to Eat

SOUTHERN COOKING FOR THE SOUTHERN AT HEART

KATIE MOSEMAN

First Edition

Text and Photographs © 2017 Katie Moseman

Cover Design by Ashley Ruggirello, www.cardboardmonet.com
Interior Design by Ashley Ruggirello, www.cardboardmonet.com

TABLE OF CONTENTS

THIS BOOK IS DEDICATED TO MY FAMILY

INTRODUCTION

To be "fixing to" means that you're planning to do something. For Southerners, "fixing to" isn't just an interesting turn of phrase—it's a whole state of mind. Others might say they're about to eat, but Southerners say they're fixin' to eat.

Whether you're new to Southern cookery, or just looking for new inspiration, this bounty of homestyle recipes from breakfast to dessert (and every meal in between) is sure to make your mouth water. Between courses, "Libation Lessons" will show you how to pair Southern food with your favorite beer, wine, and spirits.

Add a little bit of love—the secret ingredient that makes good food great—and you'll be *Fixin' to Eat*!

BREAKFAST

· BUTTERMILK DROP BISCUITS · CORNMEAL GRAVY ·
· FRESH STRAWBERRY CREAM CHEESE · SWEET POTATO MUFFINS ·
· BUTTERMILK PANCAKES & CINNAMON INFUSED MAPLE SYRUP ·
· CITRUS PECAN QUICK BREAD ·

BUTTERMILK DROP BISCUITS

More forgiving and easier to make than traditional biscuits, drop biscuits are perfect for the novice biscuit maker. Once you're familiar with the recipe, you can experiment with mix-ins. Add cheese and herbs for savory flavor, or add cut strawberries and a sprinkle of sugar on top for sweetness.

PREP TIME: 10 minutes
COOK TIME: 15 minutes
TOTAL TIME: 25 minutes
YIELD: 8 biscuits

2 cups all purpose flour
2 teaspoons baking powder
½ teaspoon baking soda
1 teaspoon salt
6 tablespoons unsalted butter, cold
¾ cup buttermilk
2 tablespoons unsalted butter, melted

1. Preheat the oven to 425°F. Whisk together the flour, baking powder, baking soda, and salt. Cut 6 tablespoons of the butter into the mixture until it resembles small breadcrumbs. Stir in the buttermilk until just combined.

2. Scoop portions of dough approximately ¼ cup in size onto a baking sheet. Brush the tops of the biscuit dough portions with the 2 tablespoons of melted butter. Bake for 10 to 15 minutes, or until the tops of the biscuits are golden brown. Serve immediately.

CORNMEAL GRAVY

This traditional Appalachian recipe makes the most of humble ingredients. It's also an excellent gluten free breakfast gravy option. For sausage cornmeal gravy, add a cup of crumbled cooked sausage and a tablespoon of dried sage after the last step in the recipe.

PREP TIME: 1 minutes
COOK TIME: 10 minutes
TOTAL TIME: 11 minutes
YIELD: 2 cups

1 cup buttermilk
1 cup hot water
½ cup cornmeal
½ teaspoon salt
½ teaspoon pepper
1 teaspoon bacon or sausage drippings (substitute unsalted butter if you don't have drippings)

1. Whisk together the buttermilk and hot water and set aside.
2. Toast the cornmeal in a large, heavy skillet over medium-high heat until browned, about 5 minutes.
3. Add the salt, pepper, and drippings to the skillet. Add the buttermilk/water mixture a little at a time, whisking constantly, until fully incorporated.
4. Bring to a boil and continue whisking constantly until the gravy has thickened. If it's too thick, add buttermilk a tablespoon at a time until the desired consistency is reached.

Fresh Strawberry Cream Cheese

Florida harvests a bounty of strawberries from December to April. This strawberry cream cheese takes full advantage of fresh strawberry flavor. Try it on bagels, biscuits, muffins, or breakfast bread.

PREP TIME: 5 minutes
TOTAL TIME: 5 minutes
YIELD: 1 cup

½ cup fresh strawberries
4 ounces cream cheese
1 tablespoon honey or more, to taste

1. Remove the stems and hulls from the strawberries. Place the strawberries in a food processor with 1 tablespoon of honey. Puree until smooth.
2. Add the cream cheese and blend until completely combined. If a sweeter taste is desired, add more honey a teaspoon at a time, blending after each addition. Cover tightly and refrigerate to store; consume within a day or two.

Sweet Potato Muffins

Whole wheat flour adds a pleasantly nutty flavor to these muffins, as well as a healthy boost of breakfast fiber. When you take out your butter to make these muffins, set aside a few extra tablespoons of butter to soften for spreading.

PREP TIME: 10 minutes

COOK TIME: 25 minutes

TOTAL TIME: 35 minutes

YIELD: 12 muffins

7 ½ ounces pureed sweet potatoes (half of a 15 ounce can)

½ cup light brown sugar

½ cup granulated sugar

1 pinch salt

1¼ cup whole wheat flour

1 heaping teaspoon baking powder

½ teaspoon cinnamon

6 tablespoons unsalted butter, melted and cooled

2 large eggs

1. Preheat the oven to 350°F and line a 12 cup muffin pan with paper liners.
2. In a large mixing bowl, stir together the sweet potato puree, sugars, and salt until well combined.
3. Add in the flour, baking powder, cinnamon, butter, and eggs, then stir together until just combined. Don't overmix. Fill the paper cups about ⅔ of the way full.
4. Bake for 20 to 25 minutes, or until a toothpick inserted in the center of a muffin comes out clean. Let the pan cool on a rack for 10 minutes, then remove the muffins from the pan and place them on a rack to finish cooling.

Buttermilk Pancakes & Cinnamon Infused Maple Syrup

Buttermilk pancakes are a traditional breakfast across the South. Adding cinnamon infused maple syrup makes them perfect for a cold fall or winter morning. If you can't find cinnamon sticks in the spice section of your grocery store, substitute 1/4 teaspoon of ground cinnamon.

PREP TIME: 5 minutes
COOK TIME: 15 minutes
TOTAL TIME: 20 minutes
YIELD: 12 pancakes

For the Cinnamon Infused Maple Syrup

1 cup real maple syrup

2 cinnamon sticks (from the spice section of your grocery store)

For the Pancakes

Dry Ingredients

1 ½ cups all-purpose flour

2 tablespoons granulated sugar

2 teaspoons baking powder

¾ teaspoon sea salt

Wet Ingredients

1 cup buttermilk

4 tablespoons unsalted butter melted and slightly cooled

1 teaspoon vanilla extract

2 large eggs

1. Place the maple syrup in a small saucepan and add the cinnamon sticks. Turn the burner on low and heat gently while you prepare the pancakes.
2. Begin preheating a large nonstick pan over medium low heat.
3. In a large mixing bowl, combine the dry ingredients and whisk together.
4. In another mixing bowl, combine the wet ingredients and whisk them.
5. Pour the wet mix into the dry mix and whisk until combined.
6. If batter is too thick to pour, add buttermilk a tablespoon at a time until a pourable consistency is reached.
7. Scoop up ½ cup of pancake batter and pour it in the center of the pan. Cook until there are many bubbles on the surface and the edges become firm (about 60 to 90 seconds). Flip the pancake and cook for another 30 seconds, then remove to a plate.
8. Repeat the last step until batter is used up. Stack all the cooked pancakes together and cover them keep them warm, or serve immediately as they come out of the pan.

Citrus Pecan Quick Bread

The combination of orange, lemon, and lime in this sweet and nutty breakfast bread will perk you right up in the morning. Slather a slice with honey and butter for an indulgent way to start your day.

PREP TIME: 20 minutes
COOK TIME: 55 minutes
TOTAL TIME: 75 minutes
YIELD: 1 loaf

¾ cup granulated sugar
2 teaspoons grated orange zest
1 teaspoon grated lemon zest
½ teaspoon grated lime zest
2 cups all-purpose flour
½ teaspoon baking soda
½ teaspoon salt
½ cup chopped pecans
⅔ cup orange juice
2 tablespoons lemon juice
1 tablespoon lime juice
1 egg
2 tablespoons vegetable or canola oil

1. Preheat oven to 350°F. Grease and flour an 8 X 4 inch or 9 X 5 inch loaf pan.
2. Put sugar and zests in a small bowl. Use your fingers to rub zest into sugar (it will begin to look like wet sand).
3. Whisk together flour, baking soda, and salt in a large bowl. Add the citrus sugar and pecans and whisk to combine.
4. Whisk together juices, egg, and oil in a medium bowl.
5. Add wet ingredients to dry ingredients and stir until just combined.
6. Spoon mixture into prepared pan and spread evenly in the pan.
7. Bake for 45 to 55 minutes or until a toothpick or cake tester inserted in the center comes out clean.
8. Cool bread in the pan for 10 minutes on a wire rack. Remove bread from pan and cool completely on a wire rack.

STARTERS

· PIMENTO CHEESE STUFFED PEPPERS · GRILLED BLT POTATO ·
· SALAD STACKS · HONEY BERRY BLUE CHEESE BALL ·
· COCA-COLA SALAD · TARRAGON GOAT CHEESE DEVILED EGGS ·
· CREAM CHEESE AND PIMENTO PEPPER STUFFED CELERY ·
· ICEBERG WEDGE SALAD · BUTTERMILK DRESSING ·
· CROUTONS · EVERYTHING CREAM CHEESE BALLS ·
· TURNIP GREEN SOUP ·

Pimento Cheese Stuffed Peppers

PREP TIME: 30 minutes

COOK TIME: 3 hours

TOTAL TIME: 3 hours & 30 minutes

YIELD: 4½ cups pimento cheese to fill the peppers

¼ cup cream cheese, at room temperature

¼ cup mayonnaise

1 teaspoon grated onion

¼ teaspoon garlic powder

2 to 3 drops Tabasco sauce

Pinch of salt

Pinch of fresh ground pepper

2 cups shredded sharp Cheddar cheese

1 cup shredded Pepper Jack cheese

1 cup shredded Monterey Jack cheese

1 jar chopped pimentos, about 4 ounces, drained

10 to 20 assorted peppers, such as jarred sweet cherry peppers or fresh jalapeño, serrano, or mini bell peppers

These stuffed peppers are well suited as a cold appetizer for holidays and gatherings. Choose your favorite type of peppers, such as sweet cherry peppers or jalapeño peppers, depending on your tolerance for spiciness. Make this dish ahead of time to allow the flavors to fully develop.

1. In the bowl of a food processor fitted with a knife blade, process cream cheese, mayonnaise, onion, garlic powder, Tabasco sauce, salt, and pepper until smooth.

2. Add the shredded cheeses and pimentos and pulse to combine. Do not over-process. Transfer pimento cheese to a bowl and stir if needed to combine ingredients thoroughly. Cover and chill for at least 3 hours.

3. Slice peppers in half horizontally and remove ribs and seeds. Fill pepper halves with pimento cheese.

Grilled BLT Potato Salad Stacks

PREP TIME: 20 minutes
COOK TIME: 22 minutes
TOTAL TIME: 42 minutes
YIELD: 6 stacks

For the tomato vinaigrette

2 large plum tomatoes chopped

¼ cup olive oil

3 tablespoons red wine vinegar

1 ½ teaspoon chopped shallot

1 teaspoon garlic

½ teaspoon salt

¼ teaspoon pepper

For the stacks:

6 red new potatoes, medium size

Olive oil

Salt and pepper

Green leaf lettuce torn into potato-width pieces

2 to 3 plum tomatoes sliced into ¼-inch thick rounds

3 slices cooked thick-cut bacon cut into width of potatoes

4- inch skewers

Well worth the effort, these potato salad stacks are an impressive sight. They combine grilled potato rounds, bacon, tomatoes, all topped with a fresh plum tomato vinaigrette.

For the tomato vinaigrette

1. Combine tomatoes, olive oil, vinegar, shallot, garlic, salt, and pepper in a blender.
2. Blend until smooth. Strain through a fine mesh sieve into a bowl.

For the stacks

1. Heat a grill to medium heat (about 400°F).
2. Slice potatoes into 1/3-inch rounds. Cook potato slices in salted water until just tender, about 5 to 8 minutes. Do not overcook, or the potato slices will fall apart.
3. Drain potatoes and place on a baking sheet. Brush both sides with olive oil. Sprinkle with salt and pepper.
4. Grill potato slices until browned on both sides, about 3 minutes per side.
5. Transfer potatoes to a cooling rack. Drizzle potatoes with vinaigrette.
6. Build the stack starting with a potato slice, then 2 pieces of lettuce, potato slice, tomato slice, potato slice, 2 pieces of bacon, and potato slice on top.
7. Insert a skewer in the center of the stack to hold it together.
8. Repeat with remaining stack ingredients.
9. Drizzle finished stacks with vinaigrette. Serve immediately with extra vinaigrette on the side.

Honey Berry Blue Cheese Ball

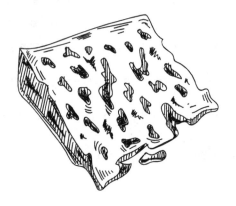

Pecans are grown in many Southern states, with the largest amount coming from Texas and Georgia. This cheese ball is rolled in toasted pecans to give it a nutty flavor alongside the sweetness of dried fruit and honey, and the piquancy of blue cheese.

PREP TIME: 15 minutes

COOK TIME: 3 hours

TOTAL TIME: 3 hours & 15 minutes

YIELD: 1 cheese ball

8 ounces crumbled blue cheese at room temperature

8 ounces cream cheese, softened

2 tablespoons honey

⅓ cup dried cranberries, chopped

¼ cup dried blueberries

½ cup chopped pecans, toasted

Crackers for serving

1. In a large bowl, beat cream cheese, blue cheese, and honey until combined. The mixture won't be smooth, as there will be lumps from the blue cheese crumbles.
2. Add cranberries and blueberries and stir to combine.
3. Shape mixture into a ball. If mixture is very soft, chill for 30 minutes before shaping into a ball.
4. Roll ball in pecans to coat the outside.
5. Chill ball at least 3 hours or overnight (wrap ball in plastic wrap after 3 hours if chilling overnight).
6. Serve cheese ball with crackers.

Coca-Cola Salad

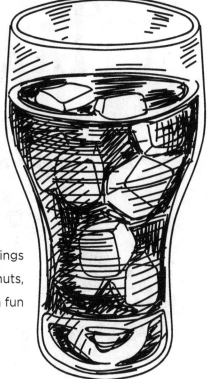

Jell-O salads, or "molded" salads, were a staple of Southern gatherings during the early to mid-twentieth century, encasing all manner of fruits, nuts, and (sometimes) vegetables. This Coke-flavored blast from the past is a fun party dish and conversation-starter.

PREP TIME: 5 minutes

COOK TIME: 30 minutes

INACTIVE TIME: 8 hours, or overnight

TOTAL TIME: 8 hours 35 minutes

YIELD: 12 servings

6 ounces cherry-flavored Jell-O, not sugar-free

1 cup boiling water

10 ounces Coca-Cola

1 can red tart pitted cherries in water, 14 ½ to 16 ounces

1 can crushed pineapple, 8 ounces

1 cup chopped pecans, raw or lightly toasted

1. Place the Jell-O in a large bowl. Pour the boiling water over it and stir until dissolved. Stir in the Coca-Cola. Refrigerate mixture until partially firm, about 30 minutes. Check and stir every 3 to 5 minutes. You want it to be thickened but not set.

2. Place the cherries and juice in a food processor fitted with a knife blade or in a blender. Pulse or blend a few times to lightly chop the cherries.

3. Once the Jell-O mixture has thickened, stir in the chopped cherries and its juice, pineapple and it's juice, and pecans. Pour into a gelatin mold. Refrigerate until set or overnight. Remove salad from the mold by inverting onto a serving platter. Serve cold.

Tarragon Goat Cheese Deviled Eggs

There's nothing more Southern than deviled eggs. This recipe incorporates tangy goat cheese and fresh tarragon. When shopping for ingredients, look for soft, spreadable goat cheese, not goat cheese crumbles.

PREP TIME: 20 minutes
COOK TIME: 20 minutes
TOTAL TIME: 40 minutes
YIELD: 24 servings

12 large eggs
¾ teaspoon salt, divided
3 ounces soft goat cheese, at room temperature
6 tablespoons mayonnaise
1 teaspoon minced fresh tarragon, plus more for garnish
⅛ teaspoon ground white pepper

1. Place eggs in a single layer in a saucepan and cover with 1 inch of water. Add ½ teaspoon salt. Bring to a boil. Cover and remove from heat.
2. Let stand for 15 minutes. Drain water and replace with cold water and ice. Let eggs cool for 5 minutes.
3. Peel eggs. After you peel each egg, lightly rinse it to make sure you remove all shell bits. Then place the egg on paper towels.
4. Slice eggs in half lengthwise. Remove yolks and place yolks in a medium bowl. Place egg whites on a serving platter.
5. Mash yolks with a fork until finely crumbled. Add goat cheese, mayonnaise, tarragon, remaining ¼ teaspoon salt, and pepper. Stir until well combined and smooth.
6. Fill egg whites with yolk mixture. Use a piping bag or spoon mixture into each one. Garnish with minced tarragon.
7. Chill deviled eggs prior to serving (cover lightly with plastic wrap or in a sealed container).

Cream Cheese & Pimento Pepper Stuffed Celery

This cream cheese and pimento pepper stuffed celery is an excellent choice when you need to quickly put together a snack or appetizer.

PREP TIME: 10 minutes
TOTAL TIME: 10 minutes
YIELD: 6 servings

Celery stalks

3 ounces cream cheese, at room temperature

1 to 1 ½ tablespoons diced pimentos

1. Clean and cut celery stalks into 3- or 4-inch pieces.
2. In a small bowl, stir together the cream cheese and pimentos.
3. Fill the celery with the cheese mixture and serve. Refrigerate leftovers.

ICEBERG WEDGE SALAD

Wedge salads are a refreshing salad for a hot summer day. Chill your salad plates in the refrigerator ahead of time, then build the salads on the chilled plates immediately before serving.

PREP TIME: 5 minutes

TOTAL TIME: 5 minutes

YIELD:4 individual salads

1 head iceberg lettuce

1 tomato

¼ cup crisp bacon crumbles

2 tablespoons roasted and salted sunflower seeds without hulls

1 cup croutons

½ cup buttermilk dressing
(see next recipe, or substitute bottled buttermilk ranch dressing)

1. Place 4 serving plates in the refrigerator to chill. Chop the tomato and set aside.

2. Wash the head of lettuce in cool water. Pull off any limp or discolored leaves. Cut the lettuce in half from top to stem, then cut each half into two wedges. Rinse the wedges in ice water to chill. You will have four wedges total.

3. Place the each wedge on a chilled plate. Drizzle each wedge with about two tablespoons of dressing. Top with chopped tomatoes, bacon crumbles, sunflower seeds, and croutons. Serve immediately.

Buttermilk Dressing

Minced green onion and fresh parsley add a spring-like flavor to this dressing. It's equally suitable for topping salads or for dipping fresh vegetables.

PREP TIME: 5 minutes
COOK TIME 1 hour
TOTAL TIME: 1 hour & 5 minutes
YIELD: 1 cup

½ cup buttermilk
½ cup mayonnaise
1 tablespoon minced green onion
1 teaspoon minced fresh parsley
1 garlic clove, pressed or minced
¼ teaspoon salt
⅛ teaspoon pepper

1. Stir together all ingredients in a medium bowl. Cover and chill for at least 1 hour (overnight for best results).
2. If a thinner dressing is preferred, stir in additional buttermilk 1 teaspoon at a time until desired consistency is reached.
3. Serve as a salad dressing or dip. Garnish with green onion slices or chopped fresh parsley.

CROUTONS

Use up leftover bakery bread loaves, whether French, Italian, or some other variety, by turning them into freshly made croutons. These croutons are delicious on salads and soups.

PREP TIME: 5 minutes
COOK TIME: 20 minutes
TOTAL TIME: 25 minutes
YIELD: 4 cups

8 ounces French baguette or other bakery-style bread

3 tablespoons butter, melted

¼ teaspoon sea salt

¼ teaspoon black pepper

1 tablespoon dried sage

1. Preheat the oven to 350°F and line a baking sheet with parchment paper for easy release and cleanup.
2. Cut the baguette down the middle into two long pieces. Cut across each long piece until you have many half-moon shaped pieces of bread.
3. In a large mixing bowl, drizzle the butter over the bread pieces and toss until thoroughly coated. Sprinkle on the salt, black pepper, and sage, then toss again until evenly coated.
4. Spread out the croutons on the baking sheet. Bake for 20 minutes, then let cool to room temperature on baking sheet. The croutons will become crispier as they cool.

Everything Cream Cheese Balls

These bagel-inspired mini cheese balls can be served with bagel chips or crackers, or used as cream cheese spread for bagels.

PREP TIME: 20 minutes

INACTIVE TIME: 3 hours

TOTAL TIME: 3 hours & 20 minutes

YIELD: 18 balls

5 tablespoons toasted sesame seeds

2 tablespoons plus 1 teaspoon poppy seeds

2 tablespoons plus 1 teaspoon dried minced onion flakes

1 ¼ teaspoon coarsely ground black pepper

¾ teaspoon salt

16 ounces cream cheese at room temperature

2 garlic cloves crushed

Bagel chips or crackers for serving

1. Combine sesame seeds, poppy seeds, onion flakes, pepper, and salt in a small bowl.
2. Beat cream cheese, garlic, and 2 tablespoons of the seed and seasoning mixture from step one, until combined. Reserve the remainder of the mixture for coating the balls.
3. Chill for at least 1 hour to firm up mixture and make it easier to roll into balls.
4. Scoop into 2 tablespoon portions and roll into balls.
5. Roll balls in remaining seed and seasoning mixture, pressing to coat.
6. Chill balls at least 2 hours prior to serving.

Turnip Green Soup

Save ham bones in the freezer for soups like this one. They add rich flavor that transforms a humble handful of ingredients into something hearty and memorable. Pair turnip green soup with fresh-baked cornbread for a complete meal that's perfect for a cold day.

PREP TIME: 45 minutes

COOK TIME: 2 hours & 30 minutes

TOTAL TIME: 3 hours & 15 minutes

YIELD: 12 cups

2 tablespoons olive oil

1 cup chopped onion

2 garlic cloves, minced

1 ham bone

1 cup frozen corn kernels

1 cup dried black-eyed peas

64 ounces low-sodium chicken broth

1 teaspoon fresh ground pepper

1 pound fresh turnip greens, thick stems removed and cut into strips

1 tablespoon vinegar pepper sauce, plus more for serving

Salt, if needed

1. Heat olive oil in a large Dutch oven or soup pot over medium heat. Add onion and cook, stirring occasionally, until soft and translucent (about 5 minutes).
2. Add garlic and cook until fragrant, about 1 minute.
3. Add ham bone, corn, black-eyed peas, broth and pepper. Stir to combine.
4. Add turnip greens and increase the heat to high. The greens will wilt as it comes to a boil. Stir or toss occasionally to combine ingredients while it is coming to a boil.
5. Once it reaches a boil, stir in pepper sauce and reduce heat to a simmer. Cover and cook for 2 ½ to 3 hours, stirring occasionally. Taste the soup and add salt if needed.
6. Serve with additional pepper sauce if desired.

LIBATION LESSON

BEER

HOW TO PAIR SOUTHERN FOOD WITH BEER

AN INTERVIEW WITH MIKE DELANCETT OF HOURGLASS BREWERY

What types of beer go best with Southern food?

The beautiful thing about beer is there is one for almost any occasion. When it comes to Southern food, there are a great number of unique and interesting flavors—but we also like to think about another major Southern element: heat. A heavy meal and a hot sun makes us want to lean on refreshing beers with unique character and approachable alcohol contents.

A hefeweizen or witbier makes a great summer treat. The hoppy character of a

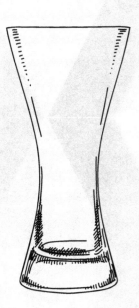 good pale ale or pils can complement a gorgeous greasy fried chicken dish. A malty brown pairs nicely with our love of smoke and savory dishes, and wild and sour brews like a Berliner Weisse or mixed fermentation saison can add just the right amount of acid and funk to play off a dish.

While it's important to consider the details, don't sweat the small stuff. Beer is about relaxing, enjoying the company of friends and family, making new friends, and sharing an experience. At the end of the day, even if the pairing wasn't perfect, you'll still have had a great meal and a great beer.

How should you serve beer?

There are a lot of options in the glassware world, and indeed, a lot of beer geeks have vast collections to suit every style. That said, we think the biggest takeaway is that glassware definitely affects the perception and quality of a pour.

If you have to stick to one glass, we'd shoot for something with a bit of flare in the body, and a tulip style rim. This should help guide proper pour, maximize carbonation, and help aromatics become more pronounced.

Can you pair beer with Southern desserts?

You most definitely can. While the typical rules of thumb for pairing are contrast or compliment, we find that with sweets we like to lean more to the latter. A nice malty brown ale or sweet stout plays to the enhancement of chocolate cake, whereas a fruited wheat beer might further enhance a tart, or pie.

Of course, if you're feeling adventurous, you can always look in the contrast direction, but it gets a bit trickier if you're looking for a sure thing.

What are some great beers currently being produced in the South?

The South is making amazing beer, and is definitely establishing itself as an authority. Here are some of our favorite notable breweries.

- Burial Beer
- Fonta Flora
- Saint Somewhere
- Creature Comforts
- Cigar City
- Yazoo
- Jester King
- Birds Fly South
- Against the Grain
- Burnt Hickory
- Prairie Artisan Ales / American Solera
- Heirloom Rustic Ales
- Walking Tree

And, of course, Hourglass Brewing.

Are there any beer cocktails that come from the South?

While not originating in the South, the shandy is a pretty popular way to beat the Southern heat.

To make a shandy, mix equal parts cold beer and lemonade. Adjust the ratio to taste.

MAIN DISHES

· KENTUCKY HOT BROWN HAM SLIDERS ·
· BAKED PECAN CHICKEN NUGGETS WITH HONEY MUSTARD ·
· DIPPING SAUCE · PIMENTO CHEESEBURGER ·
· MUFFULETTA SANDWICHES · HONEY COLA HAM ·
· CRISPY FISH STICKS WITH SPICY TARTAR SAUCE ·
· PRIME RIB ROAST · CHICKEN SALAD ·
· SLOW COOKER PORK BARBECUE SANDWICHES ·
· CREOLE BEEF TENDERLOIN · SALMON PATTIES · APPLE CIDER PORK ROAST ·
· TUNA SALAD SANDWICHES · GRILLED PIMENTO CHEESE SANDWICHES ·

Kentucky Hot Brown Ham Sliders

The Hot Brown sandwich was originally created at the Brown Hotel in Louisville, Kentucky, in the early 1920s. This recipe uses dinner rolls rather than sliced bread to turn this classic sandwich into a set of twelve hand-held sliders.

PREP TIME: 15 minutes
COOK TIME: 10 minutes
TOTAL TIME: 25 minutes
YIELD: 12 sliders

For the Mornay Sauce

1 ½ tablespoons unsalted butter
1 ½ tablespoons all purpose flour
1 ½ cups heavy cream
¼ cup Romano cheese
Pinch of nutmeg
Salt and pepper

For the Sliders

12 soft dinner rolls (do not pull apart)
1 tablespoon unsalted butter, softened
Mornay sauce
1 pound sliced ham
4 slices crisp cooked bacon
4 Roma tomatoes

For the Mornay Sauce

1. In a pot, heat the butter over medium heat until it melts. Add the flour and whisk to make a roux, or paste, and continue to cook for two minutes. Add the cream and whisk until smooth. Bring to a gentle simmer and let cook for 3 minutes. Remove from heat and whisk in the Romano cheese. Add the nutmeg and salt and pepper to taste.

For the Sliders

1. Preheat the oven to 400°F. Lay out two sheets of foil; each should be larger than one group of 6 rolls.
2. Using a serrated knife, horizontally cut through each group of rolls, creating a top and a bottom.
3. Carefully turn each group of buns so that the bottom is facing upwards. Gently rub the softened butter all over the bottom of the buns and down the sides. Once the bottom is buttered, flip each group of sliders directly onto its own piece of foil. Then rub the butter over the tops of the sliders and down the sides.
4. Open up both groups of rolls and spread Mornay sauce generously all over the inside of the top and the inside of the bottom. On each bottom, layer half of the ham, half of the bacon, and half of the sliced Roma tomatoes. Replace the top halves of the rolls.
5. Place another piece of foil over the top of each group, then pinch or roll the edges of the top and bottom foil to seal the sliders inside, making two packets of sliders.
6. Place both foil packets on a baking sheet. Bake for 7 minutes, then flip both packets over and bake for 5 more minutes. Remove from oven and let cool for 2 minutes before using your serrated knife to slice into individual sliders.

Baked Pecan Chicken Nuggets with Honey Mustard Dipping Sauce

This baked chicken nugget recipe incorporates finely chopped pecans as part of the chicken breading. A tangy honey mustard dipping sauce complements the nuggets. Serve as a main dish for children and adults alike.

PREP TIME: 10 minutes
COOK TIME: 20 minutes
TOTAL TIME: 30 minutes
YIELD: 4 servings

For the Pecan Chicken Nuggets

1 pound chicken tenderloins
Salt and pepper
¾ cup all-purpose flour
2 large eggs beaten
½ cup finely chopped pecans
½ cup plain breadcrumbs

For the Honey Mustard Dipping Sauce

¾ cup mayonnaise
½ cup prepared yellow mustard
⅓ cup honey
1 tablespoon cider vinegar

For the Chicken Nuggets

1. Preheat the oven to 375°F. Place a cooling rack in a baking sheet and set aside.
2. Use three shallow containers. Place the flour in one, eggs in another, and pecans/breadcrumbs mixed together in the third one. Cut the chicken tenderloins into 1-inch chunks. Season the chicken with salt and pepper.
3. Dip each chicken piece into the flour and shake off the excess. Dip each one in the egg mixture and then dredge into pecan/breadcrumb mixture to coat all over. Shake off the excess and place coated pieces on the rack in the baking sheet.
4. Bake for 15 to 20 minutes until the chicken is cooked through and the crust is golden. Serve warm with honey mustard dipping sauce.

For the Honey Mustard Dipping Sauce

1. In a bowl, stir or whisk together the mayonnaise, mustard, honey, and cider vinegar until smooth.

PIMENTO CHEESEBURGER

PREP TIME: 25 minutes
INACTIVE TIME: 1 hour
COOK TIME: 13 minutes
TOTAL TIME: 1 hour & 38 minutes
YIELD: 4 cheeseburgers

FOR THE PIMENTO CHEESE

¼ cup cream cheese,
at room temperature

¼ cup mayonnaise

1 teaspoon grated onion

¼ teaspoon garlic powder

2 to 3 drops Tabasco sauce

Pinch of salt

Pinch of fresh ground pepper

2 cups shredded sharp
Cheddar cheese

1 cup shredded Pepper Jack cheese

1 cup shredded Monterey
Jack cheese

1 jar chopped pimentos 4 ounces,
drained

FOR THE BURGERS

20 ounces ground beef round
or chuck

Salt and pepper

2 cups leaf or romaine lettuce

1 tomato sliced

4 slices sweet onion

4 slices cooked thick sliced bacon

4 hamburger buns, toasted
(butter buns recommended)

Despite its origins as a canned food from up north, pimento cheese was later reinvented by Southern home cooks as a freshly made spread suitable for everything from crackers, to sandwiches, to (you guessed it) burgers. For best results, don't use pre-shredded cheese.

FOR THE PIMENTO CHEESE

1. In the bowl of a food processor fitted with a knife blade, process cream cheese, mayonnaise, onion, garlic powder, Tabasco sauce, salt, and pepper until smooth.
2. Add the shredded cheeses and pimentos and pulse to combine. Do not over-process.
3. Transfer pimento cheese to a bowl and stir if needed to combine ingredients thoroughly.
4. Cover and chill for at least 1 hour.
5. You will have extra pimento cheese leftover. Keep it chilled and use it to make sandwiches, serve it with crackers or celery, or stuff in mini bell peppers or other peppers.

FOR THE BURGERS

1. Shape beef into four 1/2-inch thick patties. Sprinkle patties with salt and pepper.
2. Place patties on grid over medium, ash-covered coals. Grill, covered, 13 - 15 minutes (over medium heat on preheated gas grill, covered, 13 - 14 minutes) until instant-read thermometer inserted horizontally into center registers 160°F, turning occasionally.
3. Place lettuce, tomato, onion, and burger on bottom half of bun, top with bacon and 2 tablespoons pimento cheese. Close sandwich with top of bun.

MUFFULETTA SANDWICHES

PREP TIME: 10 minutes
INACTIVE TIME: 2 days
TOTAL TIME: 2 days & 10 minutes
YIELD: 12 sandwiches

FOR THE OLIVE SALAD

1 ½ cups pimento-stuffed olives
½ cup pitted Kalamata olives
¾ cup giardiniera Italian pickled vegetables
3 large pepperoncini top and stem removed, chopped
6 pickled onions roughly chopped
2 tablespoons capers
1 large garlic clove chopped
¼ cup chopped fresh parsley
A few grinds of pepper
¼ teaspoon red pepper flakes
Juice of 1 lemon
2 tablespoons red wine vinegar
½ cup olive oil

FOR THE SANDWICHES

12 round bakery buns about 3 to 4 inches wide
12 slices provolone cheese
12 slices capicola
12 slices Genoa salami
12 slices deli ham
12 slices deli pepperoni
12 slices swiss or mortadella cheese
Olive salad

Well worth the wait, these olive salad sandwiches are prepared ahead of time to allow the many flavors to develop and intermingle. Muffuletta sandwiches are an excellent choice for a party tray.

FOR THE OLIVE SALAD

1. Place all the salad ingredients except the olive oil into the bowl of a food processor fitted with a knife blade. Pulse a few times until roughly chopped. Transfer ingredients to a bowl and stir in the olive oil. Refrigerate overnight.

FOR THE SANDWICHES

1. Slice the buns in half. On the bottom half, layer 1 slice each of the provolone, capicola, salami, ham, pepperoni, and swiss cheese. Add about 2 tablespoons of olive salad on top of the meats and cheeses. Cover with top half of bun. Wrap each sandwich in plastic wrap or parchment paper and refrigerate overnight.

Honey Cola Ham

Sealed tightly in foil, the ham absorbs moisture and flavor of Coca-Cola and honey while baking. This ham is particularly good for large holiday gatherings.

PREP TIME: 5 minutes
COOK TIME: 3 hours
TOTAL TIME: 3 hours & 5 minutes
YIELD: 18 to 20 servings

1 fully cooked whole bone-in ham
1 ½ cups regular Coca-Cola (not diet)
1 cup honey

1. Preheat oven to 350°F.
2. Line a roasting pan or large baking pan with 2 sheets of heavy-duty aluminum foil crisscrossed and long enough to cover ham (wide foil recommended).
3. Place ham on the foil. Cut a crisscross pattern in the top of ham. Pull foil up around the ham.
4. Pour cola over ham. Pour honey on top of ham. Seal ham securely with the foil.
5. Bake for 3 hours.

CRISPY FISH STICKS WITH SPICY TARTAR SAUCE

PREP TIME: 15 minutes
COOK TIME: 10 minutes
TOTAL TIME: 25 minutes
YIELD: 16 fish sticks

Kid-friendly fish sticks get a grown-up twist with the addition of spicy tartar sauce. Oven-baking, rather than frying, means they're better for you as well.

FOR THE SPICY TARTAR SAUCE

1 cup mayonnaise
1 jalapeño pepper, seeded and minced
1 tablespoon grated onion
1 garlic clove, minced
1 tablespoon lemon juice
1 teaspoon dijon mustard
¼ teaspoon chili powder
½ teaspoon salt
2 to 3 drops hot pepper sauce

FOR THE CRISPY FISH STICKS

1 cup all-purpose flour
2 to 3 eggs, beaten
1 cup panko bread crumbs
1 teaspoon salt
½ teaspoon pepper
4 cod fillets

FOR THE SPICY TARTAR SAUCE

1. Stir together all sauce ingredients in a small bowl. Cover and refrigerate until serving. Best when made 1 or 2 days in advance.

FOR THE CRISPY FISH STICKS

1. Place a wire rack on a baking sheet.
2. Put flour in a shallow bowl.
3. Put eggs in a separate shallow bowl.
4. Combine bread crumbs, salt, and pepper in another shallow bowl.
5. Slice the cod fillets into strips, about 1/2-inch thick. Sprinkle the strips with salt and pepper.
6. Roll fish strips in flour to coat and shake off excess.
7. Dip floured strips in eggs and shake off excess.
8. Roll strips in breadcrumbs, shake off excess, and place on the wire rack.
9. Cook until golden brown and opaque throughout, about 10 minutes.
10. Serve fish sticks with tartar sauce.

Prime Rib Roast

Roast beef makes a beautiful centerpiece for a special meal. You might be surprised that it's so easy to prepare, it's equally suitable for everyday cooking. Using salt free steak seasoning allows you to control the amount of salt used in the dish.

PREP TIME: 10 minutes
COOK TIME: 3 hours
INACTIVE TIME: 15 minutes
TOTAL TIME: 3 hours & 25 minutes
YIELD: 12 servings

8 pounds bone-in prime rib roast
Sea salt
Black pepper
Salt free steak seasoning

1. Preheat the oven to 425°F and line a roasting pan with foil for easy cleanup. Place a rack in the roasting pan. (If you don't have a rack, crunch up a long piece of aluminum foil into a loose coil and place it in the roasting pan.)
2. Sprinkle all sides of the roast with sea salt, black pepper, and steak seasoning, pressing the seasonings gently into the roast as you go. If you have an oven-safe meat thermometer, you may insert it into the thickest part of the roast now, before it goes in the oven.
3. Place the seasoned roast fatty side up on the roasting rack. Roast for 15 minutes at 425°F.
4. Reduce the temperature to 325°F and continue cooking for about 2 hours and 45 minutes, or until a meat thermometer reads 135-140°F for medium doneness.
5. Remove roast from oven and let rest 15 minutes. Slice across the grain to serve.

CHICKEN SALAD

A properly made chicken salad is a delicate balance of flavors and textures. This classic Southern chicken salad uses only four ingredients. To increase the yield, use a ratio of 1 egg to 1 chicken breast to 1 teaspoon of coarse ground mustard, adding mayonnaise as needed to maintain moisture.

PREP TIME: 10 minutes
COOK TIME: 20 minutes
TOTAL TIME: 30 minutes
YIELD: 4 cups

3 large eggs

3 cups cooked chicken breast chunks (approximately 2 large cooked chicken breasts cut in chunks)

¼ cup mayonnaise

3 teaspoons coarse ground mustard, also called "country style" mustard

1. Place eggs in a single layer in a saucepan and cover with 1 inch of water. Add 1/2 teaspoon salt. Bring to a boil. Cover and remove from heat.

2. Let stand for 15 minutes. Drain water and replace with cold water and ice. Let eggs cool for 5 minutes.

3. Peel eggs. After you peel each egg, lightly rinse it to make sure you remove all shell bits. Then place the egg on paper towels.

4. Cut open each cooked egg and remove the yolk, placing all the yolks on a plate. Set the whites aside.

5. Mash the cooked yolks on the plate with the mayo and mustard until a smooth, thick paste is formed.

6. In a large mixing bowl, stir the cooked chicken breast chunks and the yolk/mayo/mustard paste together until chicken is well coated. It should stick together lightly in clumps; if it's too dry, add a bit more mayo until it's moist but not too wet.

7. Roughly chop the cooked egg whites and stir into the chicken mixture. Scoop chicken salad on sandwich bread or rolls to serve. Cover airtight and refrigerate to store.

Slow Cooker Pork Barbecue Sandwiches

Prepared in a slow cooker, pork butt roast becomes tender and easily shredded. Any leftover pork and sauce will freeze well, making this recipe as suitable for two as for a crowd.

PREP TIME: 5 minutes
COOK TIME: 8 hours & 25 minutes
TOTAL TIME: 8 hours & 30 minutes
YIELD: 6 servings

3 to 4 pound pork butt roast, tied

1 onion

18 ounces barbecue sauce

Cornstarch (optional)

12 pieces Texas toast bread
or 6 hamburger buns

Pickle slices
(optional)

1. Place the pork in the crockpot. Slice the onion into ½-inch rings and place the rings on top of the pork. Pour the sauce over the onions and pork. Place the cover on the crockpot and cook on low for 6 to 8 hours.

2. Remove the pork from the crockpot and set aside. Strain the sauce into a gravy separator. Discard cooked onions. Let the sauce sit for a few minutes to let the grease/oil float to the top. Pour the sauce only into a saucepan and discard the grease/oil. If you do not have a gravy separator, then pour the sauce into a saucepan and skim the grease/oil from the top. Cook the sauce on medium for about 20 to 25 minutes to reduce the sauce.

3. Remove and discard the tie. Using 2 forks, shred the pork. Discard any bits of fat (only use the lean meat).

4. If the sauce is too thin or you prefer a thicker sauce, stir about 1 teaspoon of cornstarch into ¼ to ⅓ cup cold water. Pour the cornstarch water into the sauce, whisking as your are adding it. Bring to a low boil, stirring occasionally.

5. Toast the Texas toast bread (or hamburger buns). Place shredded pork on 1 slice of toast. Top it with sauce and pickle slices and another slice of toast.

CREOLE BEEF TENDERLOIN

Creole seasoning is an essential kitchen staple. It instantly adds flavor to all kinds of meats. Made with just creole seasoning and olive oil, this simple beef tenderloin recipe is ideal when you don't have a lot of time for preparation.

PREP TIME: 10 minutes
COOK TIME: 30 minutes
INACTIVE TIME: 10 minutes
TOTAL TIME: 50 minutes
YIELD: 3 to 4 servings

12 ounces beef tenderloin tail end
Olive oil
1 tablespoon Creole seasoning

1. Tuck under the thinner end of the tenderloin and tie it so it is an even thickness round log.
2. Preheat oven to 450°F. Place a wire rack on a rimmed baking sheet.
3. Drizzle a small amount of olive oil on tenderloin. Rub to coat all sides with oil.
4. Sprinkle seasoning evenly on all sides of tenderloin. Place tenderloin on the wire rack.
5. Roast for 15 minutes then reduce oven temperature to 325°F.
6. Continue roasting until desired doneness, about 15 minutes for medium-rare (internal temperature is 125°F so it finishes to medium-rare after resting).
7. Remove tenderloin from the oven and transfer it to a cutting board. Allow it to rest for 10 minutes before slicing.

Salmon Patties

Salmon patties are a staple found on many Southern dinner tables. This skillet-fried fish cake can also be made with solid white albacore tuna instead of salmon.

PREP TIME: 5 minutes
COOK TIME: 6 minutes
TOTAL TIME: 11 minutes
YIELD: 6 to 8 patties

10 ounces canned boneless and skinless pink salmon, drained

2 large eggs

1 cup seasoned breadcrumbs, divided

Vegetable oil

1. Add enough oil to cover the bottom of a large nonstick skillet to a depth of ¼ inch. Preheat the pan with the oil on medium heat while you prepare the salmon.

2. Combine the salmon, the eggs, and ½ cup of seasoned breadcrumbs. Stir thoroughly until the mixture is well combined. Pour the ½ cup of remaining breadcrumbs on a plate.

3. Form the mixture into round patties about 3 inches across. Place the formed patty on the breadcrumbs on the plate; pat gently to make the breadcrumbs stick, then flip the patty and pat the other side into the breadcrumbs.

4. Slip each patty gently into the pan. Fry on one side for 2 to 3 minutes, until the cooked side is golden brown. Flip the patty and fry the other side the same way.

5. When both sides are golden brown, remove to a plate lined with paper towels to absorb excess oil. Serve warm.

Apple Cider Pork Roast

Slow-cooked with fruit and spices, this apple cider pork roast is an excellent fall or winter meal. You can save money on cardamom by buying it in whole pods and grinding the black seeds yourself.

PREP TIME: 10 minutes
COOK TIME: 3 hours
TOTAL TIME: 3 hours & 10 minutes
YIELD: 10 to 12 servings

3 to 3 ½ pound boneless pork roast, loin end

2 tablespoons canola oil

2 ½ cups apple cider

1 cup chopped onion

1 teaspoon salt

3 medium cooking apples, Granny Smith recommended

6 ounces dried apricot pieces

1 teaspoon ground cardamom

½ teaspoon ground cinnamon

1. Heat oil in a 6- to 8-quart Dutch oven for several minutes until almost smoking. Brown pork on all sides in the hot oil. Transfer browned pork to a plate and discard fat.
2. Add apple cider, onion, salt, and pork to the Dutch oven. Bring to a boil then reduce heat to simmer. Cover and simmer until meat is tender, about 2 to 2 ½ hours.
3. Remove pork and place on a cutting board. Let rest for 10 to 15 minutes. Slice and place on a serving platter. Cover with foil to keep warm.
4. Core apples and cut into wedges. Cut dried apricots in half (if not already in pieces).
5. Add apples, apricots, cardamom, and cinnamon to the Dutch oven. Bring to a boil then reduce heat to simmer. Cover and simmer until fruit is tender, about 5 minutes.
6. Use a slotted spoon to transfer apples and apricots to the serving platter. Re-cover with foil to keep warm until serving.
7. Bring the juices in the Dutch oven to a gentle boil and cook until reduced to 1 cup, about 7 to 10 minutes.
8. Spoon cider sauce over meat and fruit or serve on the side.

Tuna Salad Sandwiches

Sometimes, uncomplicated food is the best food. These tuna salad sandwiches are ready to eat in just minutes. Chow chow, a sweet Southern pickle relish, adds a unique twist. If you can't find or make chow chow, substitute your favorite pickle relish.

PREP TIME: 5 minutes
TOTAL TIME: 5 minutes
YIELD: 2 sandwiches

5 to 6 ounce canned white albacore tuna in water

1 tablespoon chow chow relish

1 teaspoon yellow mustard

2 tablespoons mayonnaise

Salt and pepper

4 slices sandwich bread

Lettuce

Tomato slices

1. Drain the water from the tuna and place tuna in a small bowl. Fluff tuna with fork if tightly packed.

2. Add the chow chow relish, mustard, mayonnaise and stir to combine.

3. Season with salt and pepper to taste. Divide into two equal portions.

4. Place lettuce and tomato on 2 bread slices. Top with tuna mixture. Place remaining bread slices on top. Serve immediately.

Grilled Pimento Cheese Sandwiches

Everything is better with pimento cheese, including grilled cheese sandwiches. The number of sandwiches yielded by this recipe will depend on how much pimento cheese you use on each sandwich.

PREP TIME: 3 hours 25 minutes
COOK TIME: 5 minutes
TOTAL TIME: 3 hours & 30 minutes
YIELD: About 4 cups of pimento cheese, enough for 4 to 6 sandwiches

¼ cup cream cheese, at room temperature

3 tablespoons mayonnaise

1 teaspoon grated onion

⅛ teaspoon garlic powder

Pinch of salt

Pinch of fresh ground pepper

2 cups shredded sharp Cheddar cheese

1 cup shredded Pepper Jack cheese

1 cup shredded Monterey Jack cheese

1 jar chopped pimentos, 4 ounces, drained

Thick slices of hearty white bread

Butter, softened for easy spreading

1. In the bowl of a food processor fitted with a knife blade, process cream cheese, mayonnaise, onion, garlic powder, salt, and pepper until smooth.

2. Add the shredded cheeses and pimentos and pulse to combine. Do not over-process. Transfer pimento cheese to a bowl and stir if needed to combine ingredients thoroughly. Cover and chill for at least 3 hours.

3. Heat a skillet or griddle to medium heat. Do not get too hot or it will burn the butter and bread.

4. Butter one side of two bread slices. Spread a thick layer of pimento cheese on the unbuttered side of a bread slice. Use about ¾ cup of pimento cheese for each sandwich.

5. Place pimento cheese covered bread slice butter side down in the skillet. Cover skillet with a lid and cook for 1 minute.

6. Remove lid and top sandwich with the other slice butter side up. Cook until bottom is lightly browned and toasted.

7. Flip sandwich over and cook until the other side is lightly browned and toasted.

8. Transfer sandwich to a plate and slice in half.

9. Repeat with remaining bread and pimento cheese or grill 2 to 4 sandwiches at a time, depending on size of skillet. Do not overcrowd the skillet.

10. Refrigerate extra pimento cheese for up to 5 days.

LIBATION LESSON
WINE

HOW TO PAIR SOUTHERN FOOD WITH WINE
BY DILEK CANER OF THE DALLAS WINE EDUCATION CENTER

Southern cooking—with its buttery flavors, flavor-intensifying cooking methods, and generous seasoning—can support some of the most intensely structured wines. Sweetness, spicy heat, and sharp cheese notes in many Southern dishes provide the opportunity for more delicate and elegant bottles to stand out.

ESSENTIAL WINE PAIRING TIPS

- The most important aspect of pairing wine with food is the intensity of the food and the wine. If their intensities are matched, neither ends up dominating the other. This approach allows the nuances of the pairing to reveal themselves.

- When pairing a dish, try to look beyond its main ingredient (which is usually a protein or a vegetable). In theory, Cabernet with meat and Pinot Noir with Pork may sound conveniently simple, but in reality, much depends on the texture of the dish, how it is cooked and what is served on the side.

- The acidity of a wine lightens a dish, and the protein, saltiness and the fat in a dish make the wine seem fuller and rounder. For example, the pure citrus fruit aromas of a Muscadet, Sancerre or an entry level Chablis match the delicate flavors of a Wedge Salad, while the acidity of the wine will be balanced by the saltiness of the bacon and the ranch dressing.

CHEESY AND CREAMY PAIRINGS

Cheese is a great friend of wine. Its saltiness and fat tames wine's acidity and tannins. A dish that contains cheese is lifted by the wine's structure.

For a cheesy dish like Squash Casserole, bring on that big California Chardonnay. A youthful Rioja Crianza, a Barbera from Northern Italy or a medium-bodied Merlot from Chile also work well by providing more structure without overwhelming the dish.

The creamy texture of a Chicken Salad calls for a medium-bodied wine with more flavor intensity such as an Albarino, a White Burgundy or a Pinot Noir from Russian River Valley. Ham and Macaroni Salad needs a similarly textured wine, but the sweetness of the pickles could use more fruitiness—even slight sweetness—in the wine. An off-dry Alsatian Gewurztraminer, an Alsatian Pinot Gris or a demi-sec Vouvray are perfect candidates.

RICH, SAVORY, MEATY, AND SPICY PAIRINGS

Umami (a savory, meaty flavor) and spicy heat in a dish can be challenging for wine pairings as both of these components tend to make a wine seem drier, more acidic, leaner, and in the case of red wines, more tannic.

When the main ingredient is a high density protein that is further intensified with roasting or any sort of cooking with dry heat, it's time to bring out the tannic reds. With Prime Rib Roast, try a prized California Cabernet Sauvignon, a red Bordeaux, or a Barolo.

With Crockpot Pork BBQ, open a rich

red Zinfandel, an Argentinian Malbec or a ripe Australian Shiraz. The relatively high tannins of these wines will pair beautifully with the rich, fat texture of the dishes. Even though the wines are not sweet, the opulent fruit aromas of Zinfandel and Shiraz will perfectly match the sweetness of the BBQ sauce.

As a principle, for dishes with strong umami flavors or spicy heat, look for wines that are not oaky, but are fruitier and lower in tannins (if red). The strong savory flavor of Tarragon Deviled Eggs will not get along with all wines, but will do well with a New Zealand Sauvignon Blanc or a Prosecco.

Succotash, with its umami flavors from the lima beans and tomatoes, works very well with the clean flavors of an Austrian Grüner Veltliner or a low tannin red such as a New Zealand Pinot Noir.

Sweet Pairings

Sweetness can be subtle. Even roasting or searing can add sweetness. Whenever you have sweetness in a dish, pair it with a wine of similar sweetness. This works even if you are not a fan of sweet wines, because once you have it with the dish, the wine will seem drier.

Your palate temporarily develops a higher threshold for sweetness once it is exposed to the sugar in the dish, and is now less sensitive to the sweetness in the wine. A slightly sweet German Riesling paired with Strawberry Cream Cheese will suddenly seem not sweet at all.

Desserts make a sweet wine seem drier than it is, and that's why they are usually served with sweet wines. For fruitier desserts, such as Apricot Hand Pies, choose similarly flavored wines. Try an icewine from Canada, a Tokaji Aszú from Hungary, or a Chenin Blanc-based sweet wine such as a Coteaux du Layon if you come across one locally.

The caramel flavors of Butterscotch Pudding pair well with the honey, saffron, and hazelnut flavors of a Sauternes. Brownies are great candidates for a Port with fig and prune flavors, especially a 30-year-Old Tawny Port, if you feel like splurging. For the Peanut Butter Ice Cream, look for a Pedro Ximenez Sherry. It is almost as thick as syrup, so pour a little on your dessert.

SIDE DISHES

· SQUASH CASSEROLE · BAKED BEANS WITH BACON ·
· CREAMY COLESLAW · SWEET CORNBREAD ·
· CREOLE SPICED POTATO BAKE · HAM AND MACARONI SALAD ·
· BOILED CORN ON THE COB · CHOW CHOW RELISH ·
· FRIED OKRA · BLACK-EYED PEAS · BROCCOLI CASSEROLE ·
· SUCCOTASH · COLLARD GREENS · ORANGE CRANBERRY SAUCE ·

SQUASH CASSEROLE

Squash casserole is a comfort food that tastes even better the second day. When you make this dish for holiday gatherings, double the recipe and enjoy the leftovers!

PREP TIME: 10 minutes
COOK TIME: 25 minutes
TOTAL TIME: 35 minutes
YIELD: 4 to 6 servings

1 ½ pounds yellow squash

3 cups shredded cheddar cheese, divided

2 cups crushed wheat crackers

2 tablespoons mayonnaise

1. Preheat the oven to 350°F.
2. Wash the squash and cut into ½ inch rounds with the skin still on. Put about a half an inch of water in a pot and bring to a boil.
3. Add the squash, cover the pot with a lid, and cook, stirring occasionally, for about 5-7 minutes. The squash is done when the middle part of the largest rounds is starting to break up and the seeds are coming loose.
4. Drain the squash with a colander. In a large mixing bowl, combine the cooked squash, 2 cups of cheese, and mayonnaise. Stir until the cheese is melted. Add 1 cup of crushed crackers crumbles and stir vigorously until well combined, allowing the squash to break up as you stir.
5. Scrape the mixture into a casserole dish and smooth out evenly. Sprinkle with the remaining cheese and the remaining crushed crackers. Bake 20 minutes and serve warm.

Baked Beans with Bacon

Every Southern cook has his or her own way of doctoring canned baked beans. The addition of mustard, ketchup, and extra brown sugar is practically traditional, but the sliced bacon on top makes it special.

PREP TIME: 10 minutes

COOK TIME: 1 hour

TOTAL TIME: 1 hour & 10 minutes

YIELD: 8 servings

Two 28-ounce cans Pork and Beans, drained

½ cup diced onion

¼ cup diced bell pepper

⅓ cup ketchup

3 tablespoons light brown sugar

1 tablespoon yellow mustard

½ teaspoon Worcestershire sauce

6 ounces bacon strips, each strip cut in half to make 2 short pieces

1. Heat oven to 400°F

2. Stir together all ingredients except bacon.

3. Spread evenly in a 2-quart baking or casserole dish.

4. Cover mixture with bacon slices.

5. Bake for 1 hour.

6. If bacon is not browned or crispier bacon is preferred, broil for a few minutes until desired bacon doneness is reached.

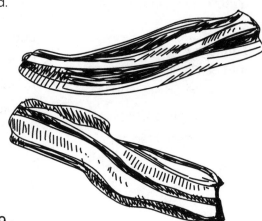

CREAMY COLESLAW

This simple Southern coleslaw uses only four ingredients. By letting the coleslaw rest for an hour or so, you give it time for the flavor to fully develop.

PREP TIME: 10 minutes

INACTIVE TIME: 1 hour

TOTAL TIME: 1 hour & 10 minutes

YIELD: 4 servings

10 ounces Angel Hair shredded cabbage

⅔ cup mayonnaise

2 tablespoons white vinegar

2 tablespoons granulated sugar

1. Place shredded cabbage in a large bowl.
2. Stir together mayonnaise, vinegar, and sugar in a small bowl until smooth.
3. Pour mayonnaise mixture over cabbage and stir to coat thoroughly.
4. Refrigerate for at least 1 hour, stirring occasionally.

SWEET CORNBREAD

Cornbread in the South comes in two varieties: sweet, and not-so-sweet. This recipe produces a cornbread that is soft, sweet, and moist. Cut it into squares and serve on a platter with butter and honey.

PREP TIME: 5 minutes
COOK TIME: 20 minutes
TOTAL TIME: 25 minutes
YIELD: 9 servings

½ cup unsalted butter, plus a little more for greasing the pan
1 cup all purpose flour
1 cup cornmeal
¼ cup granulated sugar
½ teaspoon sea salt
1 ½ teaspoons baking powder
½ teaspoon baking soda
1 cup buttermilk
2 large eggs

1. Preheat the oven to 425°F. Lightly butter an 8 inch square pan and set aside. Melt the 1/2 cup of unsalted butter, and set aside to cool slightly.
2. In a large mixing bowl, combine the flour, cornmeal, sugar, salt, baking powder, and baking soda. Whisk thoroughly to combine. Make a well in the center of the dry ingredients.
3. In another bowl, lightly beat the eggs with the buttermilk. Pour the egg/buttermilk mixture into the well in the dry ingredients, then drizzle the melted butter in as well.
4. Gently fold the mixture together until everything is moist, but do not over mix. Scrape the batter evenly into the prepared pan and very lightly smooth the top (it will still be a little uneven, but will smooth out completely when baked).
5. Bake for 15 to 20 minutes, or until a toothpick inserted in the middle comes out clean. Serve slightly warm.

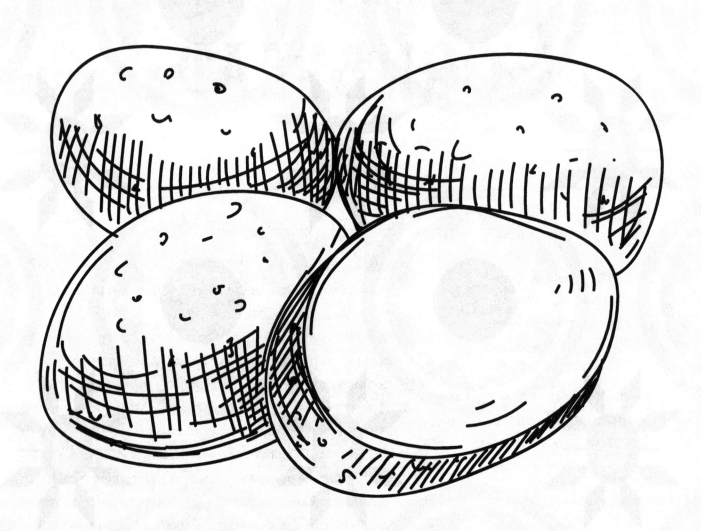

CREOLE SPICED POTATO BAKE

This Creole Spiced Potato Bake makes a great side dish during cool weather, and is a great reason (if you needed one) to keep Creole seasoning in your pantry.

PREP TIME: 10 minutes

COOK TIME: 1 hour

TOTAL TIME: 1 hour & 10 minutes

YIELD: 8 to 10 servings

4 large russet potatoes

1 small onion, chopped

2 garlic cloves, minced

2 tablespoons Creole seasoning

Zest of 1 lemon

Juice of 1 lemon

1/2 cup unsalted butter, melted

2 tablespoons chopped fresh flat-leaf parsley for garnish (optional)

1. Preheat oven to 350°F.
2. Peel potatoes and cut into bite-sized pieces. Place potato pieces in a large bowl.
3. Add onion, garlic, Creole seasoning, lemon zest, lemon juice, and butter. Toss to combine.
4. Place mixture in a lightly greased 2-quart casserole dish.
5. Bake for 1 hour, or until potatoes are tender.
6. Garnish with chopped parsley if desired.

Ham and Macaroni Salad

PREP TIME: 20 minutes

COOK TIME: 2 hours & 15 minutes

TOTAL TIME: 2 hours & 35 minutes

YIELD: 6 servings

1 ½ cups uncooked elbow macaroni pasta

6 ounces cooked ham, diced

6 ounces sharp cheddar cheese, diced

½ cup chopped sweet onion, Vidalia recommended

⅓ cup sweet pickle cubes, drained

4 ounces chopped pimento, drained

1 celery stalk, thinly sliced

½ cup sour cream, plus more if needed (see step 3)

2 tablespoons prepared mustard

This ham and macaroni salad incorporates sharp cheddar, Vidalia onions, sweet pickles, pimento, and celery, in addition to the the main ingredients of ham and macaroni.

1. Cook macaroni according to package directions. Drain and rinse with cold water until macaroni is at room temperature or cooler. Drain completely.

2. While the macaroni is cooking, place all remaining ingredients in a large bowl. Add cooked macaroni and stir to combine and coat ingredients with sour cream.

3. Cover and chill for at least 2 hours prior to serving. Pasta will tend to soak up moisture as it chills. You can stir in more sour cream if needed to make it creamier after chilling.

BOILED CORN ON THE COB

Smoked salt gives freshly boiled corn a smoky, grilled flavor Sprinkle it on after rubbing the corn with unsalted butter.

PREP TIME: 3 minutes
COOK TIME: 17 minutes
TOTAL TIME: 25 minutes
YIELD: 20 servings

6 ears fresh corn
3 tablespoons unsalted butter
Fine salt or smoked salt

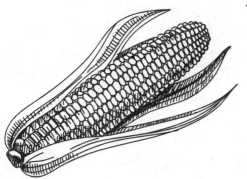

1. Remove the husks and strings of silk from the corn just before cooking. Snap off the stems. If the ears are too large to fit in your pot, break them in half.

2. Put the corn into a large pot, such as a Dutch oven, and fill it with water until the corn is floating freely. Cover the pot with a lid and bring the water to a boil over high heat.

3. Once the water is boiling, remove the lid and boil for 2 minutes.

4. Remove the pot from the heat, and let it stand uncovered for 10 minutes. Drain the water, then rub each ear of corn with butter and sprinkle it with salt.

Chow Chow Relish

Chow chow relish is a traditional pickled relish made and served throughout the South. This sweet version makes a large batch for canning, enough to stock the pantry or give as gifts.

PREP TIME: 5 minutes
INACTIVE TIME: 5 hours, or overnight
COOK TIME: 30 minutes
TOTAL TIME: 5 hours & 35 minutes
YIELD: 15 pints

4 quarts green tomatoes,
about 10 pounds

6 cups chopped onions,
about 3 ½ pounds

1 medium-large cabbage

2 quarts chopped bell pepper, about
13 green peppers and 1 red pepper

4 hot banana peppers

3 cayenne peppers

1/2 cup salt

8 cups apple cider vinegar,
5% acidity

4 cups sugar

1 tablespoon ground mustard

3 tablespoons mustard seed

1 tablespoon turmeric

2 tablespoons allspice

1. Finely chop all the vegetables in batches in a food processor fitted with a knife blade.
2. Mix chopped vegetables together in a very large non-reactive container. Sprinkle ½ cup salt over and let set at least 4 to 5 hours or overnight.
3. Drain the vegetables and squeeze out as much liquid as possible.
4. In large boiler, mix apple cider vinegar and sugar.
5. Combine the ground mustard, mustard seed, celery seed, turmeric, and allspice in a spice bag. Add the spice bag to the liquids.
6. Bring to boil then reduce heat and simmer 5 minutes.
7. Add the drained vegetables and bring back to a boil. Reduce heat and simmer 20 minutes.
8. Pack the chow chow mix while it's hot into sterilized pint canning jars. Use caution while working with the hot mix and jars. Leave about a ¼ to ½ inch headspace in each jar. Wipe the mouth of the canning jar clean and seal the jar with canning lid and rings. Lids should properly seal and make a popping sound while cooling. The seals are good if they stay depressed in the middle.

FRIED OKRA

Although it can be pickled, cooked, or eaten raw, okra is at its best when it's fried.
Adding cornmeal to the batter gives this fried okra an extra-crunchy texture.

PREP TIME: 5 minutes
COOK TIME: 10 minutes
TOTAL TIME: 15 minutes
YIELD: 4 servings

1 pound okra, stems removed
4 tablespoons cornmeal
2 tablespoons all-purpose flour
Vegetable or canola oil
Salt and pepper

1. Slice okra into ¼ to ½-inch slices. Place okra in a bowl. Add the cornmeal and flour and stir until okra is evenly coated.
2. In a skillet over medium heat, add the oil to cover the bottom of the skillet. Once the oil is heated, add the okra to the skillet and cook for a few minutes until lightly browned on the bottom. Use a spatula to turn okra over in the pan. Add more oil if needed (okra will tend to soak up the oil). Continue to cook and turn okra until evenly browned.
3. Transfer okra to a bowl or platter lined with paper towels. Season with salt and pepper. Remove paper towels and serve warm.

BLACK-EYED PEAS

Traditionally served on New Year's Day as a way to bring good luck, black-eyed peas are often paired with cornbread and collard greens. You can substitute bacon if salt pork is not available, or omit the salt pork for a lower fat version.

PREP TIME: 15 minutes

COOK TIME: 2 hours

TOTAL TIME: 2 hours & 15 minutes

YIELD: 4 to 6 servings

1 pound dried black-eyed peas

8 cups water

½ pound sliced salt pork

2 teaspoons salt

1 teaspoon pepper

OPTIONAL TOPPINGS

Chow chow relish or chopped onion

1. Rinse the peas in a colander. Pick out and discard any discolored peas along with any small stones.
2. Add all the ingredients to a large pot. Over medium heat, bring to a simmer (do not let it get to a hard boil). Turn the heat to low or medium-low to maintain a slow simmer.
3. Partially cover and cook until the peas are tender, about 2 hours. Check occasionally and add more water if needed. Remove and discard salt pork. Serve immediately.

BROCCOLI CASSEROLE

Like many homestyle Southern recipes that call for shredded cheese, it is best to use cheddar cheese hand-shredded from the block for this recipe, rather than pre-shredded. The texture and melting quality is noticeably superior.

PREP TIME: 10 minutes
COOK TIME: 30 minutes
TOTAL TIME: 40 minutes
YIELD: 4 to 6 servings

4 stalks broccoli

4 cups shredded cheddar cheese, divided

2 cups crushed wheat crackers, divided

2 tablespoons mayonnaise

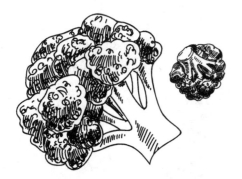

1. Preheat the oven to 350°F.
2. Cut the broccoli florets off the stalks. Trim the florets into pieces that are approximately the same size. Place the florets in a pot and add enough water to cover the bottom of the pot. Cover and bring to a boil over high heat.
3. Reduce the heat to medium and continue boiling for about 8 to 10 minutes. Cook the florets until they're tender but not mushy.
4. Drain the pot into a colander. Let the pot dry for a minute, then return the broccoli to the pot. Add 3 cups of cheese and the mayonnaise. Stir vigorously. Add 1 ½ cups of crumbs and stir vigorously again.
5. Transfer the mixture to a casserole dish. Top with remaining cheese and remaining cracker crumbs. Bake for 20 minutes, then serve while warm.

SUCCOTASH

There are many regional variations on succotash, a dish that combines beans and corn with a variety of seasonings. This version includes a kick of hot sauce and a hint of fresh basil.

PREP TIME: 15 minutes
COOK TIME: 30 minutes
TOTAL TIME: 45 minutes
YIELD: 6 to 8 servings

1 ½ cups fresh lima beans
1 tablespoon olive oil
1 tablespoon unsalted butter
1 ½ cups chopped onion
1 garlic clove minced
2 cups chopped zucchini
1 ½ cups corn kernels
2 medium red tomatoes, chopped
1 teaspoon hot sauce
1 tablespoon chopped fresh basil
Salt and pepper to taste

1. Simmer the lima beans in lightly salted water until tender, about 15 minutes. Drain.
2. In a large skillet, heat the oil and butter over medium heat.
3. Add the chopped onion and sprinkle with salt. Cook, stirring occasionally, until soft and translucent.
4. Add the garlic and cook for 1 minute.
5. Add the zucchini and cook, stirring occasionally, until slightly softened (about 5 minutes).
6. Add the lima beans, corn, tomatoes, and hot sauce. Stir to combine.
7. Reduce heat to medium-low and cover skillet. Cook until heated through and tomatoes are soft, about 10 minutes. Stir occasionally. Cook longer for softer texture, shorter for firmer texture.
8. Add chopped basil and stir to combine. Add salt and pepper to taste. Transfer to a bowl to serve.

COLLARD GREENS

Baking soda is often added to collard greens during the cooking process to reduce bitterness and toughness. It's an optional ingredient in this recipe; if your collard greens aren't too bitter, you won't need it.

PREP TIME: 5 minutes
COOK TIME: 2 hours & 45 minutes
TOTAL TIME: 2 hours & 50 minutes
YIELD: 6 to 8 servings

2 smoked ham hocks

8 cups water

2 teaspoons salt

½ teaspoon pepper

2 pounds shredded collard greens

1 teaspoon baking soda,
if needed (see step 4)

1. Look for bags of shredded collard greens in the produce section. If using whole collards, rinse thoroughly a few times to remove dirt or else the finished dish will be gritty. Remove and discard the center stalk from the leaves then cut leaves into shreds (will add to prep time).

2. Place ham hocks, water, salt, and pepper in a 7- or 8-quart soup pot or Dutch oven. Bring to a boil then reduce heat to a slow boil or fast simmer. Cover loosely and cook for 1 ¼ hours.

3. Add collard greens. Bring to a simmer and cover loosely. Cook for 1 ¼ hours.

4. Taste collards. If too bitter and still somewhat tough and firm, stir in baking soda and cook for an additional 15 minutes.

5. Remove and discard ham hocks (or you can pull the ham from the bones and add ham back to the pot).

Orange Cranberry Sauce

There's no need to resort to canned cranberry sauce when fresh cranberry sauce is so easy to make. Pair this orange cranberry sauce with turkey for Thanksgiving, or use it to top roasted pork or chicken.

PREP TIME: 2 minutes

COOK TIME: 20 minutes

TOTAL TIME: 22 minutes

YIELD: About 2 cups

12 ounces whole cranberries, frozen or fresh

½ cup plus 1 tablespoon granulated sugar

½ cup orange juice, not from concentrate

1. Combine all ingredients in a medium saucepan and bring to a boil. Reduce heat and simmer approximately 20 minutes, or until the cranberries have burst and the sauce has thickened.
2. Remove from heat and cool to room temperature. Serve, or cover and refrigerate.

Bourbon does for me what the piece of cake did for Proust.

—PERCY WALKER

Libation Lesson

SPIRITS

ALL ABOUT SOUTHERN SPIRITS

AN INTERVIEW WITH COLIN BLAKE OF MOONSHINE UNIVERSITY

What is the quintessential Southern spirit?

It's hard to argue that anything other than Bourbon would be the quintessential Southern spirit. Not only is it the spirit of choice for many people in the south, it's also the drink of choice for many famous Southern writers, like Faulkner. Some of my favorite bourbon quotes are from great Southern writers. It doesn't get better than when Percy Walker wrote, "Bourbon does for me what the piece of cake did for Proust."

Not to say that other spirits aren't popular, or becoming more popular in the modern South. Vodka is always a huge seller, no matter where you are, and rum is a fast growing category in many southern states, not to mention the resurgence of rye whiskey, but Bourbon would be hard to argue with as the spirit of the South.

What spirit is your favorite?

I love all spirits, they're all great for various different moods, food pairing, or occasion. Recently I've been enjoying many kinds of brandy and rye whiskey. I've been loving Wild Turkey 101 Rye and Copper & Kings Butchertown Brandy. But I also gravitate to a higher proof, more aggressive flavor profile. To pin down a favorite is hard. I know people always compare choosing a favorite to picking a favorite child, but I always feel like that's just a ruse. I think that every parent has a favorite child.

For me, picking a favorite spirit just melts my internal circuitry. Every time I think I might be able to name, say, a rye as my favorite, then I think of having a Navy Grog on my back porch and I change my mind...and the cycle never ends. So, I love all my children the same.

How do you pair Southern spirits with Southern food?

When pairing any spirit with food it's all about either flavor complimenting or contrasting. When looking at pairing bourbon, you have to keep in mind the proof and how robust the flavor is in the spirit. Delicate foods would get run over. Foods with lots of seasoning and flavor are ideal, like BBQ, rubs, and flavorful well-seasoned sides of baked beans or some spicy greens.

When you are thinking of your pairing you have to consider how the flavors of bourbon will match the flavor of the food or contrast in such a way that new flavors are created. Also, think about how the alcohol in the bourbon will either enhance or mellow any spiciness.

If the food is spicy enough to make your eyes water, you may want to choose a wheated bourbon, something softer and smoother to help dull that burn—or if you want to bring on the heat, go with a rye bourbon and let that heat get amplified. Take into consideration the amount of sweetness, oak, fruitiness, and other flavors of your favorite bourbon. Will those characteristics compliment what you're eating, or will it combat them?

It's all about spending time to get to know your favorite spirits and what characteristics they each have, and then thinking about how those flavor profiles will work with any given dish. It's just an extension of picking the correct spices when cooking the food.

WHERE CAN YOU FIND GOOD QUALITY SPIRITS?

I always tell people "Drink what you like." It doesn't matter who has the best ad campaign, or what celebrity drinks what, or what's rare and hard to find, that's all vanity. At the end of the day, you should enjoy what you like, it's that simple. I'm thrilled that my palate is aimed at moderately priced whiskeys, and my wallet likes it too. And if you don't know what you like, go to a good bar with a great selection and ask them to set up some flights for you, make sure you get the flights blind. Don't ask about anything just try them all. Generally people are surprised what they like once all branding and marketing is stripped away. I think that's the best way to find things that you like.

WHAT IS MOONSHINE UNIVERSITY?

Moonshine University is all about spirits education, and we focus on two different aspects of that. Most of our classes are professional distillery education where we have classes that teach people how to open, run, and operate their own distilleries. We also have in depth workshops that focus on one small aspect of the industry, like fermentation, gin production, and advanced sensory training.

The other area we offer classes in is enthusiast spirits education where we teach spirits enthusiast the unbranded story of various spirits. We house the Stave & Thief Society, which is a bourbon certification program. It's the only industry backed certification program out there for bourbon. Currently we're working on expanding Stave & Thief Society into other spirit categories.

Pear Rosemary Cocktail

This is the best spring and summer cocktail. The rosemary simple syrup is super easy
to make, and the rest of the ingredients are easy to find.

—Colin Blake

For the Rosemary Syrup

1 cup water

1 cup sugar

4-6 sprigs of fresh rosemary

For the Cocktail

1 ½ ounce pear brandy

½ ounce rosemary syrup

½ ounce ginger liqueur

½ ounce freshly squeezed lemon juice

2-inch sprig of rosemary

For the Rosemary Syrup

1. Bring one cup of water to a boil.

2. Add 1 cup of sugar and 4-6 sprigs of rosemary.

3. Bring down to a simmer for 7-10 minutes, or until the liquid starts to become syrupy.

For the Cocktail

1. Shake the first four cocktail ingredients together, strain into a glass, and garnish with rosemary.

DESSERTS

· BLACKBERRY CRUMBLE · OLD-FASHIONED PEANUT BUTTER ICE CREAM ·
· BOURBON WHITE CHOCOLATE BROWNIES ·
· TRADITIONAL BREAD PUDDING · APRICOT HAND PIES ·
· CRUSTLESS PUMPKIN PIE · THE PERFECT BROWNIES ·
· BUTTERSCOTCH PUDDING · APPLE DUMPLINGS ·
· OVEN BAKED S'MORES · UPSIDE DOWN PEACH BREAD PUDDING ·
· SELF-CRUST COCONUT PIE · SPICED PECANS · BOURBON HONEY MILK ·

BLACKBERRY CRUMBLE

Southern blackberries are at season's peak during the summer months. This blackberry crumble takes full advantage of their juicy sweetness and allows the berries to shine. You can also substitute 3 cups of blueberries for the blackberries to make a blueberry crumble.

PREP TIME: 5 minutes
COOK TIME: 30 minutes
TOTAL TIME: 35 minutes
YIELD: 4 servings

12 ounces blackberries, fresh or frozen, about 3 cups

6 tablespoons unsalted butter, softened

⅔ cup brown sugar

½ cup old fashioned oats

½ cup all purpose flour

¼ teaspoon cinnamon

1 pinch sea salt

1. Preheat the oven to 375°F and take out a 1 quart casserole dish.
2. Place the butter, sugar, oats, flour, cinnamon, and salt in a medium sized bowl. Stir vigorously until the ingredients have formed into small clumps. At this point, there should be no loose flour or sugar in the bowl and no visible bits of butter.
3. Using the back of the fork, compact the mixture firmly into the bowl until it sticks together in one large clump. Then, use the tines of the fork to gently break it into clumps of various sizes- some large, some small. Carefully tip the bowl sideways over the pan of berries and use the fork to scoot the clumps out of the bowl evenly over the top of the berries.
4. Place the pan in the oven and bake for 30 minutes, or until the top is golden brown. Let cool until just slightly warm so that the topping can firm up properly.

Old-Fashioned Peanut Butter Ice Cream

This peanut butter ice cream is made the old fashioned way, by creating a custard base of sugar, eggs, and cream. It's well worth the effort.

PREP TIME: 2 hours & 5 minutes

COOK TIME: 10 minutes

INACTIVE TIME: 16 hours (overnight, twice)

TOTAL TIME: 18 hours 15 minutes

YIELD: 6 servings

1 cup sugar

2 eggs plus 1 egg yolk

1 ½ cups half-and-half

1 cup heavy whipping cream

1 teaspoon vanilla extract

½ cup creamy peanut butter

SPECIAL EQUIPMENT:

Instant read thermometer

1. In a medium bowl, whisk together sugar, eggs, and egg yolk until lighter in color.

2. In a saucepan over medium heat, bring the half-and-half and whipping cream to 160°F. Remove from the heat. Use a ladle to add a little of the cream to the egg/sugar mixture and whisk to combine. Continue adding cream until at least half of it has been mixed with the eggs.

3. Add the eggs/cream mixture back to the pan and whisk to combine.

4. Over medium heat, cook the mixture until it reaches 170 to 175°F, stirring constantly.

5. Pour the mixture into a medium bowl. Add the vanilla and peanut butter and whisk to combine until smooth.

6. Cover the mixture directly on top with plastic wrap to prevent a skin from forming. Cool to room temperature. Once it has cooled, place it in the refrigerator to chill overnight.

7. Pour chilled mixture into an ice cream maker and freeze according to the manufacturer's instructions. Transfer ice cream to a container and place it in the freezer for at least one hour or overnight.

Bourbon White Chocolate Brownies

Bourbon is the quintessential Southern spirit. It adds a hint of complexity and smokiness to these rich white chocolate brownies. Look for white chocolate made with cocoa butter, not vegetable oil, for the very best flavor.

PREP TIME: 10 minutes
COOK TIME: 25 minutes
TOTAL TIME: 35 minutes
YIELD: 9 brownies

8 ounces white chocolate
6 tablespoons unsalted butter
½ cup granulated sugar
¼ teaspoon salt
2 teaspoon bourbon
2 eggs
1 cup all purpose flour

1. Preheat the oven to 350°F. For easy cleanup, line your 8 inch square pan with parchment paper or foil.
2. Put the sugar and salt in a large mixing bowl and set aside.
3. Chop the white chocolate into small pieces and cut up the butter. Place both in a microwaveable bowl. Microwave at 50% power for one minute, or until the butter has melted (it may take 2 to 3 minutes total, but check after each minute). Once the butter has melted, remove the bowl from the microwave and stir gently until the white chocolate has melted completely and the mixture is smooth.
4. Add the butter and chocolate mixture to the large mixing bowl with the sugar and salt. Stir until combined. Add the eggs and the bourbon, then stir until combined.
5. Sprinkle the flour over the batter and stir together until just combined. Pour the batter into the prepared pan.
6. Bake at 350°F for 25 to 30 minutes or until a toothpick inserted in the middle comes out with moist crumbs but no wet batter on it. Let cool to room temperature before serving.

Traditional Bread Pudding

This classic bread pudding recipe is assertively flavored with nutmeg. It's equally delicious served warm or cold, and can be enjoyed as dessert... or breakfast!

PREP TIME: 10 minutes
COOK TIME: 30 minutes
TOTAL TIME: 40 minutes
YIELD: 8 servings

2 tablespoons unsalted butter
6 cups bread chunks
2 cups milk
1 teaspoon vanilla extract
2 tablespoons plus ½ cup granulated sugar, divided
¼ teaspoon salt
½ teaspoon nutmeg
½ teaspoon cinnamon
2 eggs
OPTIONAL INGREDIENTS
½ cup raisins

1. Preheat the oven to 400°F. Put the butter in a 9 inch cake pan or pie plate, and place the pan in the oven for a minute or two to melt the butter.
2. Remove the pan and swirl the butter evenly over the bottom of the pan.
3. Sprinkle 2 tablespoons of granulated sugar evenly over the bottom of the pan. Set the pan aside.
4. In a large mixing bowl, combine the milk, sugar, salt, nutmeg, cinnamon, vanilla, and eggs. Whisk briefly until just combined.
5. Add the bread chunks to the mixing bowl. If you are using raisins, add them now as well.
6. Stir until the bread is well saturated with liquid, then use your fingers to massage the mixture and break up any large chunks.
7. Gently place the soaked bread chunks in the pan, on top of the butter/sugar coating. Fill in any gaps in the bread and gently press down on the top to make it even. Pour any remaining liquid evenly over the top.
8. Place the pan in the oven. Bake for 15 minutes at 400°F, then turn the oven down to 300°F and bake another 15 minutes. The bread pudding is done when the temperature in the middle reaches 175°F, or when the center jiggles but does not slosh.

Apricot Hand Pies

Hand pies are a well-known Southern treat that can be made with a variety of fruit fillings. This version uses dried apricots that are rehydrated and softened before being made into a jam-like filling. You can refrigerate leftover apricot filling in a sealed container, and use it as preserves.

PREP TIME: 25 minutes
COOK TIME: 45 minutes
TOTAL TIME: 1 hour & 10 minutes
YIELD: 16 servings

6 ounces dried apricots
⅓ cup granulated sugar
1 tablespoon unsalted butter
⅛ teaspoon ground cinnamon
2 packages refrigerated pie crusts
Vegetable oil for frying

1. Place apricots in a saucepan and cover with at least 1 inch of water. Bring to a boil then reduce heat to simmer. Cook until apricots have softened, about 20 to 25 minutes. Drain apricots.
2. Place warm apricots, sugar, butter, and cinnamon in a food processor fitted with a knife blade. Process until combined and mixture looks like jam.
3. Cut pie crusts into 4- to 5-inch rounds.
4. Place about 1 tablespoon of apricot filling on each round. Moisten edges with water.
5. Fold rounds in half and press edges together with a fork.
6. Pour enough oil into a large cast iron skillet or sauté pan to be about 1-inch deep.
7. Heat oil to 375°F.
8. Fry pies a few at a time until golden brown, turning once or twice while frying for even browning. Transfer pies to a platter or baking sheet lined with paper towels.
9. Add more oil to the skillet if needed between batches.

CRUSTLESS PUMPKIN PIE

By making pumpkin pie without a crust, it becomes a much lighter treat. Indulge by topping it with whipped cream flavored with fresh orange zest.

PREP TIME: 15 minutes
COOK TIME: 45 minutes
INACTIVE TIME: 90 minutes
TOTAL TIME: 2 hours & 30 minutes
YIELD: 8 servings

For the Pie
¾ cup granulated sugar
1 teaspoon pumpkin pie spice
½ teaspoon sea salt
2 large eggs
1 large egg yolk
15 ounces canned pureed pumpkin
(not pumpkin pie mix)
12 ounces evaporated milk

For the Orange Flavored Whipped Cream
Zest of one orange
(use the finest grater you have)
½ cup heavy whipping cream
1 tablespoon powdered sugar

1. Place the zest and whipping cream together in a mixing bowl. Stir together, then cover the bowl and let it sit in the refrigerator while the pie cooks and cools.
2. Preheat the oven to 400°F. Mix the sugar, pumpkin pie spice, and salt together in a small bowl. In a large mixing bowl, beat the eggs and yolk lightly. Add the sugar mixture to the beaten eggs and whisk together.
3. Whisk in the pumpkin. Gradually whisk in the evaporated milk. Pour into a 9 inch springform pan.
4. Bake for 15 minutes at 400°F, then reduce heat to 300°F and continue baking for 20 to 35 minutes, or until an instant read thermometer reads 175°F when inserted in the middle of the pie.
5. Remove the pie from the oven and let cool for 90 minutes. Place in the refrigerator to cool completely.
6. When you're ready to serve the pie, prepare the whipped cream. Strain the cream through a fine mesh strainer to remove the zest. Whip the cream with a whisk until soft peaks form, then add the powdered sugar and whip a little more. Garnish slices of pie with the whipped cream and serve immediately

THE PERFECT BROWNIES

These decadent brownies are baked in an 8 inch square pan to make them much thicker than the average brownie. One taste, and you'll understand why they are called "the perfect brownies."

PREP TIME: 10 minutes

COOK TIME: 40 minutes

TOTAL TIME: 50 minutes

YIELD: 9 very thick brownies

1 ¼ cups unsweetened cocoa powder, natural or Dutch process

¾ cup all purpose flour

16 tablespoons unsalted butter, melted

2 ¼ cups granulated sugar

½ teaspoon salt

1 teaspoon vanilla extract

4 eggs

1. Preheat the oven to 350°F and prepare an 8 inch square pan by lining it with parchment or foil.
2. In a small bowl, stir together the flour and the cocoa until well combined, then set aside.
3. In a large bowl, combine the melted butter, sugar, salt, and vanilla, and whisk together. Mixture will be grainy but uniform. Add the eggs one at a time, whisking thoroughly after each addition.
4. Set aside the whisk and add the flour/cocoa mixture to the large bowl. Stir with a large spoon or spatula until just combined, scraping down the sides of the bowl as needed.
5. Scrape the batter into the prepared pan and smooth out the top. Bake for 40 to 45 minutes, or until a toothpick inserted in the middle comes out with moist crumbs but no liquid batter attached. Set the pan on a rack to cool for 15 minutes, then use the pan liner to lift the brownies out. Set the brownies on a rack to finish cooling.

Butterscotch Pudding

Blending the pudding base and straining the liquid makes this butterscotch pudding silky smooth. Garnish with a dollop of freshly whipped cream for an extra treat.

PREP TIME: 15 minutes
COOK TIME: About 10 minutes
INACTIVE TIME: 4 hours
TOTAL TIME: 4 hours & 25 minutes
YIELD: 4 cups

½ cup firmly packed light brown sugar

1 tablespoon light corn syrup

2 tablespoons unsalted butter

2 cups plus 3 tablespoons whole milk

¼ cup cake flour

¼ teaspoon salt

5 egg yolks

½ vanilla bean, split lengthwise

½ cup heavy whipping cream

1 teaspoon rum

1. Bring brown sugar, corn syrup, butter, and 3 tablespoons milk to a boil over medium heat, stirring constantly to prevent scorching.
2. Reduce heat to low and simmer until slightly thickened, about 2 minutes. Remove from heat and cool for 5 minutes.
3. Put hot butterscotch syrup, remaining 2 cups milk, flour, salt, and egg yolks in a blender. Blend until smooth.
4. Pour mixture into a saucepan and add vanilla bean. Slowly bring to a boil over medium heat, stirring constantly. It will become very thick. Boil for 30 seconds.
5. Press pudding through a fine mesh sieve/strainer into a medium bowl.
6. Scrape the seeds from the vanilla bean and add seeds to the mixture. Discard outer bean.
7. Add cream and rum and whisk to combine.
8. Lay plastic wrap directly on top of pudding to prevent a skin from forming. Cool to room temperature then chill thoroughly, at least 4 hours.

Apple Dumplings

Allowing the dough for these apple dumplings to rest for one hour will make it easier to roll out into squares. Look for turbinado sugar in your grocery store; its large, shiny crystals make it ideal for decorating baked goods.

PREP TIME: 1 hour & 10 minutes
COOK TIME: 45 minutes
TOTAL TIME: 1 hour & 55 minutes
YIELD: 6 apple dumplings

For the Dough
3 cups all-purpose flour
2 teaspoons baking powder
1 teaspoon salt
1 cup shortening
¾ cup milk

For the Sauce
1 cup sugar
1 cup water
½ teaspoon cinnamon
Pinch of nutmeg
Pinch of salt
6 tablespoons unsalted butter

For the Dumplings
3 medium tart baking apples (such as Granny Smith or Honeycrisp apples)
½ cup sugar
¾ teaspoon cinnamon
Additional sugar or turbinado sugar for decoration

For the Dough
1. In a large bowl, whisk together the flour, baking powder, and salt. Cut in the shortening using a pastry blender until mixture resembles a coarse meal. Gradually add milk, stirring to make a soft dough. Shape dough into a rectangular disk, wrap with plastic wrap, and refrigerate for at least 1 hour.

For the Sauce
1. In a sauce pan, combine the sugar, water, cinnamon, nutmeg, salt, and butter. Bring to a boil, remove from heat, and set aside. Stir occasionally to melt butter if it has not melted.

For the Dumplings
1. Preheat oven to 375°F.
2. Lightly grease a 13 X 9 X 2-inch baking dish.
3. In a small bowl, combine ½ cup sugar and ¾ teaspoon cinnamon. Set aside.
4. Peel, core, and cut apples in half across the equator.
5. Divide dough into thirds. Roll each out on a lightly floured surface to 1/4-inch thickness and about a 7 by 14-inch rectangle. Cut in half to get 7-inch squares. Place an apple half on the center of each square. Sprinkle apple with cinnamon-sugar mixture. Paint the edges of the dough with a little water and wrap the dough around each apple half, pinching edges to seal. Place dumplings in the baking dish. Repeat with remaining dough and apples.
6. Pour the sauce over the apples. Sprinkle apples with sugar if desired. Bake for 45 to 50 minutes until golden. Serve warm with whipped cream or ice cream.

Oven Baked S'Mores

This recipe for oven baked s'mores will save the day when the weather is not cooperative for making s'mores outdoors. You can adjust the amount of ingredients to make as many s'mores as you want.

PREP TIME: 5 minutes
COOK TIME: 10 seconds
TOTAL TIME: 5 minutes & 10 seconds
YIELD: Will vary

Graham crackers
Large marshmallows
Chocolate bars

1. Move an oven rack to a position about 6 inches from the broiler element at the top of the oven.
2. Turn on the broiler (on high, if you have a choice between low and high).
3. Prepare a baking sheet by lining it with foil for easy cleanup.
4. Place as many graham crackers as you want on the baking sheet.
5. Break or cut the chocolate into large pieces that will fit on top of each graham cracker without hanging off.
6. Place the marshmallows on top of the chocolate, on a flat end not a round side (so they don't roll), enough to cover the graham cracker without hanging over the edge.
7. Slide the baking sheet onto the oven rack by the broiler. Close the oven door and count to 10. Remove the baking sheet. The tops of the marshmallows should be brown; if not, return to oven for a couple more seconds.
8. Top each s'more with another graham cracker and serve immediately, while warm.

Upside Down Peach Bread Pudding

If you like upside down cake, you'll love upside down bread pudding. Opt for fresh Georgia peaches, if they are available in your local grocery store.

PREP TIME: 25 minutes
COOK TIME: 45 minutes
TOTAL TIME: 1 hour & 10 minutes
YIELD: 6 to 8 servings

¼ cup unsalted butter, melted

¾ cup light brown sugar, divided

1 large peach, peeled, seed removed, cut into 16 equal slices

¼ cup granulated sugar

1 teaspoon cinnamon

1 pinch sea salt

2 cups whole milk

4 large eggs

8 ounces white bread, cut into 1-inch pieces (soft dinner rolls, or something similar, work well)

1. Preheat the oven to 400°F. Mix ½ cup of the brown sugar into the butter and spread the mixture evenly over the pan bottom.

2. Arrange the peach slices like flower petals on top of the butter/sugar mixture in the pan. If you have more slices than you need to fill the pan, you don't need to squeeze in the extra pieces.

3. In a large mixing bowl, combine the granulated sugar, ¼ cup brown sugar, cinnamon, and salt. Add the milk and stir to combine. Beat in the eggs. Drop in the bread pieces and massage with your hands to get them to absorb the most liquid.

4. Scoop the bread and custard mixture into the cake pan and pat it down evenly on top of the peaches. Place the pan in the oven and bake for 15 minutes.

5. After 15 minutes, reduce the heat to 300°F and continue baking for about 30 minutes, or until the temperature in the middle of the bread pudding reaches 175°F. Remove from the oven and let cool for 30 minutes.

6. Run a knife around the edge of the pan to loosen the pudding, then top the pan with a platter and invert. The bread pudding should drop neatly onto the platter. Continue cooling for another 30 minutes. Serve slightly warm, or place in the refrigerator and chill completely.

SELF-CRUST COCONUT PIE

PREP TIME: 10 minutes

COOK TIME: 35 minutes

INACTIVE TIME: 2 hours

TOTAL TIME: 2 hours & 45 minutse

YIELD: 12 servings

¼ cup self-rising flour

1 cup plus 2 tablespoons sugar

Pinch of salt

2 eggs, beaten, at room temperature

2 tablespoons unsalted butter, melted

½ teaspoon vanilla extract

4 ounces sweetened coconut (measured by weight, not volume)

1 cup whole milk, at room temperature

This clever coconut pie makes its own crust and is remarkably easy to assemble. Remember to let it cool completely before chilling in the refrigerator prior to serving.

1. Preheat the oven to 325°F.
2. In a medium bowl, whisk together flour, sugar, and salt. Add eggs to flour mixture and stir to combine. Add melted butter, vanilla, coconut, and milk. Stir to combine.
3. Pour mixture into an ungreased 9-inch pie plate. Bake for 30 to 35 minutes or until the top is lightly browned. Remove pie from the oven and cool completely on a wire rack. Refrigerate pie for at least 2 hours before serving.

SPICED PECANS

These spiced pecans are especially good when made with farm-fresh mammoth pecans. Double the recipe to make enough to share with family and friends.

PREP TIME: 10 minutes

COOK TIME: 20 minutes

TOTAL TIME: 30 minutes

YIELD: 4 cups

2 cups sugar

1 tablespoon ground cinnamon

¼ teaspoon cream of tartar

½ cup hot water

1 tablespoon vanilla extract

1 pound pecan halves

1. Lay 3 strips of wax paper (about 2 feet long) on a counter or work surface.

2. Combine sugar, cinnamon, cream of tartar, and water in a 2 ½ to 3 quart pot (do not use non-stick). Bring to a boil and cook to a semi-hard ball stage when tested in cold water. Remove from heat and add the vanilla and pecans. Stir to coat all the pecans with the syrup. When syrup begins to sugar, transfer the pecans to waxed paper. Separate the pecans and allow to dry. Store in an airtight container.

BOURBON HONEY MILK

Flavorful honey and smoky bourbon are a delicious complement to warm milk. Try this soothing concoction with a varietal honey of Southern origin, such as orange blossom, tupelo, or sourwood.

PREP TIME: 1 minutes
COOK TIME: 5 minutes
TOTAL TIME: 6 minutes
YIELD: 2 servings

2 cups milk
2 teaspoons bourbon
2 teaspoons honey

1. Combine the milk, bourbon, and honey in a small saucepan. Warm the mixture gently over low to medium heat, whisking to combine, until the honey is completely dissolved.
2. Serve warm, or chill until cold.

Contributors

MATTIE ADAMS is a retired educator who enjoys good food, gardening, and spending time with her grandchildren. She is also the author's mother, and her Southern cooking was one of the original inspirations for this cookbook.

COLIN BLAKE runs the educational endeavors of Moonshine University, an educational distillery in downtown Louisville, KY. He is the Director of Spirits Education and the head of the Stave & Thief Society, a bourbon certification program.

DILEK CANER is one of the 46 Masters of Wine in the US, and the only Master of Wine residing in Texas. She also holds the title of Advanced Sommelier, given by the Court of Master Sommeliers. Her wine school, Dallas Wine Education Center, provides Wine & Spirit Education Trust (WSET) courses to wine industry members and individuals with a deep interest in wine in Texas.

MIKE DELANCETT is the co-head brewer (along with Matt Gemmell) for Hourglass Brewing in Longwood, Florida. He cut his teeth as a volunteer and homebrewer and has worked his way up to his current position. He has a deep love and appreciation for beer, its breadth of style, its depth of history, and the wild west mentality of craft beer with infinite opportunities to explore and create.

RENEE DOBBS is a self-proclaimed Domestic Goddess who loves to eat, drink, and dig in the dirt. She is enjoying life in the South and experiencing flavors from around the world. Cooking will always be one of her passions along with gardening and spoiling her whippets. You can read more of her food adventures on Magnolia Days, a blog she created and filled with recipes until retiring from it in 2017.

Acknowledgments

I would like to express profound gratitude to my team of readers, who gave valuable feedback during the creation of this cookbook. Thank you to Jason Moseman, Mattie Adams, John Adams, Dawn DeBlois, Steve DeBlois, Susan Moseman, and Alice Moskola.

ABOUT THE AUTHOR

KATIE MOSEMAN is a freelance writer, photographer, and recipe developer whose work can be found on her blogs, Recipe for Perfection and Magnolia Days, as well as in numerous national publications. She lives in Florida with her family.

RECIPE INDEX

CPSIA information can be obtained
at www.ICGtesting.com
Printed in the USA
LVHW061125260219
608781LV00018B/222/P

David Sprigings MA, MRCP

Clinical Lecturer and Honorary Senior Registrar,
John Radcliffe Hospital, Oxford

John Chambers MA, MD, MRCP

Senior Lecturer and Honorary Consultant,
UMDS (Guy's Hospital), London

Oxford

Blackwell Scientific Publications

London Edinburgh Boston

Melbourne Paris Berlin Vienna

Acute Medicine

A practical guide to the
management of medical emergencies

Acute Medicine

A practical guide to the
management of medical emergencies

© 1990 by
Blackwell Scientific Publications
Editorial Offices:
Osney Mead, Oxford OX2 0EL
25 John Street, London WC1N 2BL
23 Ainslie Place, Edinburgh EH3 6AJ
238 Main Street, Cambridge
  Massachusetts 02142, USA
54 University Street, Carlton
  Victoria 3053, Australia

Other Editorial Offices:
Librairie Arnette SA
2, rue Casimir-Delavigne
75006 Paris
France

Blackwell Wissenschafts-Verlag
Meinekestrasse 4
D-1000 Berlin 15
Germany

Blackwell MZV
Feldgasse 13
A-1238 Wien
Austria

First published 1990
Reprinted 1991, 1992, 1993

Set by Times Graphics,
  Singapore
Printed and bound in Great
Britain by William Clowes Ltd.,
  Beccles

DISTRIBUTORS

Marston Book Services Ltd
PO Box 87
Oxford OX2 0DT
(*Orders:* Tel: 0865 791155
         Fax: 0865 791927
         Telex: 837515)

USA
Blackwell Scientific Publications, Inc
238, Main Street
Cambridge, MA 02142
(*Orders:* Tel: 800 759-6102
         617 876-7000)
Canada
Times Mirror Professional
  Publishing, Ltd
130 Flaska Drive
Markham, Ontario L6G 1B8
(*Orders:* Tel: 800 268-4178
         416 470-6739)
Australia
Blackwell Scientific Publications
  Pty Ltd
54 University Street
Carlton, Victoria 3053
(*Orders:* Tel: 03 347-5552)

British Library
Cataloguing in Publication Data

Sprigings, David
  Acute Medicine.
  A practical guide to
  the management of
  medical emergencies
  1. Medicine. Emergency
  treatment
  I. Title II. Chambers, John
  616'.025

ISBN 0–632–02169–1

Contents

Contents

Acknowledgements

We are grateful to Dr Vicky Reeders of Blackwell Scientific
Publications who encouraged us to write this book.

We also wish to thank the following colleagues for expert
criticism of sections of the manuscript: C Bass, Professor
A J Bellingham, D A Chamberlain, E A Fagan, A Forbes,
W N Gardner, J Henry, Professor M C Lessof, Professor
A A McGregor, W J Marshall, F C Martin, B A Millward, A Pagliuca,
Professor D J Parkes, V Parsons, K N Robinson, M M Sharr,
G E Sowton, A D Timmis, D E Ward, J S Weinberg, D Westaby.

Section 1
Common Presentations

1 Cardiac Arrest

- **Sudden loss of consciousness with absent femoral or carotid pulses.**
- The commonest cause is **ventricular fibrillation (VF)**.

Priorities

If you witness the onset of ventricular fibrillation:
1 Thump the sternum firmly.
2 If this fails, **immediately apply DC countershock (200 J)** before starting ventilation and chest massage.
In other patients:
1 **Quickly check the diagnosis** — shake and call to the patient whilst feeling for the femoral or carotid pulses — **and summon help.**
2 **Start ventilation and chest massage (Table 1.1).**
3 **As soon as the defibrillator arrives, apply a 200 J countershock** (even if ECG monitoring is not yet available).
4 **Attach an ECG monitor.**
5 **Establish venous access** via an antecubital fossa or central vein.

Further management

This depends on the cardiac rhythm:
1 Ventricular fibrillation/ventricular tachycardia (VT) with no pulse (Tables 1.2 and 1.3)
2 Asystole (Table 1.4).
3 Bradycardia (Table 1.5).
4 Electromechanical dissociation: organized cardiac rhythm, but no femoral pulse (Table 1.6).

■ **Table 1.1.** Priority management of cardiac arrest

1 Airway	• Extend the neck, lift the chin and clear the mouth (by finger and suction)
	• Insert an oropharyngeal airway
	• Endotracheal (ET) intubation only if experienced
2 Breathing	• Ventilate with oxygen (flow 10 l/min) using a mask and Ambubag, one ventilation for every five compressions if airway, 12–15/min if ET tube
3 Circulation	• Sternal compression by 5 cm about 80/min
4 Countershock	• 200 J as soon as defibrillator arrives
5 Drugs	• Prepare adrenaline, atropine, lignocaine and calcium; give according to cardiac rhythm (Tables 1.2–1.6)

■ **Table 1.2.** Ventricular fibrillation/ventricular tachycardia with no pulse

1 **200 J shock**

2 **200 J shock**

3 **Maximal (320–400 J) shock**

4 **Adrenaline** 1 mg i.v. (10 ml of one in 10 000 solution/1 ml of one in 1000 solution) (repeat every 5 min until a spontaneous output is restored to maintain aortic diastolic pressure)

5 **Maximal shock**

6 **Lignocaine** 100 mg (1 mg/kg) (10 ml of 1% solution) as an i.v. bolus
Continue chest massage for 1–2 min to allow for the prolonged circulation time then:

7 **Maximal shock**

8 **Sodium bicarbonate** 50 mmol (50 ml of 8.4% solution) i.v. over 10 min

9 **Lignocaine** 50 mg (0.5 mg/kg) (5 ml of 1% solution) as an i.v. bolus

10 **Maximal shock**

11 **If ventricular fibrillation still persists, try other antiarrhythmics (Table 1.3):** repeat maximal shock after each dose

■ **Table 1.3.** Alternative drug therapy of ventricular fibrillation/ventricular tachycardia (in conjunction with DC countershock)

- **Procainamide:** 100 mg by slow i.v. injection every 5 min up to a total dose of 1 g
- **Amiodarone:** 150–300 mg i.v. over 1–2 min
- **Bretylium:** 5 mg/kg i.v. bolus, followed by 10 mg/kg i.v. after 5 min if VF persists

■ **Table 1.4.** Asystole

1 Give **adrenaline 1 mg i.v.** (10 ml of one in 10 000 solution/1 ml of one in 1000 solution) followed by **atropine 1 mg i.v.** Give further doses at 5-min intervals until a spontaneous output is restored (or up to a total dose of 4 mg atropine)

2 Give **sodium bicarbonate 50 mmol (50 ml of 8.4% solution) i.v.** over **10 min**

3 Pacing is rarely effective in the treatment of asystole except when due to isolated conducting system disease. However, if an **external cardiac pacing system** is available, this should be tried

4 If a spontaneous output is restored, a **transvenous pacing wire** should be inserted

■ **Table 1.5.** Bradycardia

1 Give **atropine 1 mg i.v.,** with further doses at 5-min intervals up to a total dose of 4 mg if bradycardia persists

2 Insert a **transvenous pacing wire** as soon as possible. To maintain a satisfactory rate whilst the patient is being transferred to an area with screening facilities, either use an **external cardiac pacing system,** or:

3 Start an **isoprenaline i.v. infusion (2–20 µg/min)**
- Add isoprenaline 1 mg to a 100 ml bag/5 mg to a 500 ml bag of dextrose 5% or saline to give a concentration of 10 µg/ml
- Start the infusion at 1 ml/min and adjust it as required to maintain a ventricular rate over 60/min

■ **Table 1.6.** Electromechanical dissociation

1 Give **adrenaline 1 mg i.v.** (10 ml of one in 10 000 solution/1 ml of one in 1000 solution). This should be repeated every 5 min until a spontaneous output is restored

2 Give **calcium chloride 10 ml of 10% solution i.v. over 5 min**

3 Give **sodium bicarbonate 50 mmol (50 ml of 8.4% solution) i.v. over 10 min**

4 **Consider the potentially treatable causes**
- Hypovolaemia from acute massive haemorrhage
- Tension pneumothorax (p. 144)
- Cardiac tamponade (p. 118)
- Severe hypoxia
- Severe acidosis

NB

• Calcium and bicarbonate must not be given together through the same line

• The place of calcium in resuscitation is controversial. Calcium should unquestionably be given if arrest occurs in a patient with hypocalcaemia, hyperkalaemia or calcium antagonist poisoning

Problems

Cardiac arrest for longer than 5 minutes

1 **Give sodium bicarbonate 50 mmol (50 ml of 8.4% solution) by i.v. infusion over 10 minutes (if not already given).** Further doses should ideally be guided by measurement of arterial pH (aiming to keep it between 7.3 and 7.5) but if this is not possible, give 25–50 ml every 10 minutes while resuscitation continues.

2 **Take arterial blood for gases, pH and potassium.**

3 **If the patient is hypoxic ($Pa o_2$ <10 kPa), check that the endotracheal tube is in the trachea.** Other causes of hypoxia are given in Table 1.7.

■ **Table 1.7.** Causes of hypoxia in the patient ventilated via an endotracheal tube

- Endotracheal tube in oesophagus
- Endotracheal tube in right main bronchus (giving absence of breath sounds over the left lung)
- Pulmonary oedema, pneumonia or inhalation of vomit
- Massive pulmonary embolism
- Pneumothorax

4 If plasma potassium is high (>6 mmol/l): Table 1.8.

If plasma potassium is low (<3.5 mmol/l): give potassium chloride 20 mmol (1.5 g) in 100 ml of dextrose 5% via a central vein, over 15 minutes.

■ **Table 1.8.** Cardiac arrest with hyperkalaemia (plasma potassium >6 mmol/l)

1 **Give 10 ml of calcium chloride 10% i.v. over 5 min.** This can be repeated every 5 min up to a total dose of 40 ml
2 **Correct metabolic acidosis with sodium bicarbonate 50 mmol (50 ml of 8.4% solution) over 10 min**
3 **Give 25 g of dextrose (50 ml of dextrose 50%) with 10 units of soluble insulin i.v. over 15–30 min.** This will usually reduce plasma potassium for several hours

When to stop resuscitation

- There is no universally applicable rule.
- In most cases resuscitation should be stopped after 30 minutes if there is **refractory asystole or electromechanical dissociation.** Other rhythms may imply a potentially salvageable heart.
- Where cardiac arrest is due to **hypothermia** (p. 222) or **poisoning,** patients have survived neurologically intact after even longer resuscitation attempts.

- Resuscitation should not be stopped because the pupils are dilated: this may be due to atropine or adrenaline.
- In patients without myocardial disease, do not stop resuscitation unless the arterial pH and potassium are normal, and core temperature is >36°C.

What to do after successful resuscitation
(Table 1.9)

1 Decide why the arrest occurred. **Correct high or low plasma potassium, hypoxia and acidosis.** Consider prophylactic antiarrhythmic therapy in patients in whom arrest was due to VF/VT.

2 Transfer the patient to a Coronary Care or Intensive Care Unit for ECG monitoring.

3 Treat hypotension and pulmonary oedema (Chapters 3 and 16).

4 Mechanical ventilation should be continued for:
- coma;
- severe pulmonary oedema;
- Pao$_2$ < 9 kPa (on 60% oxygen) or Paco$_2$ > 6.5 kPa.

5 Intravenous lines inserted without sterile technique during the resuscitation should be changed.

■ **Table 1.9. Urgent investigation after successful resuscitation**

- **ECG** (?acute myocardial infarction)
- **Chest X-ray** (?pulmonary oedema, pneumothorax, rib fracture)
- **Arterial gases and pH**
- **Plasma potassium**
- **Blood glucose** (by stick test)

2   Cardiac Arrhythmias

The initial classification of arrhythmias is based on the
ventricular rate:

1 Tachycardia (ventricular rate >120/min); Fig. 2.1.
2 Bradycardia (ventricular rate <50/min); Table 2.2 (p. 14).
3 Rhythm looks abnormal, but the ventricular rate is 50–120/min;
 Table 2.3 (p. 16).

Regular broad complex tachycardia — VT or SVT? (Figs 2.2 and 2.3)

• Do not give verapamil as this may cause fatal hypotension in
patients with VT. If there is doubt about the diagnosis, use
synchronized DC countershock.

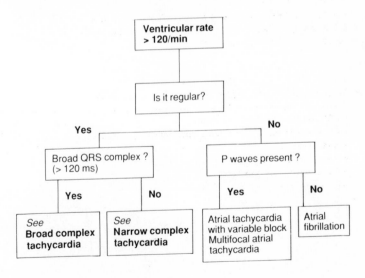

Fig. 2.1. Classification of tachycardia.

9

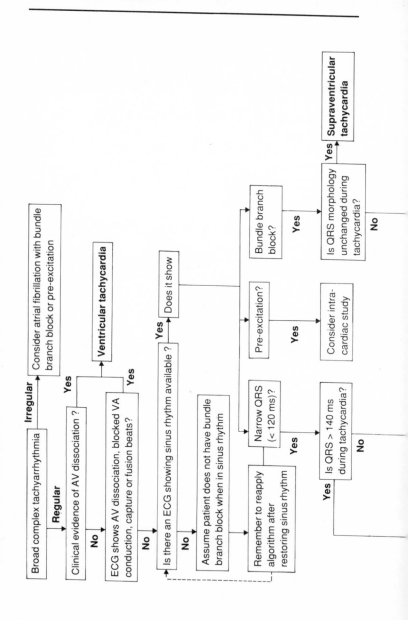

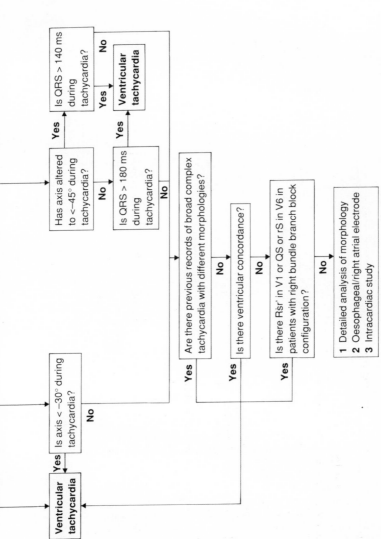

Fig. 2.2. Algorithm for the diagnosis of a broad complex tachycardia. Reproduced from Dancy M, Ward D. *Br Med J* 1985; **291**: 1036–8.

a

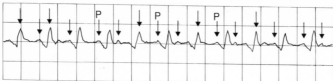

b

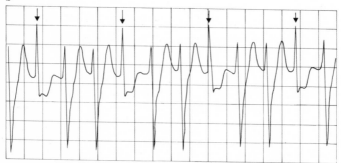

c Rsr in VT

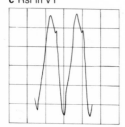

d rsR in SVT

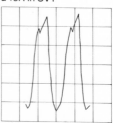

Fig. 2.3. Diagnosis of ventricular tachycardia. VT is confirmed by:
• AV dissociation (P waves occurring regularly at a different rate to QRS complexes) (**a**).
• capture or fusion beats (**b**).
  VT is supported by:
• QRS duration >140 ms (3.5 small squares).
• left axis deviation further than − 30° (QRS in lead II predominantly negative).
• 'ventricular concordance' — QRS complex looks similiar in all chest leads.
• Rsr' in V1 (compared with rsR in SVT) (**c, d**).

- If the patient has myocardial disease, e.g. myocardial infarction, a regular broad complex tachycardia is almost invariably VT.
- A normal blood pressure does not exclude VT.

Regular narrow complex tachycardia (Table 2.1, Fig. 2.4)

- Atrial activity is the key to diagnosis. If you cannot see P or flutter waves, try carotid sinus massage (Table 2.8, p. 20). Look at the shape of the atrial wave and its relationship to the QRS complex.
- If the ventricular rate is 150/min, suspect atrial flutter with 2 : 1 block.

■ **Table 2.1.** Diagnosis of narrow complex tachycardia

	QRS rate (/min)	Atrial rate	Regular QRS?	Atrial activity	Effect of vagotonic manoeuvres
Sinus tachycardia	100–200	100–200	Yes	P wave precedes QRS	+
Atrial fibrillation	< 200		No	Chaotic (f waves)	+
Atrial flutter	75–175	250–350	Yes	'Saw tooth' in the inferior leads/V1	+
SVT	150–250	150–250	Yes	Usually not seen or inverted P after QRS	+ +
Atrial tachycardia	100–200	120–250	Yes	Abnormal shaped P wave May outnumber QRS	+ +
MAT	100–130	100–130	No	Variable P wave morphology and PP interval	+ / −
Junctional tachycardia	70–130	70–130	Yes	Preceded or followed by an inverted P wave	+ / −

+, Slowing of ventricular rate; + +, may terminate tachycardia; + / −, no effect or slight slowing; MAT, multifocal atrial tachycardia; SVT, re-entrant tachycardia involving the AV node or an accessory pathway.

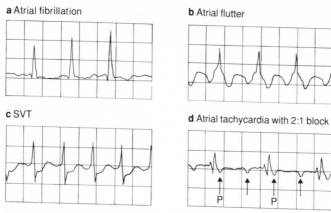

a Atrial fibrillation   **b** Atrial flutter

c SVT   **d** Atrial tachycardia with 2:1 block

Fig. 2.4. Examples of narrow complex tachycardia (see Table 2.1).

• If the ventricular rate is >200/min, suspect an accessory pathway (e.g. Wolff–Parkinson–White syndrome) or AV nodal re-entrant tachycardia.

■ **Table 2.2.** Diagnosis of bradycardia and atrioventricular block

Diagnosis	ECG features
Sinus bradycardia	Constant PR interval <200 ms
Junctional bradycardia	P wave absent or position constant either after, immediately before or hidden in the QRS complex
First degree AV block	Constant PR interval >200 ms
Second degree AV block	
Mobitz type I (Wenckebach)	Progressively lengthening PR interval followed by dropped beat
Mobitz type II	Constant PR interval with dropped beats
Third degree AV block (complete heart block)	Relationship of P wave to QRS varies randomly PP and RR intervals constant but different

Bradycardia and atrioventricular block

• Record a long rhythm strip. Look at the PR interval and the relationship between the P wave and QRS complex (Table 2.2, Fig. 2.5).

• A non-conducted atrial extrasystole is often misdiagnosed as second degree AV block (Fig. 2.6).

• A regular ventricular rate <50/min in a patient with atrial fibrillation indicates complete heart block (not 'slow AF'): always consider digoxin toxicity (p. 26).

a Second degree AV block (Wenckebach)

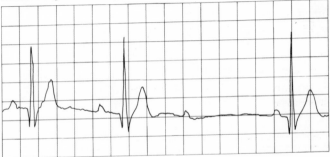

b Second degree AV block (Mobitz II)

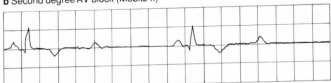

c Third degree AV block (complete heart block)

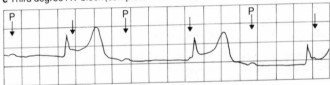

Fig. 2.5. Examples of bradycardia and AV block (see Table 2.2).

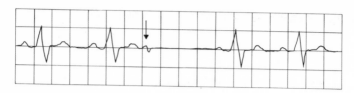

Fig. 2.6. Non-conducted atrial extrasystole.

Rhythm abnormal — ventricular rate 50–120/min

The possible causes are given in Table 2.3.

■ **Table 2.3.** Abnormal rhythms with ventricular rate 50–120 /min

Diagnosis	ECG features
Sinus arrhythmia	Normal P waves (upright in lead II) PP interval varies cyclically Constant PR interval
Multifocal atrial tachycardia	Variable P wave morphology Totally irregular PP interval Most P waves conducted
Atrial tachycardia with block	Abnormal P waves (inverted in lead II)
Atrial fibrillation	No P waves Baseline shows fibrillation waves Irregular RR interval
Atrial flutter with block	'Saw tooth' flutter waves in the inferior leads/V1
Junctional tachycardia	Abnormal P waves (inverted in lead II)
Accelerated idioventricular rhythm	P waves not seen Broad QRS complex Regular RR interval
Intermittent second degree AV block	Normal P wave not followed by QRS

Part II: Management

Arrhythmias must be corrected urgently if causing severe haemodynamic compromise:

- systolic BP <90 mmHg with cold extremities;
- reduced conscious level;
- pulmonary oedema;
- angina at rest.

TACHYARRHYTHMIAS

Ventricular tachycardia

Conscious but severe haemodynamic compromise
Urgent synchronized DC countershock (see p. 268).

Systolic BP > 90 mmHg
1 Record a 12 lead ECG.
2 Give **lignocaine 100 mg (5 ml of 2% solution) i.v. over 30 seconds.**
3 If this fails, give **procainamide 200 mg over 1 minute.**
4 If this also fails, use **synchronized DC countershock.** This is preferable to giving further antiarrhythmics.

Temporary pacing wire in place
You may be able to convert VT by **overdrive pacing:**
1 Pace at up to 50/min faster than the rate of the VT in demand mode for about 10 seconds.
2 Either switch off the box or gradually reduce the pacing rate to 100/min.

After correction of VT
1 **Clinical assessment:** see p. 28 and p. 110 for further management of **hypotension** and **pulmonary oedema.**
2 **Establish the cause** from the history and investigation (Table 2.4).

■ **Table 2.4.** Urgent investigation after correction of VT

- **ECG** — ?myocardial infarction. ?long QT interval
- **Chest X-ray** — ?pulmonary oedema, ?cardiomegaly
- **Plasma potassium**
- Consider **plasma magnesium** (if taking diuretics)
- **Cardiac enzymes** (for later analysis)
- **Arterial blood gases** (if there is pulmonary oedema or reduced conscious level)

3 Plasma potassium should be kept in the range 4–5 mmol/l.

4 Correct hypoxia (Pa_{O_2} should be kept >8kPa).

5 Correct persistent severe acidosis: if pH <7.2 after restoration of spontaneous output, give bicarbonate 50 mmol i.v. over 10 min.

6 Insert a temporary pacing wire if VT was associated with a slow ventricular rate due to sinus bradycardia or AV block, and pace at 90–110/min.

7 Maintenance antiarrhythmic therapy will usually be indicated. The following are guidelines:

- **VT in the first 24–48 hours after acute myocardial infarction:** give lignocaine by i.v. infusion for 12–24 hours (Table 2.5). If VT

■ **Table 2.5.** Lignocaine regimen

1 Loading dose	• 100 mg (5 ml of 2% solution) i.v. over 30 s
2 Maintenance dose	• 4 mg/min for 30 min • 2 mg/min for 2 hours • 1 mg/min for 12–24 hours
3 If VT recurs	• Give a further bolus of 50 mg and increase the infusion rate by 1–2 mg/min

4 If VT recurs despite infusion at maximum dose	• Recheck plasma potassium
	• Options are:
	  to change to procainamide
	  to add amiodarone
	• If these fail, ask for cardiological advice

5 Toxic effects	• Confusion, seizures

■ **Table 2.6.** Amiodarone regimen

• **Loading dose:** 300 mg (5 mg/kg) in dextrose 5% by i.v. infusion over 30 min (preferably via a central vein to avoid thrombophlebitis), followed by 600–1200 mg over 24 hours
• **Start oral therapy at the same time:** initially 200 mg 8-hourly

does not recur during this period, further antiarrhythmic therapy is not required;
• **VT late after myocardial infarction** (usually taken arbitrarily as > 2 days) **or due to other ventricular muscle disease:** give lignocaine by infusion and start oral therapy;
  a amiodarone if left ventricular function is poor (Table 2.6);
  b either a Class 1 drug (e.g. mexiletine) or sotalol if left ventricular function is fair.

Atrial fibrillation or flutter

Conscious but severe haemodynamic compromise
• **Urgent DC countershock** (see p. 268); *or*
• **Rapid digitalization** (Table 2.7) depending on the clinical state.

■ **Table 2.7.** Digoxin regimen

Rapid digitalization (systolic **BP** <90 mmHg)	• **Loading:** give 0.75–1.0 mg digoxin in 50 ml of dextrose 5% or normal saline i.v. over 2 hours • **Maintenance:** see below
Standard digitilization	• **Loading:** give 0.5 mg 12-hourly orally for 2 doses, followed by 0.25 mg 12-hourly for 2 days • **Maintenance:** 0.0625–0.25 mg/day. Take into account age, renal function and drug interactions
Therapeutic range	• 0.8–2.0 ng/ml (1.0–2.6 nmol/l) (blood taken >6 hours after last dose)
Important drug interactions	• Quinidine, quinine, amiodarone and verapamil increase plasma level: halve dose of digoxin

Systolic BP >90 mmHg

To control the ventricular rate, options are:

- oral digitalization (Table 2.7); *or*
- verapamil or a beta-blocker if left ventricular function is good.

To restore sinus rhythm, options are:

- flecainide 2 mg/kg i.v. over 10 minutes; *or*
- elective DC countershock.

Supraventricular tachycardia (AV nodal re-entrant tachycardia)

Conscious but severe haemodynamic compromise

- Treat with urgent synchronized DC countershock.
- If the QRS complexes are broad, have you misdiagnosed VT?
- Significant haemodynamic compromise can occur in the absence of structural heart disease, but arrange echocardiography to look for ventricular or valvular disease.

Systolic BP >90 mmHg

- Vagotonic manoeuvres may help the differentiation of tachycardias and may terminate them (Table 2.1).
- Try carotid sinus massage (Table 2.8), a Valsalva manoeuvre or sucking ice (not eyeball pressure which carries the risk of retinal detachment).

■ **Table 2.8.** Carotid sinus massage for SVT

---

1 Connect to an ECG monitor (preferably with a printer)

2 Check that there is no evidence of carotid artery disease (previous stroke, TIA or carotid bruit)

3 The carotid sinus lies at the level of the upper border of the thyroid cartilage just below the angle of the jaw

4 Massage first one side and then the other for up to 15 s, pressing over the artery with your thumb or index and middle fingers

5 Stop massage if sinus rhythm supervenes or there is a ventricular pause >2 s

- If the patient is well, no treatment need necessarily be given and the tachycardia can be allowed to resolve spontaneously.
- Treatment options are given in Fig. 2.7. Doses are given in Table 2.9.

Atrial tachycardia or junctional tachycardia

1 Both may occur as a result of digoxin toxicity.

2 Check the plasma potassium and maintain at 4.0–5.0 mmol/l. Withdraw digoxin.

3 If the arrythmia does not resolve spontaneously and digoxin toxicity is likely, treatment is with phenytoin (5 mg/kg i.v. over 5 minutes) or beta-blockers (Table 2.9).

4 If the patient is not taking digoxin, and the tachycardia does not resolve spontaneously, use synchronized DC countershock, digoxin or lignocaine.

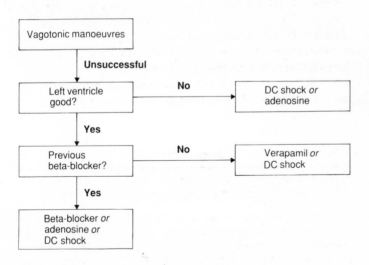

Fig. 2.7. Treatment of supraventricular tachycardia (AV nodal re-entrant tachycardia).

■ **Table 2.9.** Drug doses in supraventricular tachycardia

Verapamil	• 5 mg i.v. over 20 s repeated if necessary after 5 min • Maximum total dose 20 mg (or 10 mg in patients with ischaemic heart disease or aged >60 years)
Adenosine	• 0.05 mg/kg by i.v. bolus • If this is unsuccessful, give further boluses every 2 min at the following doses: 0.1 mg/kg, 0.15 mg/kg, 0.2 mg/kg, 0.25 mg/kg
Beta-blockers	• Atenolol 5 mg i.v. • Sotalol 20–60 mg i.v. • Propranolol 1 mg i.v.

Multifocal atrial tachycardia

• Most commonly occurs in elderly patients with chronic airflow limitation.

• Treatment is directed at the underlying disease and correction of hypoxia. Consider verapamil if the ventricular rate is consistently >110/min. DC cardioversion is ineffective.

BRADYARRHYTHMIAS

Sinus or nodal bradycardia

Symptomatic or rate <40/minute

1 Give atropine 0.6–1 mg i.v. with further doses at 5-minute intervals up to a total dose of 4 mg if the heart rate remains below 60/min.

2 Reverse beta-blockade (see Appendix 2.1).

3 If bradycardia is unresponsive or recurs, put in a temporary pacing wire. If necessary, whilst transferring the patient to the screening room:

• either start an isoprenaline infusion (Table 2.10); *or*

• use an external cardiac pacing system.

■ Table 2.10. Isoprenaline infusion for bradyarrhythmias

1 Add 1 mg to a 100 ml bag or 5 mg to a 500 ml bag of dextrose 5% or saline (10 µg/ml)
2 Start the infusion at 1 ml/min
3 Adjust the infusion to keep the heart rate over 50/min

First degree atrioventricular block (PR interval >200 ms)

• As an isolated abnormality, no treatment is required.

Second and third degree atrioventricular block

Related to acute MI
• **Inferior MI:** pacing is needed only if the patient is hypotensive or has signs of low cardiac output (cool extremities, low urine output or rising blood urea, drowsy).
• **Anterior MI:** pacing always indicated.

Second degree block unrelated to MI
1 Exclude digoxin toxicity (Appendix 2.2) or beta-blockade.
2 If the patient has experienced syncope or presyncope, put in a temporary pacing wire.
3 If asymptomatic, record a 24-hour ECG and discuss with a cardiologist whether permanent pacing is indicated.

Third degree AV block unrelated to MI
• Even in asymptomatic patients, this carries the risk of sudden death.
• Put in a temporary pacing wire and arrange for a permanent system to be implanted.

Problems

Ventricular extrasystoles — to treat or not to treat?

Early after acute MI
• There is conflicting evidence that suppression of ventricular extrasystoles will prevent VF.
• Maintain plasma potassium >4.0 mmol/l, relieve pain and anxiety.
• Give lignocaine (Table 2.5) only if extrasystoles are occurring so frequently as to cause hypotension.

Other situations
• The significance of ventricular extrasystoles is largely related to the underlying cardiac disease. Drug therapy to suppress them may in fact worsen prognosis.

Suspected pacemaker malfunction

1 Check the details of the pacemaker: is it a standard VVI system (ventricular pacing and sensing, inhibited in response to a sensed beat)?
2 Obtain a 12-lead ECG, a long rhythm strip (with and without a magnet over the pulse generator (Table 2.11) and a penetrated chest X-ray (for the position of the lead).
3 If these show no abnormality:
  • Record a 24-hour ECG.
  • Consider other causes of syncope or presyncope (see Table 7.1, p. 51).

■ **Table 2.11.** Diagnosis of pacemaker malfunction

1 No spikes*	• Normal sensing
	• Generator malfunction
	• Spike 'buried' in QRS
	• Electromagnetic interference
2 Spikes without ventricular capture (failure to capture)	• High threshold
	a Malposition of lead
	b Fibrosis
	c Cardiac perforation
	• Generator malfunction
	• Lead not properly connected to generator
	• Spike in ventricular refractory period
3 Spikes without sensing (failure to sense)	• Malposition of lead
	• Low intrinsic QRS current (i.e. not at sensing threshold)

* Placing a magnet over the pulse generator converts nearly all units to fixed rate pacing.

Appendices

2.1. Reversal of beta-blockade

Beta-blockade must be reversed if contributing to pulmonary oedema, hypotension or low cardiac output:

• give atropine and isoprenaline (Table 2.10, p. 23) until the heart rate is over 60/min;

• if the blood pressure remains low, start a dobutamine infusion at 10 μg/kg per min, increasing the dose as required;

• glucagon can be combined with isoprenaline or dobutamine.

Give an i.v. bolus of 50 μg/kg followed by an infusion of 1–5 mg/hour.

2.2. Digoxin toxicity and poisoning

Digoxin toxicity
- A clinical diagnosis, supported by measurement of plasma digoxin level. Hypokalaemia (<3.5 mmol/l) predisposes to toxic effects.
- Common symptoms: anorexia, nausea, vomiting, diarrhoea, confusional state (in the elderly).
- Common arrhythmias: atrial tachycardia with AV block, junctional tachycardia, multiform ventricular extrasystoles.
- Toxicity is likely if plasma digoxin level is >3.0 ng/ml (>3.8 nmol/l).

Management
1 Stop digoxin.
2 Check plasma potassium and give potassium i.v. to keep it in the range 4.5–5 mmol/l.
3 Treat arrhythmias:
  - **atrial tachycardia and junctional tachycardia:** p. 21;
  - **ventricular tachycardia:** lignocaine (procainamide or phenytoin if lignocaine fails);
  - **second or third degree AV block:** atropine and temporary pacing (avoid isoprenaline because of the risk of provoking ventricular arrhythmias).

NB In digoxin toxicity, **DC countershock** can result in ventricular arrhythmias. Start with a 10 J shock.

Poisoning with digoxin

Management
1 Gastric lavage followed by activated charcoal (p. 75).
2 Check plasma potassium (hyperkalaemia indicates severe toxicity and should be treated with dextrose and insulin (p. 188) if >6 mmol/l).

3 Admit to the Coronary Care Unit for ECG monitoring.

4 Treat arrhythmias as above.

5 Give digoxin antibody fragments (Table 2.12) if:

- plasma potassium is >5 mmol/l or rising;
- ventricular arrhythmias or complete heart block occur.

6 Check plasma potassium hourly as hypokalaemia often occurs following antibody treatment.

■ **Table 2.12.** Calculation of the dose* of digoxin antibody fragments

Digoxin load (mg)	= dose ingested (mg) × 80% (to take account of incomplete absorption)
Dose of digoxin antibody fragments (mg)	= 60 × digoxin load, rounded up to the nearest 40 mg

* **If the dose ingested is not known:** give 480 mg (six vials of Digitalis Antidote BM, 12 vials of Digibind).

3   Hypotension

Hypotension (Table 3.1) must be corrected immediately if:
- systolic BP is <75 mmHg; *or*
- there are associated signs of low cardiac output: oliguria; confusion or drowsiness; cold skin.

■ **Table 3.1. Causes of hypotension**

1 Cardiac pump failure	• Arrhythmia
	• Acute myocardial infarction
	• Acute valvular lesion
	• Massive pulmonary embolism
	• Tamponade
	• Tension pneumothorax
2 Hypovolaemia	• Haemorrhage
	• Urinary loss
	• Gastrointestinal fluid loss
	• Cutaneous loss (e.g. burns)
	• Third-space sequestration (e.g. pancreatitis)
3 Vasodilatation	• Sepsis
	• Drugs/poisoning
	• Anaphylaxis
	• Acute adrenal insufficiency

Priorities

1 Lie the patient flat. Elevate the foot of the bed if hypovolaemia or vasodilatation are likely.

2 Give oxygen.

3 Connect to an ECG monitor: correct cardiac arrhythmias.

4 Put in a venous cannula.

Initial management is given in Fig. 3.1. Investigations needed urgently are given in Table 3.2.

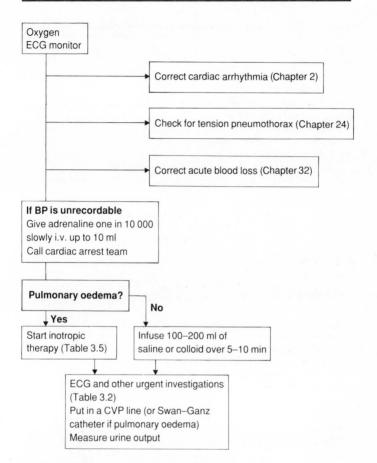

Fig. 3.1. Priority management of hypotension.

■ **Table 3.2. Urgent investigation in unexplained hypotension**

- **ECG**
- **Chest X-ray**
- **Urea, sodium and potassium**
- **Full blood count**
- **Blood glucose** by stick test
- **Arterial blood gases and pH**
- **Group and save** (cross-match if haemorrhage suspected)
- **Culture blood and urine** if suspected sepsis
- **Echocardiography** if:
  a enlarged cardiac shadow and high JVP (? tamponade)
  b suspected surgically correctable lesion, e.g. acute VSD, severe aortic stenosis

JVP, jugular venous pressure; VSD, ventricular septal defect.

Further management (Table 3.3)

■ **Table 3.3. Key points in the management of hypotension**

- Correct cardiac arrhythmias
- Optimize the blood volume
- Inotrope/vasopressor agents if indicated
- Correct hypoxia and biochemical abnormalities
- Specific treatment of the underlying condition

1 **Correct cardiac arrhythmias:**
  - treat ventricular tachycardia with synchronized DC countershock;
  - for atrial fibrillation or flutter, consider synchronized DC countershock (systolic BP < 75 mmHg) or rapid digitalization (systolic BP 75–90 mmHg);
  - for bradycardia unresponsive to atropine or isoprenaline, insert a temporary pacing wire (set the rate at 90 bpm).
2 **Optimize the blood volume:**
  - put in a central venous pressure (CVP) line;

- the CVP is a clue to the diagnosis (Table 3.4) and guides fluid therapy;
- infuse colloid until the CVP is +10 cmH$_2$O. Use blood if the haemoglobin is <10 g/dl.

■ **Table 3.4. The CVP in hypotension**

1 High	• Biventricular failure
	• Pulmonary embolism
	• Right ventricular infarction
	• Cardiac tamponade
	• Tension pneumothorax
2 Low or normal with warm skin	• Sepsis
	• Drugs/poisoning
3 Low or normal with cold skin	• Hypovolaemia
	• Left ventricular failure
	• Sepsis

3 Inotrope/vasopressor agents:

- reverse beta-blockade (p. 25).
- if the systolic BP remains <90 mmHg despite adequate fluid therapy (CVP around +10 cmH$_2$O, pulmonary artery (PA) wedge pressure 15–20 mmHg), start an inotrope/vasopressor (Table 3.5);
- put in a urinary catheter: the urine output is an index of renal blood flow and cardiac output.

■ **Table 3.5. Inotrope/vasopressor therapy for hypotension**

1 Systolic BP 80–100 mmHg	• **Dobutamine,** initially 5–10 µg/kg per min (p. 294)
2 Systolic BP < 80 mmHg	• **Dopamine,** 15–20 µg/kg per min via central line (p. 293)
3 If this fails:	• **Noradrenaline,** initially at 2 µg/min via central line (p. 293)
	• Reduce dopamine to 2.5 µg/kg per min (renal vasodilator dose)

4 Correct hypoxia and biochemical abnormalities:
- maintain Pa_{O_2} > 8kPa (60 mmHg), arterial saturation >90%;
- if arterial pH is <7.2, give bicarbonate 50 mmol i.v. over 30 minutes and recheck pH.

Problems

When to put in a Swan–Ganz catheter?

This is not of use in the priority management of hypotension. Measurement of the wedge pressure can guide further management where there is:
- **persisting hypotension despite CVP +10 cmH₂O;**
- **suspected VSD after myocardial infarction** if echo-Doppler is not available (p. 97);
- **hypotension with pulmonary oedema** (cardiogenic or ARDS): initial therapy is with an inotrope/vasopressor. Measurement of the wedge pressure allows titration of subsequent therapy including i.v. fluid and vasodilators (p. 93).

When to give corticosteroid?

Hydrocortisone 200 mg i.v. should be given if:
- **previous long-term steroid treatment** (prednisolone >7.5 mg daily);
- suspected **acute adrenal insufficiency** (p. 216) (preceding anorexia, nausea, vomiting and weight loss; pigmentation; low plasma sodium and raised potassium; or at risk of adrenal haemorrhage);
- suspected **anaphylaxis** (hypotension following i.v./i.m. injection; rash, abdominal cramps and wheeze) (p. 231).

4   Acute Chest Pain

Your main aim is to confirm or exclude potentially lethal causes of pain:

- myocardial infarction or unstable angina;
- pulmonary embolism;
- aortic dissection;
- oesophageal rupture.

If you cannot make a confident diagnosis of a minor and self-limiting disorder, admit the patient.

Priorities

1 Check the pulse and blood pressure and listen over the lungs.
- Give oxygen by mask.
- Connect to an ECG monitor.
- Put in a venous cannula.
- Relieve severe pain with diamorphine 2.5–5 mg i.v. plus an anti-emetic, e.g. prochlorperazine 12.5 mg i.v.

■ **Table 4.1. 'Pattern recognition' in acute chest pain**

Myocardial infarction (p. 89)	• Pain at rest for >30 min • ST segment elevation in at least two adjacent leads
Unstable angina (p. 101)	• Pain at rest or on minimal exertion • No ST elevation • Relief with sublingual or i.v. nitrate
Pulmonary embolism (p. 123)	• Pleuritic pain and breathlessness • Hypoxia despite clear chest X-ray • At risk of DVT (Chapter 19)
Aortic dissection (p. 103)	• Severe pain of sudden onset • Asymmetric pulses or aortic regurgitation • Widened mediastinum
Oesophageal rupture (p. 38)	• Pain following vomiting, worse on swallowing • Mediastinal gas • Pleural effusion

• Obtain an ECG and chest X-ray.

2 The diagnosis is often obvious from 'pattern recognition' (Table 4.1).

3 If the diagnosis is not clear within a few minutes, you need to adopt a systematic approach based on a full history and examination (Table 4.2).

■ **Table 4.2. Clinical assessment in chest pain: points not to miss**

History	• Its speed of onset and duration
	• Exacerbating and relieving factors: ask specifically about swallowing, meals, exercise, deep breathing and movement of the trunk
	• Associated symptoms particularly breathlessness, haemoptysis, vomiting, neurological symptoms
	• Risk factors for ischaemic heart disease (smoking, strong family history, hyperlipidaemia, hypertension, diabetes), pulmonary embolism (recent surgery, immobility, previous deep vein thrombosis) and aortic dissection (hypertension)
Examination	• Blood pressure in both arms (>15 mmHg difference in systolic pressure is abnormal)
	• All peripheral pulses
	• Friction rub — pleural or pericardial?
	• Localized chest wall tenderness?
	• Cardiac murmurs — especially early diastolic (aortic regurgitation as a result of dissection)
	• Lungs — ?pneumothorax, ?effusion

4 Take another look at the ECG and chest X-ray (Table 4.3). The first sign of myocardial infarction may be hyperacute peaking of the T wave, which is often overlooked. If present, relieve pain, give i.v. nitrate (p. 101) and repeat the ECG in 1 hour.

■ **Table 4.3. Abnormalities easily missed in 'normal' chest X-rays**

• Small apical pneumothorax
• Mediastinal gas (pneumothorax or oesophageal rupture)
• Small pleural effusion (which may occur in pulmonary embolism, aortic dissection or oesophageal rupture)
• Mediastinal widening (aortic dissection, oesophageal rupture)

5 Other causes of chest pain are given in Table 4.4.

■ **Table 4.4. Other causes of chest pain**

Common	• Oesophageal motility disorders and acid reflux (associated dysphagia or waterbrash, precipitation by lying down)
	• Chest wall pain, e.g. costochondritis or fractured rib (localized tenderness)
	• Pericarditis (p. 115)
	• Hyperventilation (p. 147)
	• Cervical spondylosis (neck movement restricted and reproduces pain)
	• Pleurisy (flu-like prodrome, pleural friction rub)
Rare	• Vertebral collapse (associated 'girdle' pain)
	• Herpes zoster (before the rash appears)
	• Vaso-occlusive crisis of sickle cell disease (p. 233)
	• Intra-abdominal inflammation (e.g. cholecystitis, pancreatitis)

Problems

Unstable angina vs oesophageal pain

1 Unstable angina and oesophageal pain may be indistinguishable on the history because:
  • the pain of both may be either burning or gripping in quality, with identical site and radiation;
  • angina may be noticed after meals, although usually during exercise after meals:
  • angina may be relieved transiently by belching;
  • acid reflux may be precipitated by heavy exercise.

2 The presence of ST depression during pain strongly favours (but is not diagnostic) of unstable angina.

3 If in doubt, admit the patient and treat for unstable angina (p. 101).

Pericarditis vs other causes of chest pain

1 The diagnosis of pericarditis is based on:

- pain worse on inspiration and worse lying than sitting;
- characteristic ECG appearances (Table 4.5).

2 A pericardial friction rub may not be heard.

3 Further management is given in Chapter 17.

Chest pain in an unusual distribution

1 The working diagnosis must be unstable angina, however atypical in site or quality if:
- it has previously occurred reliably on exertion with relief on resting;
- there are important risk factors for ischaemic heart disease — strong family history, heavy smoking or familial hypercholesterolaemia;
- the history is difficult to obtain.

2 Early repolarization ('high take-off of the T wave') (Table 4.5) is a normal ECG variant and may lead to the erroneous diagnosis of myocardial infarction.

Hyperventilation

1 The suspicion of hyperventilation is based on:
- pain in a distribution atypical for myocardial ischaemia;
- a thoracic sighing respiratory pattern.

2 Further management is given in Chapter 25. A firm diagnosis should only be made in the Emergency Department if the following features are also present:
- exact pain reproduction by palpation, breath-holding or a hyper-ventilation provocation test (p. 149);
- normal ECG and chest X-ray with no hypoxia on arterial blood gas analysis.

■ **Table 4.5a.** The ECG in pericarditis compared with myocardial infarction

	Acute MI	Pericarditis
ST morphology	Usually convex	Usually concave
Distribution	Inferior, anterior or lateral patterns	Commonly both limb and chest leads
Q waves	Usual	Never occur
ST and T wave evolution	Uniform in all affected leads	Various stages occur concurrently
QT prolongation	May occur	Does not occur

■ **Table 4.5b.** The ECG in pericarditis compared with 'early repolarization' normal variant

	Early repolarization	Pericarditis
ST morphology	Concave	Concave
Leads showing ST elevation	Commonly septal, rarely limb	Both limb and chest
ST elevation V6	Uncommon	Common
ST depression V1	Rare	Common
PR depression in precordial leads	Rare	Common

Based on

Goldberger AL. *Myocardial infarction: electrocardiac differential diagnosis*. St. Louis: CV Mosby 1975.

Spodick DH. Differential characteristics of the electrocardiogram in early repolarisation and acute pericarditis. *N Engl J Med* 1976; **295:** 523–6.

Appendix

4.1 Oesophageal rupture

Suspect the diagnosis where there is severe chest or epigastric pain, which is worse on swallowing, after:

• oesophageal instrumentation, particularly dilatation of a stricture;
• vomiting;
• swallowing a sharp object.

Oesophageal rupture can lead to mediastinitis or haemorrhage requiring initial resuscitation from circulatory collapse.

Management

1 Obtain a chest X-ray (preferably with a lateral film as well) and look for:

• **mediastinal gas** (a crescentic radiolucent zone — may be retrocardiac or along the right cardiac border);
• **pleural effusion** (blood, gastrointestinal contents or the digestion of mediastinal pleura);
• **widened mediastinum** (haematoma).

2 If the chest X-ray supports the diagnosis:

• give i.v. fluids (no oral fluids or food);
• start antibiotic therapy against Gram-negative rods and entero-cocci:

   a ampicillin 500 mg 6-hourly i.v.; *plus*
   b gentamicin i.v. (p. 71); *plus*
   c metronidazole 500 mg 8-hourly i.v.

3 Discuss further management with a surgeon. A large tear or continued bleeding may require repair. Small tears following oesophageal instrumentation commonly heal spontaneously.

5   Acute Breathlessness

Priorities

1 Give oxygen 35–50% (or 28% if suspected chronic airflow
limitation) and **attach an ECG monitor**. Make a clinical assessment of
the patient (Table 5.1).

■ **Table 5.1.** Clinical assessment of the breathless patient

History	• Preceding chest pain or palpitation?
	• Increase in volume or change in colour of sputum?
	• Associated wheeze?
	• Past history of airways or cardiac disease?
	• Risk factors for deep vein thrombosis (p. 121)?
	• Usual exercise capacity?
Examination	• Stridor?
	• Blood pressure (check for pulsus paradoxus: p. 118)
	• JVP — raised in pulmonary embolism, cardiac tamponade and right ventricular failure
	• Heart — valvular lesion or VSD?
	• Lungs
	• Legs — evidence of deep vein thrombosis (DVT)? — oedema?
	• Sacral oedema?
	• Temperature

2 If there are signs of a **pneumothorax with impending cardiac
arrest** insert a wide bore needle into the second intercostal space
in the midclavicular line (p. 144).
3 If there is wheeze give nebulized salbutamol 5 mg (1 mg of
nebulizer solution) diluted in 2 ml of normal saline or sterile water.
4 If there is **severe pulmonary oedema** (the patient is exhaling
froth):
  • correct arrhythmias;
  • give:
    a diamorphine 2.5–5.0 mg by slow i.v. injection;

    b frusemide 40–80 mg i.v.;

    c glyceryl trinitrate spray two puffs sublingually (if systolic BP
>90 mmHg);

    d an **anti-emetic,** e.g. metoclopramide 10 mg i.v.

5 Investigations required urgently are given in Table 5.2.

■ Table 5.2. Urgent investigation in acute breathlessness

---

1 **Chest X-ray**
2 **ECG** except in patient <40 with pneumothorax or acute asthma
3 **Arterial blood gases** for breathlessness with
 • Normal chest X-ray
 • Wheeze
 • Reduced conscious level
4 **Peak flow before and after bronchodilator** for
 • Wheeze
 • Overexpanded lung fields
5 **Echocardiogram** for
 • Cardiomegaly and high JVP
 • Possible surgically-correctable cause of pulmonary oedema (e.g. VSD, aortic stenosis)

---

6 You should now be able to make a working diagnosis (Table 5.3).

    Further management of specific problems is given in Section 2.

■ Table 5.3. Features pointing to a diagnosis in the breathless patient

Common	
Asthma (p.126)	• Wheeze with reduced peak flow rate
	• Previous similar episodes responding to bronchodilator therapy
	• Diurnal and seasonal variation in symptoms
	• Symptoms provoked by exercise or allergen exposure
Pulmonary oedema (p. 110)	• Cardiac disease
	• Bilateral interstitial or alveolar shadowing on chest X-ray

■ **Table 5.3.** (Continued)

Pneumonia (p. 137)	• Fever • Cough, pleuritic chest pain • Alveolar shadowing on chest X-ray
Acute exacerbation of chronic airflow obstruction (p. 132)	• Increase in sputum volume or the development of purulent sputum • Previous chronic bronchitis: sputum production on most days for 3 months of the year, for 2 or more consecutive years
Pulmonary embolism (p. 123)	• Risk factors for DVT (p. 121) (**NB** signs of DVT commonly absent) • Pleuritic chest pain, haemoptysis
Uncommon	
Cardiac tamponade (p. 118)	• Markedly raised JVP • Pulsus paradoxus >20 mmHg • Enlarged cardiac silhouette • Known carcinoma of the bronchus or breast
Tracheobronchial obstruction	• Stridor (inspiratory noise) or monophonic wheeze (expiratory 'squeak') • Known carcinoma of the bronchus • History of inhaled foreign body • $Paco_2 > 5$ kPa • Breathlessness unresponsive to bronchodilators
Laryngeal obstruction	• History of smoke inhalation or the ingestion of corrosives • Palatal or tongue oedema • Anaphylaxis (following i.v. drug, associated urticaria and hypotension: Chapter 45)
Large pleural effusion	• Distinguished from pulmonary consolidation/collapse by: • Shadowing higher laterally than medially • Shadowing does not conform to that of a lobe or segment (p. 305) • No air bronchogram • Trachea and mediastinum pushed to opposite side

Problems

Breathlessness with a normal chest X-ray

The history and arterial blood gases (Table 5.4) give the clue.

■ Table 5.4. Arterial blood gases in breathlessness with a normal chest X-ray

	P_{O_2}	P_{CO_2}	pH*
Pulmonary embolism	Normal/low	Low	High
Preradiological pneumonia[†]	Low	Low	High
Acute asthma	Normal/low	Low	High
Metabolic acidosis	Normal	Low	Low
Hyperventilation without organic disease	High/normal	Low	High

* Respiratory alkalosis may be offset by a metabolic acidosis: Fig. 58.1, p. 304 allows identification of mixed acid-base disturbances.

[†] Most commonly due to viruses or *Pneumocystis carinii* (p. 143).

Infection vs pulmonary oedema

Differentiation may occasionally be difficult:
• wheeze may occur in both;
• pulmonary oedema may sometimes be localized and when severe (alveolar) may produce an air-bronchogram;
• the radiological signs of pulmonary oedema are modified by the presence of lung disease, e.g. chronic airflow limitation;
• the two may coexist.

Management

1 Recheck the history, signs and ECG.

2 Nebulized salbutamol or aminophylline i.v. can be used as initial treatment for wheeze whichever the cause.

3 If fever and productive cough are absent, and the white cell

count is less than $15 \times 10^9/l$, give frusemide and assess the response. Repeat the chest X-ray the following day.

4 Consider:

- echocardiography;
- pulmonary artery catheterization.

These should always be done if the patient is seriously ill.

Tamponade vs cardiomyopathy

1 Confusion may occur because both cause:

- enlargement of the cardiac shadow on the chest X-ray;
- a raised JVP.

2 **Points in favour of tamponade:**

- pulsus paradoxus >20 mmHg;
- absence of pulmonary oedema;
- ECG normal apart from sinus tachycardia and reduced voltages;
- straight left heart border on chest X-ray.

Management

1 Echocardiography should be obtained urgently.

2 Never attempt pericardiocentesis (p. 265) without echocardiographic confirmation of a pericardial effusion except when there is imminent cardiac arrest.

Upper airways obstruction

Clues to the diagnosis are given in Table 5.3.

Management

1 Discuss management with an ENT surgeon or chest physician.

2 If there is stridor with the strong suspicion of carcinoma of the bronchus, start dexamethasone 4 mg 8-hourly i.v.

6 The Unconscious Patient

Your first aim is to maintain adequate respiration and circulation to prevent further neurological damage.

Priorities

1 **Clear the airway and give oxygen. If there is no femoral or carotid pulse, start external cardiac massage. Put in a peripheral i.v. cannula.**
   • Remove false teeth if loose and aspirate the pharynx, larynx and trachea with a suction catheter.
   • Insert an airway and give 60% oxygen by mask: if the patient is not breathing, ventilate with an Ambubag.
   • If there is no reflex response (gagging or coughing) to the suction catheter, a cuffed endotracheal tube should be inserted, preferably by an anaesthetist (Table 6.1).

■ **Table 6.1.** Indications for intubation/ventilation of the unconscious patient

Clinical	• Coma due to cardiorespiratory arrest
	• Respiratory rate <8/min*
	•ˇNo gag reflex
	• To protect the airway before gastric lavage (if gag/cough reflex severely depressed)
Arterial gases	• Pa_{O_2} <8 kPa (60 mmHg) breathing 60% oxygen
	• Pa_{CO_2} >7.3 (55 mmHg)

* Give naloxone if narcotic poisoning suspected (Table 6.2).

2 **If the patient is fitting,** give diazepam, i.v. 2 mg/min up to 20 mg or until seizures stop.
3 **Attach an ECG monitor, check the blood pressure and respiratory rate and listen over both lung bases.**
   • Correct arrhythmias.
   • If the respiratory rate is less than 10/min, if the pupils are

pinpoint or there is other reason to suspect narcotic poisoning, give naloxone (Table 6.2).

• If systolic BP is <80 mmHg (despite correction of arrhythmias) give adrenaline 0.5–1 mg i.v. (5–10 ml of one in 10 000 solution).

• If systolic BP is 80–100 mmHg, and there are no signs of pulmonary oedema, give i.v. fluid (saline or colloid) 500 ml over 30 minutes, with further fluid if required.

■ **Table 6.2. Naloxone**

1 Naloxone should be given if
  • Respiratory rate <10/min
  • Pupils pinpoint
  • Narcotic poisoning suspected

2 Give up to four doses of 800 µg i.v. every 2–3 min until the respiratory rate is around 15/min

3 If there is a response, start an i.v. infusion: add 2 mg to 500 ml dextrose 5% or saline (4 µg/ml) and titrate against the respiratory rate and conscious level. The plasma half-life of naloxone is 1 hour: shorter than that of most narcotics

4 If there is no response, narcotic poisoning is excluded

4 Check blood glucose by stick test.

• If blood glucose is less than 5 mmol/l, give dextrose 25 g i.v. (50 ml of the 50% solution) and start an infusion of dextrose 10%. Recheck blood glucose immediately and after 30 minutes.

• In chronic alcoholics, there is a remote risk of precipitating Wernicke's encephalopathy by a glucose load; prevent this by giving thiamine 100 mg before or shortly after the glucose (Parentrovite Intravenous High Potency (IVHP) contains 250 mg thiamine).

5 Check arterial blood gases.

• Increase inspired oxygen concentration if Pao_2 is <8kPa (60 mmHg).

• If $Paco_2$ is >7.3 kPa (55 mmHg), consider intubation and ventilation: discuss this with an anaesthetist.

• A low $Paco_2$ is an important clue to several causes of coma (Table 6.3).

■ **Table 6.3.** Causes of coma plus hyperventilation (low Pa_{CO_2})

- Ketoacidosis — diabetic or alcoholic
- Liver failure
- Renal failure
- Bacterial meningitis
- Poisoning with salicylate, ethylene glycol or methyl alcohol
- Stroke complicated by pneumonia or pulmonary oedema
- Brainstem stroke

Further management

At this stage you should obtain a full history and perform a systematic examination. Your further management depends on the neurological signs (Table 6.4 and Fig. 6.1).

■ **Table 6.4.** Neurological examination of the unconscious patient

1 Document the level of consciousness in objective terms (the Glasgow Coma Scale is given in Appendix 6.1)
2 Examine for signs of head injury (e.g. scalp laceration, bruising, blood at external auditory meatus or from nose)
3 If there are signs of head injury, assume additional cervical spine injury until proven otherwise: the neck must be immobilized in a collar and X-rayed before you test neck stiffness and the oculocephalic responses
4 Test for neck stiffness
5 Record the size of pupils and their response to bright light
6 Test the oculocephalic response: this is a simple but important test of an intact brainstem. Rotate the head to left and right. In an unconscious patient with an intact brainstem, both eyes rotate counter to movement of the head
7 Examine the limbs: tone, response to painful stimuli (nailbed pressure), tendon reflexes and plantar responses
8 Examine the fundi

The patient can now be placed in one of four groups:
1 Signs of head injury (with or without focal neurological signs).
- An intracranial haematoma must be excluded.
- Check for injury to other bones and organs.

- Eyes directed straight ahead
- Pupils reactive
- Normal oculocephalic reflex (OCR)

- **Toxic/metabolic cause** (NB barbiturate, phenytoin and tricyclic poisoning can abolish OCR)

- Pinpoint pupils

- **Narcotic poisoning** (OCR intact)
- **Pontine haemorrhage** (OCR absent, quadriplegia)

- Dysconjugate deviation of eyes (vertical or lateral)

- **Structural brainstem lesion** (haemorrhage, infarction or compression)

- Conjugate lateral deviation of eyes

- **Ipsilateral cerebral haemorrhage or infarction** (looking away from hemiplegic side)
- **Contralateral pontine infarction** (looking towards hemiplegic side)

- Unilateral dilated pupil

- **Supratentorial mass lesion** (haematoma/cerebral infarction with oedema) with uncal herniation and compression of III nerve

- **Midbrain lesion** (haemorrhage, infarction, compression)

- Bilateral midposition, fixed pupils

Fig. 6.1. Eye signs in the comatose patient.

- Correct hypotension (systolic BP <100 mmHg) with i.v. fluid or blood.
- X-ray skull, cervical spine and chest.
- Discuss further management with a neurosurgeon.

2 Neck stiffness (with or without focal neurological signs) (Table 6.5).

- If the clinical features suggest bacterial meningitis, take blood for culture and start antibiotic therapy (Table 28.3, p. 160).
- Malaria must be excluded in patients who have recently travelled to an endemic area (p. 236).
- Discuss urgent CT scanning with a neurologist.

■ **Table 6.5.** Causes of coma with neck stiffness

- Bacterial meningitis
- Encephalitis
- Primary subarachnoid haemorrhage
- Cerebral or cerebellar haemorrhage with extension into the subarachnoid space
- Cerebral malaria

NB In any of these conditions, neck stiffness may be lost with increasing coma

3 Focal neurological signs but no head injury or neck stiffness (Table 6.6).

- Exclude hypoglycaemia.
- The likely diagnosis is a stroke (p. 150).

■ **Table 6.6.** Causes of coma with focal neurological signs but no head injury or neck stiffness

With brainstem signs (deviation of the eyes/abnormal pupils)	• Brainstem compression due to large intracerebral haemorrhage or infarction with oedema • Brainstem stroke • Cerebellar stroke
Without brainstem signs	• Hypoglycaemia (in some cases) • Liver failure (in some cases)

4 No head injury, neck stiffness or focal neurological signs.
- The likely diagnosis is poisoning with psychotropic drugs or alcohol intoxication, but other metabolic causes must be excluded.
- Urgent investigation is given in Table 6.7.

■ **Table 6.7.** Urgent investigation of the comatose patient without head injury, neck stiffness or focal neurological signs

- **Blood glucose**
- **Urea, sodium and potassium** (?hyponatraemia ?renal failure)
- **Plasma osmolality** (raised in poisoning with ethanol, methanol or ethylene glycol)
- **Full blood count**
- **Prothrombin time** if suspected liver failure
- **Arterial blood gases and pH**
- **Gastric lavage** (p. 75) if poisoning suspected or coma remains unexplained
- **Chest X-ray**
- **Blood culture** if temperature <36 or >37.5°C

Appendix

6.1. Glasgow Coma Scale

This is a scale based on the assessment of three clinical signs: eye opening, verbal response and motor response. It provides a simple, rapid, objective and reproducible measure of the level of consciousness.

Eye opening
1 Nil: the eyes remain closed.
2 To pain: the eyes open in response to a painful stimulus applied to the trunk or a limb (a painful stimulus to the head usually provokes closing of the eyes).
3 To voice.
4 Spontaneous: the eyes are open, with blinking.

Verbal response

1 **Nil:** no sound whatsoever is produced.

2 **Incomprehensible:** mutters or groans only.

3 **Inappropriate:** intelligible but isolated words.

4 **Confused speech.**

5 **Oriented speech.**

Motor response

1 **Nil.**

2 **Extensor.**

3 **Flexor.**

4 **Withdrawal.**

5 **Localizing:** uses limb to locate or resist the painful stimulus.

6 **Voluntary:** obeys commands.

1 **Ask the patient to move the limb. If there is no response, apply firm pressure to the nailbed.**

2 **Test for a localizing response by pressure on the supraorbital notch or sternal rub.**

3 **Test and record for each of the limbs.** For the purpose of assessment of conscious level, the best motor response is taken. Differences between the limbs will be important in localizing a neurological lesion.

Reference

Teasdale G, Jennett B. Assessment of coma and impaired consciousness: a practical scale, *Lancet* 1974;**2**:81–4.

7 Transient Loss of Consciousness

Your aim is to distinguish the more common benign causes from others which require specific treatment (Table 7.1).

■ **Table 7.1.** Causes of transient loss of consciousness

	Common	Rare
Benign	Vasovagal syncope Micturition/cough/ defaecation syncope Primary hyperventilation	
Cardiovascular	Arrhythmias Postural hypotension	Aortic stenosis Aortic dissection Pulmonary embolism Pacemaker malfunction Carotid sinus hypersensitivity Pulmonary hypertension
Neurological	Major seizure	Transient ischaemic attack Subclavian steal Subarachnoid haemorrhage
Others	Hypoglycaemia	Rapid haemorrhage

Priorities

1 **Check the conscious level, pulse and blood pressure.**
Hypotension and **arrhythmias** must be corrected.
2 **Take a full history (Table 7.2) from the patient and preferably a witness as well.**

- Does the history point to vasovagal syncope or hyperventilation (Table 7.3)?
- Was there evidence of a major seizure?

    a Tonic/clonic activity (a brief seizure can follow syncope of any cause).

■ **Table 7.2. Checklist history after syncope**

1 Before the attack	• Prodromal symptoms, e.g. gradual fading of consciousness, vertigo, aura, chest pain, palpitation • Circumstances, e.g. exercising, standing, sitting or lying • Precipitants, e.g. head movement
2 The attack	• Duration • Tonic/clonic movements? • Associated tongue biting or micturition? • Facial colour changes? • Abnormal pulse? (must be assessed in relation to the reliability of the witness)
3 After the attack	• Immediately well or delayed recovery?
4 Background	• Any previous similar attacks • Other illness, e.g. diabetes, previous myocardial infarction (at risk of VT), pacemaker (p. 25) • Drugs, e.g. antiarrhythmics, antihypertensives, nitrates

■ **Table 7.3. Points in favour of benign diagnoses**

Vasovagal syncope	• Circumstances, e.g. hot room, hungry, anxious, tired; sometimes a specific precipitant, e.g. venepuncture, dental surgery • Sights and sounds gradually diminishing often over a few minutes • Associated nausea and sweating • Often prolonged malaise afterwards
Micturition/cough/ defaecation syncope	• Syncope occurring in these circumstances, without another cause apparent on examination or ECG
Primary hyperventilation (p. 147)	• Prodromal breathlessness and chest tightness • Irregular thoracic respiratory pattern • Associated symptoms (Table 25.1, p. 148) • Symptoms reproduced by voluntary overbreathing

b Associated tongue biting and micturition (these are not specific features).

c Postictal confusion or somnolence.

See Chapter 31 for further management after a seizure.

3 The examination (Table 7.4) is directed at excluding structural heart disease or residual neurological signs.

4 Initial investigation is given in Table 7.5.

■ **Table 7.4. Points not to be missed on examination**

- Systolic BP sitting or lying and after 2 min standing (fall >20 mmHg abnormal; note if symptomatic or not)
- Pulses — asymmetry? carotid bruit?
- JVP (if raised, consider pulmonary embolism or cardiac tamponade)
- Heart murmurs (aortic stenosis, pulmonary stenosis and hypertrophic cardiomyopathy may all cause exertional syncope)
- Neck mobility (does neck movement induce dizziness?)
- Abnormal neurological signs?

■ **Table 7.5. Initial investigation after loss of consciousness**

ECG in all patients	• Signs of infarction?
	• Left ventricular hypertrophy? If so, check again for aortic stenosis
	• Wolff–Parkinson–White syndrome (short PR interval, delta wave)?
	• Long QT interval?
	• Heart block?
	• Evidence of sinoatrial disease (Table 7.6)?
Postural hypotension	• Urea and electrolytes
Cause uncertain	• Full blood count
	• Urea and electrolytes
	• Blood glucose
	• Chest X-ray

Further management

1 **Admit or discharge?** Patients with benign causes of syncope
and no significant abnormalities on clinical examination or ECG do
not need admission.

2 **When is temporary pacing indicated?**
   - Second degree or complete AV block.
   - Sinus pauses >3 seconds.
   - Sinus or nodal bradycardia <40/min unresponsive to atropine (p. 22).
   - Failure of permanent pacemaker system (Table 2.11, p. 25).

3 **Who should be monitored on the Coronary Care Unit?**
   - Patients with evidence of conducting system disease, but without
   absolute indications for temporary pacing:
     a sinus bradycardia, not due to beta-blockade;
     b sinus pauses of 2–3 seconds;
     c left bundle branch block.
   - Patients at risk of ventricular tachycardia (Table 7.6).

4 **Further investigation.**
   - In the absence of features pointing to an alternative cause, a
   cardiac arrhythmia is the commonest cause found. Clinical features
   and abnormalities on the resting ECG may point to a specific
   diagnosis (Table 7.6).
   - Arrange ambulatory ECG monitoring.
   - Test for carotid sinus hypersensitivity. Before doing this, put in a
   venous cannula and draw up atropine in case prolonged asystole
   occurs. Check the blood pressure. Perform carotid sinus massage
   (p. 20) whilst recording a rhythm strip. An abnormal response is
   defined by a sinus pause >3 seconds or a drop in systolic BP
   >50 mmHg. If these occur, discuss with a cardiologist whether
   pacemaker implantation is indicated.

■ **Table 7.6.** Clinical and ECG features suggesting sinoatrial disease or ventricular tachycardia as causes of syncope

Sino-atrial disease	• Clustering of attacks • Syncope at rest • Facial pallor during the attack with subsequent flushing • Occasionally observed abnormalities of the pulse • Age usually >60 • ECG: may show sinus bradycardia, sinus arrhythmia, sinus pauses, variable P wave morphology, atrial extrasystoles, episodes of atrial fibrillation/flutter
Ventricular tachycardia	• Previous myocardial infarction or other ventricular disease • Syncope during or after exertion • May complicate antiarrhythmic therapy • ECG: evidence of infarction; long QT interval

8   Acute Confusional State

- Consider in any patient labelled as difficult, uncooperative or a 'poor historian'.
- Usually caused by acute illness (most commonly infection) or an adverse effect of drugs (Appendix 8.1).

Priorities

1 **Assess the mental state.**
   - An acute confusional state is characterized by:
     a 'clouding of consciousness' — reduced alertness, impaired attention and concentration;
     b disorientation in time (and often also for place and person);
     c impaired short term memory (Appendix 8.2).
   - Vivid auditory or visual hallucinations suggest alcohol withdrawal (Appendix 8.3).
2 **Check the blood glucose** by stick test.
3 Specific points to be covered in the examination are given in Table 8.1, and investigations required urgently in Table 8.2.
4 **Check the drug chart:** many drugs may cause an acute confusional state in the elderly, notably benzodiazepines, tricyclics and drugs for Parkinsonism.

Further management

1 **Specific treatment** is directed at the underlying cause.
2 **Sedation** should only be used if the patient is at risk of self-injury or if aggressive behaviour prevents treatment. Oral administration (syrup may be easier than tablets) is usually preferable to i.m. or i.v. Options include:
   - **haloperidol** 0.5–10 mg 8 to 12-hourly p.o./i.m.;

■ **Table 8.1. Examination in acute confusional state**

1 Check the pulse, blood pressure and respiratory rate

2 Are there signs of infection?
- Fever or reduced temperature (rectal temperature more reliable in the confused patient if feasible)
- Neck stiffness
- Focal chest signs
- Abdominal tenderness/rigidity
- Cellulitis

3 Are there focal neurological signs? As a minimum, check
- Pupils
- ?Facial asymmetry. ?Orofacial dyskinesia
- Limb power — ?lateralized weakness
- Tendon reflexes and plantar responses

4 Are there signs suggesting hepatic encephalopathy?
- Stigmata of liver disease
- Asterixis (liver 'flap')

5 In patients with suspected alcohol abuse, check for signs of Wernicke's encephalopathy
- Nystagmus
- Gaze palsy (unable to abduct the eye)
- Ataxia (wide-based gait; may be unable to stand or walk)

6 Check for urinary retention and faecal impaction

■ **Table 8.2. Urgent investigation in acute confusional state**

- **Blood glucose**
- **Urea and electrolytes**
- **Plasma calcium** in patients with malignancy
- **Full blood count**
- **Prothrombin time** if suspected liver disease
- **Blood culture** if temperature <36 or >37.5°C or if difficult to measure
- **Urine stick test, microscopy and culture**
- **ECG** if age >50 years
- **Chest X-ray** if new focal signs, tachypnoea or fever
- **Arterial blood gases** if cyanosed or chest signs

• **thioridazine:** in the elderly start at a dose of 12.5–25 mg at night or 12-hourly p.o.;

• **chlormethiazole** p.o. or by i.v. infusion (Appendix 8.3): specifically indicated for confusional states due to alcohol- or drug-withdrawal. withdrawal.

Problems

Confusional state associated with alcohol abuse.

• Consider the causes in Table 8.3.

• The management of alcohol withdrawal is given in Appendix 8.3.

■ **Table 8.3. Causes of a confusional state associated with alcohol abuse**

• Hypoglycaemia
• Acute intoxication
• Alcohol withdrawal
  a Tremulousness after 8–24 hours
  b Confusional state
  c Hallucinations
  d Delirium tremens usually after 2–4 days
• Wernicke's encephalopathy
• Hepatic encephalopathy
• Other intercurrent illness, particularly pneumonia

Appendices

8.1   Common causes of an acute confusional state

1 Infection, usually of the urinary or respiratory tract. Endocarditis and biliary tract sepsis should be considered in the febrile patient without localizing signs.

2 Drugs, e.g. benzodiazepines, tricyclics and drugs for Parkinsonism.

3 Metabolic/endocrine disease:

  • hypoglycaemia;

- hyponatraemia;
- hypercalcaemia;
- diabetic ketoacidosis (DKA) or hyperosmolar non-ketotic hyperglycaemia (HONK);
- liver failure;
- renal failure.

4 **Primary neurological disease:**
  - postictal state;
  - non-dominant parietal lobe stroke;
  - subarachnoid haemorrhage.

5 **Others:**
  - hypoxia;
  - hypotension/low cardiac output;
  - dehydration;
  - hypothermia;
  - alcohol withdrawal;
  - urinary retention;
  - faecal impaction.

8.2. Abbreviated mental status examination of the elderly

Item

1 Age.

2 Time (to nearest hour).

3 Address for recall at end of test — this should be repeated by the patient to ensure it has been heard correctly: 42 West Street.

4 Year.

5 Name of institution.

6 Recognition of two people (doctor, nurse, etc.).

7 Date of birth (day and month sufficient).

8 Year of First World War.

9 Name of present Monarch.

10 Count backwards, 20 to 1.

Each correct answer scores one mark. The healthy elderly score 8–10.

Reference

Qureshi KN, Hodkinson HM. Evaluation of a 10-question mental test in the institutionalized elderly. *Age and Ageing* 1974;**3**:152–7.

8.3. Alcohol withdrawal

- **Can give rise to a wide spectrum of neurological abnormalities** (tremulousness, confusional state, fits and, uncommonly, delirium tremens (Table 8.4)).

■ **Table 8.4. Features of delirium tremens**

- Agitation often with shouting
- Tremulousness
- Picking at imaginary objects
- Truncal ataxia
- Vivid auditory or visual hallucinations
- Paranoid misinterpretations
- Sympathetic overactivity — tachycardia, hypertension, sweating, dilated pupils
- Fever

■ **Table 8.5. Chlormethiazole in the management of alcohol withdrawal**

Oral regimen using 192 mg capsules*	• Day 1: three capsules 6-hourly • Day 2: two capsules 6-hourly • Day 3–4: two capsules 8-hourly • Day 5–6: two capsules 12-hourly • Day 7–8: two capsules at night • Subsequently nil
Intravenous regimen (0.8% infusion)	• Start at 60 standard drops/min (3 ml/min); stay with the patient • When drowsy, reduce to the minimum rate at which mild sedation is maintained (usually 8–15 drops/min) • Monitor respiratory rate: stop the infusion if <10/min

* Reduced doses are necessary in patients with hepatic impairment (stigmata or prolonged prothrombin time). Initially give one capsule only and observe the response.

- **Give i.v. fluid** if the patient is unable to maintain an adequate oral intake (avoid saline if there are signs of liver disease).
- **If there is severe agitation** with serious risk of injury start chlormethiazole i.v. (Table 8.5). Otherwise, start either oral chlormethiazole or chlordiazepoxide or diazepam.
- **Give Parentrovite** IVHP: two pairs of ampoules 8-hourly for 3 days then one pair once daily for 5 days.
- **If the prothrombin time is prolonged >1.5 × normal,** start a liver failure regimen (Table 33.4, p. 185).

9   Headache

On the basis of the clinical assessment (Table 9.1), the patient with headache can be placed in one of five groups:

1 Febrile, but no focal neurological signs.
2 Reduced conscious level and/or focal neurological signs.
3 Papilloedema but no focal neurological signs.
4 Local signs.
5 No abnormal signs.

■ **Table 9.1. Clinical assessment of the patient with headache**

History	• Is the headache acute, or chronic and recurrent?
	• If acute, was the onset sudden?
	• Associated loss of consciousness?
	• Distribution (unilateral, diffuse, localized?)
	• Associated visual symptoms (blurring, transient blindness, scotomata, fortification spectra?)
	• Recent travel abroad?
	• Is the patient immunocompromised?
Examination	• Temperature
	• Blood pressure
	• Conscious level
	• Neck stiffnesss?
	• Focal neurological signs?
	• Visual acuity and fields
	• Fundi (?papilloedema, ?retinal haemorrhages)
	• Sinus tenderness?
	• Temporal artery thickening or tenderness?

Febrile but no focal neurological signs (Table 9.2)

Neck stiffness present

A lumbar puncture should be performed to exclude **meningitis** or **subarachnoid haemorrhage** (p. 274).

No neck stiffness

• Lumbar puncture is indicated in immunocompromised patients. Neck stiffness is not an invariable feature of **cryptococcal meningitis** (p. 164).

• Consider **malaria** and **typhoid** in patients who have returned from abroad (Chapter 47).

■ **Table 9.2.** Causes of headache with fever but no focal neurological signs

• Meningitis
• Acute sinusitis
• Malaria and typhoid
• Other infectious diseases including benign viral illnesses
• Subarachnoid haemorrhage

Reduced conscious level and/or focal neurological signs (Table 9.3)

• The mode of onset of symptoms will help distinguish between vascular (acute onset), infectious (subacute) and neoplastic (slow) disease.

• If the patient is febrile, take blood cultures and start antibiotic therapy to cover **bacterial meningitis** (Table 28.3, p. 160). Computed tomography (CT) should be performed before lumbar puncture.

• Discuss further management with a neurologist.

■ **Table 9.3.** Causes of headache with reduced conscious level and/or focal neurological signs

• Stroke
• Subarachnoid haemorrhage
• Chronic subdural haematoma
• Meningitis
• Encephalitis
• Brain abscess
• Subdural empyema
• Brain tumour

Papilloedema but no focal neurological signs

(Table 9.4)

• If the diastolic BP is >120 mmHg and there are retinal haemorrhages or exudates, start antihypertensive therapy (pp. 106–107).

• If the BP is normal, discuss further management with a neurologist.

■ **Table 9.4. Causes of headache with papilloedema but no focal neurological signs**

• Accelerated phase hypertension
• Brain tumour (e.g. in non-dominant frontal lobe)
• Benign intracranial hypertension

Local signs

Acute sinusitis

• Suspect from associated fever, facial pain especially on bending over, mucopurulent nasal discharge and tenderness on pressure over the affected sinus.

• Obtain X-rays of the sinuses (to look for mucosal thickening, a fluid level or opacification).

• Discuss management with an ENT surgeon.

Acute angle-closure glaucoma

• Suspect from blurred vision with reduced visual acuity due to corneal clouding, red eye, pupil fixed in the mid-position.

• Refer urgently to an ophthalmologist.

Temporal arteritis

• Consider in any patient aged >50 years.

• If the erythrocyte sedimentation rate (ESR) is >50 mm/hour and/or the temporal artery is thickened or tender (feel 2 cm above and 2 cm forward from the external auditory meatus), start prednisolone, initially 60 mg daily p.o.

• Arrange a temporal artery biopsy within 48 hours.

Cervical spondylosis
- Suspect from subacute occipital headache associated with pain on rotation of the neck.
- Check for signs of root or cord compression (p. 165).
- X-ray the cervical spine. Treat with a non-steroidal anti-inflammatory drug (NSAID).

No abnormal signs (Table 9.5)

- **Subarachnoid haemorrhage** should be excluded by CSF examination in patients with **unexplained headache of sudden onset.**

- **Migraine** is diagnosed on the **history** of a recurrent throbbing headache with headache-free intervals, and two or more of the following features:

    a prodromal visual, sensory or motor symptoms;

    b nausea;

    c hemicranial distribution;

    d family history of similar headache.

The first migraine headache usually occurs from age 10–30 years.

- **Temporal arteritis** should be considered in any patient aged >50 years. Check the ESR.

■ **Table 9.5. Causes of headache with no abnormal signs**

- Muscle contraction ('tension') headache
- Migraine
- Drugs (e.g. nitrates, calcium antagonists)
- Toxin exposure
- Temporal arteritis
- Subarachnoid haemorrhage

10   Septicaemia

- **Make a working diagnosis of septicaemia** if a patient has unexplained **hypotension, oliguria or confusional state** associated with **fever or reduced body temperature (<36°C).**
- *Escherichia coli, Staphylococcus aureus and S. epidermidis,* and *Streptococcus pneumoniae (pneumococcus)* are the commonest pathogens.

Priorities

1 If the systolic BP is <90 mmHg, give colloid i.v. 500 ml over 15–30 minutes.

2 Give oxygen and measure arterial blood gases and pH.
Both Pao_2 and $Paco_2$ are usually low: increase the oxygen concentration if Pao_2 is <8 kPa (60 mmHg).

3 Decide the likely source of infection. Check for:
- neck stiffness;
- focal lung crackles/bronchial breathing;
- heart murmur;
- abdominal tenderness/guarding;
- soft tissue abscess: check the perineum and, in diabetics, the feet.

4 Investigations required urgently are given in **Table 10.1.**

5 Start antibiotic therapy as soon as blood has been taken for culture. Guidelines are given in **Table 10.2.** Gentamicin dosages are given in **Appendix 10.1.**

Take into account previous isolates from the patient and the local pattern of antibiotic resistance; in patients with hospital-acquired septicaemia:
- substitute aztreonam or ciprofloxacin for gentamicin if gentamicin resistance is prevalent;
- substitute vancomycin for flucloxacillin if methicillin-resistant

■ **Table 10.1. Urgent investigation of the septicaemic patient**

- **Full blood count** (the white cell count may be low in overwhelming bacterial sepsis).
- **Clotting screen** if purpura, prolonged oozing from puncture sites, or bleeding from surgical wounds
- **Urea and electrolytes**
- **Glucose** by stick test
- **Blood culture** (two sets)*
- **Urine microscopy and culture**
- **Chest X-ray**
- **Arterial pH and gases**
- **CSF examination** if suspected meningitis (p. 159)
- **Joint aspiration** if suspected septic arthritis (p. 227)
- **Blood film for malaria** if recent travel to or through an endemic area

*If suspected intravascular line-related sepsis** (central venous line, Swan–Ganz catheter, Hickman line):
- take one culture via the line and the other via a peripheral vein;
- change the central venous line/Swan–Ganz catheter and send the tip for culture.

■ **Table 10.2. 'Blind' antibiotic therapy for septicaemia**

Suspected primary infection	Antibiotic therapy
Meningitis	Table 28.3 p. 160
Pneumonia	Table 23.2 p. 138
Endocarditis	Gentamicin + benzylpenicillin
Peritonitis	Gentamicin + metronidazole
Urinary tract	Gentamicin + ampicillin
Intravascular line related	Flucloxacillin
Cellulitis	Benzylpenicillin + flucloxacillin
No localizing signs	
Immunocompetent	Gentamicin + flucloxacillin
Neutropenic*	Gentamicin + azlocillin
i.v. drug abuse*	Gentamicin + flucloxacillin

*See under **Problems** for further management of these patients.

Staphylococcus aureus (MRSA) infection is possible. Serum levels of vancomycin should be measured.

6 Obtain a surgical opinion if you suspect an abdominal or pelvic source of sepsis.

7 Transfer the patient to Intensive Care Unit if:

- Pao_2 is <8 kPa despite an inspired oxygen concentration of 60%; *or*
- Systolic BP is <90 mmHg after fluid replacement.

8 Give sucralfate 1–2 g 6-hourly orally/via nasogastric tube **as prophylaxis against stress ulceration** in severely ill patients.

Problems

1 Circulatory failure ('septic shock').

- **Put in a CVP line** and give further i.v. colloid (or blood if haemoglobin is <10 g/dl) until CVP is + 5 to 10 cmH$_2$O.
- **A Swan–Ganz catheter** should be inserted in patients with heart disease or if ventilation is required. Wedge pressure should be kept at 12–16 mmHg.
- If systolic BP remains <90 mmHg despite an adequate CVP or wedge pressure, **inotropic/vasopressor therapy** should be started **(Table 10.3).**
- **Put in a urinary catheter:** urine output provides a measure of renal blood flow and ideally should be >0.5 ml/kg per hour.
- **High-dose corticosteroid therapy** has not been shown to improve the outcome of septic shock in large trials.

■ **Table 10.3.** Inotropic/vasopressor therapy in septic shock

1 Give **dopamine** up to 20 μg/kg per min. If systolic BP remains <90 mmHg

2 Add **noradrenaline,** starting at 2–10 μg/min, and reduce dopamine to 'renal' dose of 1–5 μg/kg per min

- Both drugs should be given via a **central vein** to avoid the risk of extravasation
- See **Tables 57.3 and 57.4 (p. 293)** for preparation of infusions

- **Naloxone** infusion has proved beneficial in some patients: the results of large trials are awaited.

2 **Respiratory failure.**

- **Adjust the inspired oxygen concentration to keep Pa_{O_2} 8-10 kPa (60-70 mmHg)**
- If Pa_{O_2} is <8 kPa despite an inspired oxygen concentration of 60%, ventilation is likely to be needed: discuss this with an anaesthetist.

3 **Metabolic acidosis.**

- **If arterial pH is <7.2, give sodium bicarbonate 50 mmol (50 ml of 8.4% solution) over 30 minutes** and recheck pH.

4 **Acute renal failure.**

- If oliguria (urine output <30 ml/hour or 0.5 ml/kg per hour) persists despite adequate fluid replacement, start 'renal dose' dopamine and give frusemide (p. 190).
- See Chapter 34 for further management.

5 **Disseminated intravascular coagulation.**

- Suspect in patients with **purpura, prolonged oozing from puncture sites, or bleeding from surgical wounds.**
- Confirm by a **low platelet count, prolonged prothrombin and kaolin-cephalin clotting times,** and increased concentration of fibrin degradation products.
- **If there is active bleeding, give fresh frozen plasma and platelets:** seek advice from a haematologist.
- **Heparin** is not of proven benefit.

6 **Hypoglycaemia** can complicate severe infection, especially in patients with liver disease. Blood glucose should always be rechecked if there is any deterioration in conscious level.

7 **Infection in the neutropenic patient.**

- Patients with **neutrophil counts <0.5 $\times$ 10.9/l** are at high risk of bacterial infection, particularly from Gram-negative rods and *Staphylococcus aureus* and *S. epidermidis.*
- If the neutropenic patient has **unexplained fever >2 hours duration,** the likely cause is bacterial infection and antibiotic therapy should be started.

- Check for a possible focus of infection. Examination should include:
  - **a** the entire skin including perineum and perianal region;
  - **b** Hickman line site and other i.v. sites;
  - **c** mouth, teeth and sinuses.
- **Investigation** as in **Table 10.1.**
- Several **antibiotic regimens** have been shown to be effective in neutropenic patients without localizing signs:
  - **a** an **aminoglycoside** plus an **antipseudomonal penicillin** (e.g. gentamicin plus azlocillin); *or*
  - **b** monotherapy with a **third generation cephalosporin** (e.g. ceftazidime).
  - **c** **vancomycin** should be added if Hickman line infection is suspected.
- **If cultures are negative,** continue antibiotic therapy until the patient has been afebrile for 5 days or the neutrophil count is $>0.5 \times 10.9/l$.
- **Add antifungal therapy** if fever persists >72 hours despite antibiotics with no clinical or laboratory evidence of bacterial infection. Discuss this with a microbiologist.

8 **Infection in the i.v. drug abuser.**
- Several causes of fever must be considered (Table 10.4).
- Right-sided endocarditis may not give rise to abnormal cardiac signs.
- If septicaemic, antibiotic therapy must cover staphylococci (Table 10.2).

■ Table 10.4. Possible causes of fever in the i.v. drug abuser

- Infection at injection sites
- Thrombophlebitis
- Endocarditis (especially right-sided)
- Pulmonary tuberculosis
- Hepatitis B
- Septic arthritis
- Pyrogen reaction
- AIDS-related infection, e.g. cryptococcal meningitis, *Pneumocystis carinii* pneumonia

Appendix

10.1 Gentamicin

• **Aminoglycoside principally active against Gram-negative rods.**
• Can be given i.m. or i.v. (the preferred route in severe infection).
• **Loading dose:** based on body weight — give 2 mg/kg.
• **Maintenance dose and dosage interval:** based on renal function. Table 10.5 serves as a guide, but **serum levels should be checked daily after the third dose.**

■ **Table 10.5. Gentamicin dosages**

Blood urea (mmol/l)	Dose (mg)		Interval
	< 60 kg	**> 60 kg**	
<7	60	80	8-hourly
7–10	60	80	12-hourly
11–15	60	80	18-hourly
16–20	60	80	24-hourly
>20	Check serum level 24 hours after loading dose		

Serum levels

• **Trough level** reflects the renal excretion of the preceding dose. Take blood just before the next dose. The level should be 1–2 mg/l: if >2 mg/l, decrease the dose or increase the interval between doses.
• **Peak level:** reflects the adequacy of the dose. Take blood 1 hour after i.m. dose or 15–20 minutes after i.v. dose. The level should be in the range 5–10 mg/l: modify the dose as required.
• **Toxic effects (ototoxicity and renal failure)** may occur if trough levels are persistently >2 mg/l or peak levels >12 mg/l.

11 Poisoning

- Should be considered in any comatose patient.
- If you need advice about the management of poisoning, contact the **National Poisons Information Service** (see Appendix 11.1 for telephone numbers).

Priorities

The unconscious patient

1 Resuscitation (p. 44).
- **Clear the airway and give oxygen** 60% (100% if carbon monoxide poisoning is suspected).
- Put in a peripheral i.v. cannula.
- Attach an ECG monitor and correct arrhythmias.

■ **Table 11.1. Urgent investigation of the comatose patient with suspected poisoning***

- **Urea and electrolytes**
- **Blood glucose** (by stick test)
- **Full blood count**
- **Paracetamol and salicylate levels** (mixed poisoning common)
- **Plasma osmolality**[†]
- **Arterial blood gases**[‡]
- **Chest X-ray**
- **ECG** if there is hypotension, coexistent heart disease or suspected ingestion of cardiotoxic drugs (antiarrhythmics, tricyclic antidepressants)

---

* **If the substance ingested is not known, save serum** (10 ml), **urine** (50 ml) **and vomit or gastric aspirate** (50 ml) at 4°C for subsequent analysis.
[†]normal range 280-300 mosmol/kg. Raised plasma osmolality occurs in poisoning with ethanol, methanol or ethylene glycol.
[‡] Low Pa_{CO_2} occurs in poisoning with aspirin (respiratory alkalosis/metabolic acidosis), methanol and ethylene glycol (metabolic acidosis).

- **Give naloxone** if the respiratory rate is <10/min or the pupils are pinpoint (Table 6.2, p. 45).
- **Correct hypotension:** give colloid or normal saline 500 ml i.v. over 15–30 minutes if systolic BP is <90 mmHg (<80 mmHg if aged less than 40 years). If hypotension persists: see Chapter 3.
- **Check blood glucose** and correct hypoglycaemia (p. 196).

2 **Perform a systematic examination.** The clinical features may give clues to the poison (Appendix 11.2). Points in the neurological examination are given in Table 6.4, p. 46.

3 **Investigations** required urgently are given in Table 11.1.

The conscious patient

1 **Check the pulse, blood pressure, and respiratory rate.**
2 **Establish:**
- which poisons were taken, in what amount, and over what period?
- has the patient vomited since ingestion?
- what symptoms?
- other illness?

3 **Investigations** required will depend on the poison and the presence of other illness.
- **Plasma levels** should be checked after poisoning with drugs given in Table 11.2.

Further management

Is gastric lavage indicated?

1 Lavage is indicated if a potentially dangerous overdose has been ingested within the previous 4 hours (or within 8 hours if the drug delays gastric emptying; Table 11.3), or the patient is unconscious and the time of ingestion is not known.

2 Gastric lavage should not be performed:
- after ingestion of **corrosives** (acids, alkalis, kettle descaler, bleach) or **petroleum derivatives** (paraffin);

■ **Table 11.2.** Poisoning in which plasma levels should be measured

Poison	Plasma level at which elimination is indicated	Elimination technique
Aspirin	Appendix 11.4	
Paracetamol	Appendix 11.5	
Lithium (plain tube)	>5 mmol/l	HD, PD
Iron	>3.5 mg/l*	Desferrioxamine
Theophylline	>50 mg/l	RAC, HP
Digoxin	>4 ng/ml	(p. 27)
Barbiturates	Discuss with Poisons Unit	
Methanol	>500 mg/l	HD, PD
Ethylene glycol	>500 mg/l	HD, PD

* Also if clinical evidence of severe toxicity (hypotension, nausea, vomiting, diarrhoea) or if massive ingestion (>200 mg elemental iron/kg body weight; one 200 mg tablet of ferrous sulphate contains 60 mg elemental iron).
HD, haemodialysis; HP, haemoperfusion; PD, peritoneal dialysis; RAC repeated activated charcoal.

■ **Table 11.3.** Indications for gastric lavage

Drug or poison	Amount (in adults) over:	Within the previous:
Aspirin	10 g	12 hours
Paracetamol	10 g (5 g)*	4 hours
Benzodiazepines	Lavage not indicated†	
Digoxin	5 mg	8 hours
Tricyclic antidepressants	750 mg	8 hours
Methanol	25 ml	8 hours
Ethylene glycol	100 ml	4 hours
Phenobarbitone	1000 mg	8 hours
Phenytoin	Lavage not indicated†	
Sodium valproate	Lavage not indicated†	
Theophylline	2.5 g	4 hours (8 hours)‡
Dextropropoxyphene	325 mg	8 hours
Cyanide	Any case with symptoms	1 hour

*If patient alcoholic, on anticonvulsants or on starvation diet.
†Except in massive overdose, when each case should be considered on its merits.
‡ If delayed release preparation taken.

Based on
Henry J, Volans G. ABC of poisoning: preventing absorption. *Br Med J* 1984;**289**:304–5.

• in patients with oesophageal varices or stricture or previous gastric surgery.

3 The procedure is described in Table 11.4: if the patient is conscious, verbal consent must be obtained. If unconscious, a cuffed endotracheal tube should be inserted first (by an anaesthetist) to protect the airway.

■ **Table 11.4. Technique of gastric lavage**

1 If the patient is unconscious, a cuffed endotracheal tube should be inserted first to protect the airway

2 Tip the trolley head down, with the patient lying on their left side.

3 Use a wide bore tube (Jacques gauge 30 in adults) which has been lubricated (e.g. with KY jelly)

4 Insert the tube. Confirm that it is in the stomach by aspirating and test with litmus paper. The gastro-oesophageal junction is about 40 cm from the incisor teeth

5 Run in 300–600 ml of water warmed to 38° C and then drain out. Repeat 3–4 times or more if the washings still contain tablets or debris.

6 Leave activated charcoal (see below) in the stomach

Is activated charcoal indicated?

• Activated charcoal reduces the absorption of most ingested drugs and poisons. In some cases it also increases the elimination (Table 11.5).

• Give 50 g with 200 ml of water (by mouth, gastric lavage tube or nasogastric tube), followed by 50 g 4-hourly until recovery or until plasma drug levels have fallen to within the safe range.

■ **Table 11.5. Drugs whose elimination is increased by repeated dosing with activated charcoal**

• Aspirin and other salicylates
• Digoxin
• Phenobarbitone
• Theophylline
• Carbamazepine

Based on
Editorial. Repeated oral activated charcoal in acute poisoning.
Lancet 1987;**1**:1013–5.

Is a specific antidote or treatment indicated?

• Poisoning with aspirin and paracetamol; Appendices 11.3 and 11.4.

• Specific antidotes for other poisons are given in Appendix 11.5.

Supportive treatment

1 Monitoring of the patient after severe poisoning is given in Table 11.6.

2 Unconscious patients should be nursed in the recovery position.

■ **Table 11.6. Monitoring of the patient after severe poisoning**

• **Conscious level** (Glasgow Coma Scale; Appendix 6.1, p. 49)
• **Respiratory rate**
• **Minute volume** if intubated, or if respiratory depression suspected
• **Blood pressure and heart rate** (ECG monitor)
• **Blood glucose**
• **Arterial blood gases** if the poison can cause a metabolic acidosis (aspirin, ethylene glycol, ethanol, methanol, tricyclic antidepressants) or there is suspected acute respiratory distress syndrome (ARDS) (p. 111) or after inhalation injury
• **Urine output** via catheter if poison potentially nephrotoxic, forced diuresis indicated or patient hypotensive or comatose
• **Temperature** (consider inhalation pneumonia if fever develops; Table 23.2, p. 138 for antibiotic therapy)

Common problems

• **Hypotension:** this usually responds to elevation of the foot of the bed and i.v. fluids. For further management see Chapter 3.

• **Respiratory depression:** the half-life of most opiates is longer than that of naloxone and repeated doses or an infusion may be required (p. 45). Alternatively, ventilate electively.

• **Fits:** these are a particular feature of poisoning with tricyclic antidepressants and theophylline. Give diazepam 5 mg i.v. then further doses up to 20 mg. Exclude hypoglycaemia and hypoxia. For further management, see Chapter 31.

Psychiatric assessment

This should be performed when the patient has recovered from the physical effects of the poisoning. Establish:

• the circumstances of the overdose — the underlying reasons and precipitants, and whether it was impulsive or planned;

• past psychiatric history;

• whether there is a high suicidal risk (Table 11.7) or evidence of a psychiatric disorder (Table 11.8): these patients should be referred to a psychiatrist before discharge;

• social circumstances: where will the patient go on leaving hospital?

■ **Table 11.7. Patients at high risk of suicide after self-poisoning**

• Middle-aged or elderly men
• Widowed, divorced or separated
• Unemployed
• Psychiatric or chronic physical illness
• Chronic alcohol or drug abuse
• Self-poisoning massive, planned, note left, discovery evaded

■ **Table 11.8. Evidence of major psychiatric disorder in patients with self-poisoning**

• Biological evidence of depression — e.g constipation, insomnia, psychomotor retardation
• Psychotic ideation — e.g. paranoid thoughts, feelings of bodily corruption
• First-rank symptoms of schizophrenia — e.g. thought insertion or withdrawal, auditory hallucinations

Appendices

11.1. National Poisons Information Service

For information and advice in cases of poisoning, contact one of the centres listed in Table 11.9 and ask for Poisons Information.

■ **Table 11.9. Poisons Information centres**

London	New Cross Hospital	071 635 9191
Belfast	Royal Victoria Hospital	0232 240503
Cardiff	Landough Hospital	0222 709901
Dublin	Beaumont Hospital	0001 379966
Edinburgh	Edinburgh Royal Infirmary	031 229 2477
Birmingham	Dudley Road Hospital	021 554 3801
Leeds	Leeds General Infirmary	0532 430715
Newcastle	Royal Victoria Infirmary	091 232 1525 (9 am–5 pm) or 091 232 5131 (after 5pm)

11.2. Poisoning — clues to the substance ingested

Coma	Barbiturates, benzodiazepines, ethanol, glutethimide, opiates, trichloroethanol, tricyclics
Fits	Amphetamine, phenothiazines, theophylline, tricyclics
Constricted pupils	Organophosphates, opiates, trichloroethanol
Dilated pupils	Cocaine, glutethimide, phenothiazines, quinine, sympathomimetics, tricyclics
Cardiac arrythmias	Antiarrhythmics, anticholinergics, phenothiazines, quinine, sympathomimetics, tricyclics
Pulmonary oedema	Aspirin, ethylene glycol, irritant gases, opiates, organophosphates, tricyclics, paraquat
Metabolic acidosis	Aspirin, ethanol, ethylene glycol, methanol, tricyclics
Hyperthermia	Anticholinergics, MAO inhibitors

11.2. (Continued)

Renal failure (not due to hypotension or rhabdomyoysis)	Ethylene glycol, methanol, paracetamol, aspirin

11.3. Poisoning with aspirin and other salicylates

1 Ingestion of 15 g of aspirin (50 × 300 mg tablets) causes moderate to severe poisoning in an adult.

2 Gastric lavage should be performed if the patient is seen within 12 hours of ingestion, followed by treatment with activated charcoal (p. 75).

3 Investigation is given in Table 11.11.

4 Further management depends on the degree of poisoning.

■ **Table 11.11. Investigation in aspirin poisoning**

- **Full blood count**
- **Prothrombin time** (may be prolonged)
- **Urea and electrolytes** (hypokalaemia is common)
- **Blood glucose** (hypoglycaemia may occur)
- **Arterial blood gases** (respiratory alkalosis in early stage, progressing to metabolic acidosis)
- **Plasma salicylate level** (sample taken >6 hours after ingestion; Table 11.12. Repeat 4 hours later as levels may continue to rise for 24 hours or more)
- **Chest X-ray** (pulmonary oedema may occur)

■ **Table 11.12. Interpretation of plasma salicylate level (sample taken >6 hours after ingestion)**

Plasma level (mg/l)	Interpretation
150–250	Therapeutic
250–500	Mild poisoning
500–750	Moderate poisoning
>750	Severe poisoning

Mild poisoning
Fluid replacement (oral or i.v.).

Moderate or severe poisoning
• Fluid replacement, preferably guided by measurement of CVP (always put in a CVP line if the patient is over 60 years).
• Urinary catheter to monitor urine output.
• Correct hypokalaemia with i.v. potassium.
• Correct hypoglycaemia with i.v. dextrose.
• Give vitamin K 10 mg i.v. to reverse hypoprothrombinaemia.
• Forced alkaline diuresis **(Fig. 11.1)** in an ITU for moderate poisoning.
• Patients with severe poisoning (plasma level >750 mg/l after rehydration or >1000 mg/l before rehydration) arterial pH <7.3, renal failure or pulmonary oedema should be referred urgently for haemodialysis.
Peritoneal dialysis can be used but is less effective.

11.4. Paracetamol poisoning

• The threshold dose for severe hepatic toxicity is 150–250 mg/kg.
• Management is outlined in Fig. 11.2.
• Gastric lavage should be performed if the patient is seen within 6 hours of ingestion of >10 g (>5 g if alcoholic, on anticonvulsants or on starvation diet).
• Patients who might have taken >7.5 g of paracetamol within 8–12 hours should be treated immediately with oral methionine or i.v. acetylcysteine (see below). This can be stopped if the plasma level is below the treatment line.
• Prolongation of the prothrombin time is the first sign of hepatic necrosis. Severe liver damage is indicated by a prothrombin time >45 seconds at 48 hours. Prothrombin time, liver function tests and plasma urea and creatinine should be checked daily in patients who present >15 hours after ingestion of a significant amount. See Chapter 33 for further management of fulminant hepatic failure.

Treatment regimens in paracetamol poisoning

Methionine (total dose 10 g)
Supplied as 250 mg tablets. Give ten tablets on admission followed by three doses of ten tablets 4-hourly.

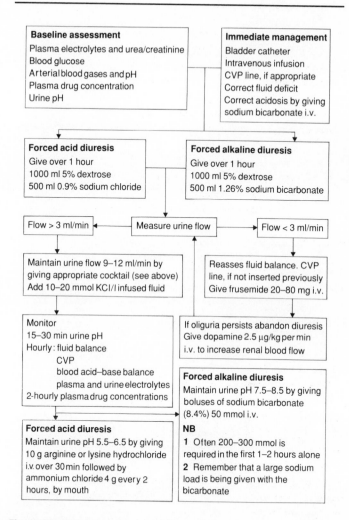

Baseline assessment
Plasma electrolytes and urea/creatinine
Blood glucose
Arterial blood gases and pH
Plasma drug concentration
Urine pH

Immediate management
Bladder catheter
Intravenous infusion
CVP line, if appropriate
Correct fluid deficit
Correct acidosis by giving
sodium bicarbonate i.v.

Forced acid diuresis
Give over 1 hour
1000 ml 5% dextrose
500 ml 0.9% sodium chloride

Forced alkaline diuresis
Give over 1 hour
1000 ml 5% dextrose
500 ml 1.26% sodium bicarbonate

Flow > 3 ml/min   Measure urine flow   Flow < 3 ml/min

Maintain urine flow 9–12 ml/min by
giving appropriate cocktail (see above)
Add 10–20 mmol KCl/l infused fluid

Reasses fluid balance. CVP
line, if not inserted previously
Give frusemide 20–80 mg i.v.

Monitor
15–30 min urine pH
Hourly: fluid balance
          CVP
          blood acid–base balance
          plasma and urine electrolytes
2-hourly plasma drug concentrations

If oliguria persists abandon diuresis
Give dopamine 2.5 µg/kg per min
i.v. to increase renal blood flow

Forced alkaline diuresis
Maintain urine pH 7.5–8.5 by giving
boluses of sodium bicarbonate
(8.4%) 50 mmol i.v.

Forced acid diuresis
Maintain urine pH 5.5–6.5 by giving
10 g arginine or lysine hydrochloride
i.v. over 30 min followed by
ammonium chloride 4 g every 2
hours, by mouth

NB
1 Often 200–300 mmol is
required in the first 1–2 hours alone
2 Remember that a large sodium
load is being given with the
bicarbonate

Fig. 11.1 Forced diuresis in adults. Redrawn from Vale A, Meredith T, Buckley
B, *Br Med J* 1984;**289**:367.

a

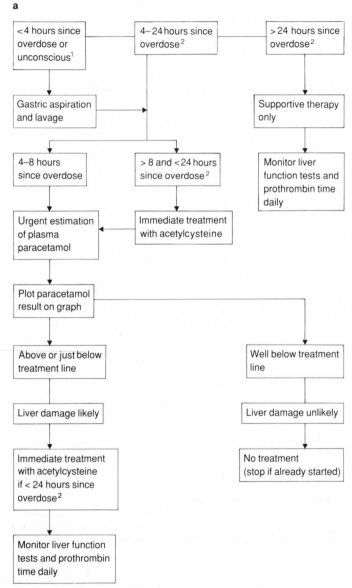

b

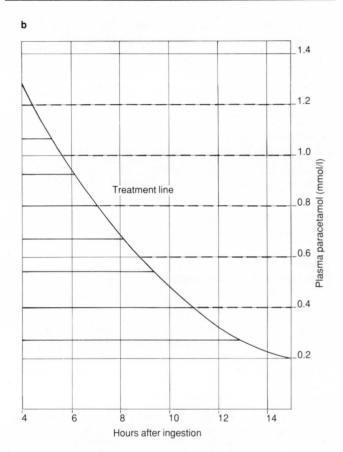

Fig. 11.2. a Management of suspected paracetamol poisoning.
[1] Results of plasma paracetamol estimation cannot be interpreted less than 4 hours after ingestion of the overdose.
[2] Trials are in progress to test the efficacy and safety of acetylcysteine given up to 36 hours after overdose.
b Plasma paracetamol concentration in relation to time after overdosage as a guide to prognosis. Acetylcysteine is indicated in patients with values above or just below the treatment line. Reproduced from Prescott LF. *Health Bull* 1978;**4**:204.

Acetylcysteine (total dose 300 mg/kg)

Supplied as 10 ml ampoules containing 2 g (200 mg/ml).

Start infusion as soon as possible:

- 150 mg/kg over 15 minutes, then;
- 50 mg/kg in 500 ml 5% dextrose over 4 hours, then;
- 100 mg/kg in 1 litre 5% dextrose over 16 hours.

Acetylcysteine should be given

- If the overdose is very large or plasma level very high.
- If activated charcoal has been given.
- If the patient is vomiting before or after administration of methionine.
- If the patient is comatose.
- If the patient is seen 12–24 hours after ingestion.

11.5. Specific antidotes

Poison	Antidote
Arsenic	**Dimercaprol** 2.5–5 mg/kg by deep i.m. injection 4-hourly for 2 days then 2.5 mg/kg 12-hourly on day three then 2.5 mg/kg once daily
Benzodiazepines	**Flumazenil** 1–2 mg i.v. (for respiratory arrest)
Beta-blockers	Appendix 2.1, p. 25
Cyanide	**Dicobalt edetate** 600 mg i.v. over 1 min then 300 mg if recovery does not occur within 1 min; *or* **Sodium nitrite** 10 ml of 3% solution i.v. over 3 min followed by **sodium thiosulphate** 25 ml of 50% solution i.v. over 10 min
Digoxin	**Digoxin specific antibody** (Table 2.12, p. 27)
Ethylene glycol	**Ethanol** 50 g p.o. or i.v. followed by 10–12 g/hour p.o. or by i.v. infusion of 10% ethanol in normal saline to maintain plasma ethanol level 1–2 g/l. For patients with induced liver enzymes (phenytoin therapy or chronic alcohol abuse) give at 12–15 g/hour, or if haemodialysed at 17–22 g/hour

11.5. (Continued)

Iron	**Desferrioxamine** 15 mg/kg per hour slow i.v. infusion (maximum 80 mg/kg in 24 hours). Gastric lavage with desferrioxamine 2 g in 1 litre water
Lead	**Dimercaprol** (see under arsenic) *or* **penicillamine** 250 mg to 2 g p.o. daily
Mercury	**Dimercaprol** (see under Arsenic) *or* **penicillamine**
Methanol	**Ethanol** (see under Ethylene glycol)
Opiates	**Naloxone** (Table 6.2, p. 45)
Organophosphates	**Atropine** 1.2–2.4 mg i.v. every 10 min until heart rate >70/min and mouth dry. Give further doses for 2–3 days
Paracetamol	**Methionine or acetylcysteine** (Appendix 11.4)
Paraquat	**Fuller's earth** 250 ml of 30% suspension p.o. 4-hourly for 24–48 hours. Give with magnesium sulphate as a purgative (250 ml of 5% solution until diarrhoea occurs)
Thallium	**Prussian blue** 10 g 12-hourly p.o. with a magnesium sulphate purgative (see under Paraquat) until thallium is no longer detected in the faeces
Warfarin	**Vitamin K** (Table 57.10, p. 298)

Based on

Drugs of special value in the treatment of poisoning in accident and emergency departments. DHSS circular HN (78) 23.

Section 2
Specific Problems

12 Acute Myocardial Infarction

- Acute central chest pain is the commonest symptom but may be absent or overshadowed by other clinical features (Table 12.1), particularly in elderly patients.

■ **Table 12.1.** Presentations of myocardial infarction without chest pain

- Acute pulmonary oedema
- Syncope (from an arrhythmia)
- Acute epigastric pain and vomiting
- Post-operative hypotension or oliguria
- Acute confusional state
- Stroke
- Diabetic hyperglycaemic states

- **The working diagnosis is based on the history and ECG** (Fig.12.1). Confirmation of myocardial infarction requires a twofold or greater rise in cardiac enzymes (Appendix 12.1). For prolonged angina without ECG changes of infarction see Chapter 13.
- **Remember that chest or upper abdominal pain with ECG abnormalities can occur in several conditions other than myocardial infarction** (aortic dissection, pericarditis, pulmonary embolism, and occasionally pancreatitis and biliary tract disease).

Priorities

1 Connect the patient to an ECG monitor. **Make sure a defibrillator is near because VF is a common early complication.**
2 Give oxygen and put in a peripheral i.v. cannula.
3 Relieve pain with diamorphine (Table 12.2).
4 Is the patient suitable for thrombolytic therapy?
   - **Clinically definite MI.**
   - **ST elevation of >2 mm in chest leads or >1 mm in limb leads.**
   - **No major contraindication** (Table 57.6, p. 295).

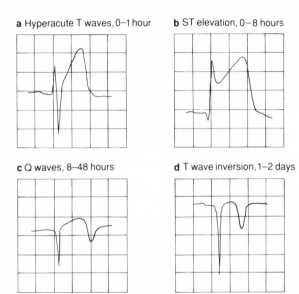

a Hyperacute T waves, 0–1 hour   **b** ST elevation, 0–8 hours

c Q waves, 8–48 hours   **d** T wave inversion, 1–2 days

Fig. 12.1. ECG changes in myocardial infarction.

■ **Table 12.2. Pain relief after myocardial infarction**

- Give diamorphine 5 mg (2.5 mg if the patient is small or elderly) i.v. over 3–5 min
- Give further doses of 2.5 mg every 10–15 min until the patient is free of pain
- An anti-emetic should also be given (e.g. prochlorperazine 12.5 mg or metoclopramide 10 mg i.v.)
- Avoid i.m. injections as absorption is unpredictable and they can result in a misleading elevation of plasma creatine kinase

- **Within 6 hours of the onset of pain, or within 24 hours if regional ST elevation is still present.**

    If so, give streptokinase 1.5 megaunits by i.v. infusion over 1 hour (p. 294) **and aspirin 150 mg p.o.**

5 Investigations required urgently are given in Table 12.3.

■ **Table 12.3.** Urgent investigation in suspected myocardial infarction

- **ECG** (repeat daily for 3 days or if pain recurs)
- **Chest X-ray**
- **Plasma potassium:** maintain at 4–5 mmol/l (recheck if significant arrhythmia occurs or after large diuresis)
- **Blood glucose** by stick test: insulin-dependent diabetes should be managed by insulin infusion (Table 38.1, p. 207)
- **Save plasma for cardiac enzymes** (check daily for 3 days or if pain recurs)

6 Are there complications of infarction — pulmonary oedema, hypotension, mitral regurgitation, VSD, arrhythmia or heart block? See **Problems** below.

Further management of uncomplicated infarction

1 Bed rest with ECG monitoring for 24–48 hours followed by a programme of mobilization. Discharge 7–10 days after admission.
2 Prophylaxis against deep vein thrombosis with heparin 5000 units 8-hourly s.c. until ambulant. In patients at high risk of thromboembolism (previous DVT or pulmonary embolism), consider full anticoagulation with i.v. heparin (1000 units/hour).
3 Oxygen can be discontinued if the chest X-ray shows clear lungs and there are no complications of infarction.
4 Consider a **benzodiazepine** (e.g. diazepam 5 mg 8-hourly p.o.) to reduce anxiety caused by the infarction and the atmosphere of the Coronary Care Unit.

Other points

What to do after thrombolytic therapy
- Start a heparin infusion (1000 u/hour) 4–6 hours after streptokinase and continue for 24 hours.
- Continue aspirin 150 mg daily for (at least) 1 month.

• In patients whose course is uncomplicated, further management is guided by a pre-discharge exercise test, as for non-Q wave infarction.

'Non-Q wave' infarction

• In one-third of patients, myocardial infarction occurs without the development of pathological Q waves on the ECG.

• Non-Q wave infarction is associated with a lower early mortality but a higher rate of reinfarction.

• A symptom-limited exercise test should be done before discharge in patients who would be candidates for angioplasty or bypass grafting.

• If any of the following occur: angina, ST segment depression >1 mm, or a fall in systolic BP of >10 mmHg (relative to the previous stage):

  a start a beta-blocker (e.g. timolol 5–10 mg 12-hourly) or diltiazem (60–120 mg 8-hourly);

  b refer to a cardiologist.

Secondary prevention

• Important modifiable risk factors are smoking, hypertension and hypercholesterolaemia.

• The routine use of beta-blockade (e.g. timolol 5–10 mg 12-hourly) in asymptomatic patients remains controversial.

Who should be referred to a cardiologist?

• Patients with suspected mitral regurgitation or VSD (see below).

• Unstable angina before discharge.

• Abnormal exercise test (defined above).

• Arguably all patients aged <50 years (who may occasionally have three vessel or left main stem disease in the absence of symptoms or an abnormal exercise test).

Problems

• **Pulmonary oedema.**

• **Hypotension and low cardiac output.**

- Arrhythmias and heart block.
- Further chest pain.
- New systolic murmur.
- Fever.

Pulmonary oedema

1 Give oxygen.
2 Correct arrhythmias.
3 Further treatment depends on the blood pressure.

Systolic BP > 100 mmHg

- Give **frusemide** 40–100 mg i.v.
- Start a **nitrate infusion**, e.g. isosorbide dinitrate ('Isoket') 2 mg/hour increasing by 2 mg/hour every 15–30 minutes until breathlessness is relieved or the systolic BP falls below 100 mmHg.
- If there is wheeze, give **aminophylline** 250 mg (5 mg/kg) by slow injection or infusion over 10 minutes watching for ventricular extrasystoles.

Systolic BP < 100 mmHg

Treatment is initially directed at improving the cardiac output and blood pressure.

Hypotension and low cardiac output (Table 12.4, Fig. 12.2)

■ **Table 12.4. Signs of a low cardiac output**

- **Heart rate:** usually >100/min
- **Skin:** cool or cold, sweating
- **Mental state:** agitated/confused
- **Urine output:** <30 ml/hour
- **Arterial pH:** metabolic acidosis

1 Give oxygen.
2 Correct arrhythmias.
3 Further treatment depends on whether or not the patient has pulmonary oedema.

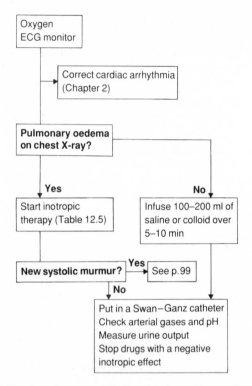

Fig. 12.2. Summary of management of hypotension and low cardiac output after myocardial infarction.

No pulmonary oedema

The two possibilities are **hypovolaemia** and **right ventricular infarction.** Hypovolaemia may be due to sweating, vomiting, reduced fluid intake or diuretic therapy.

● Check the JVP — low in hypovolaemia and high in right ventricular infarction.

● For both, initial treatment is a **fluid challenge: give 100–200 ml of normal saline or colloid over 5–10 minutes and assess the response.** This can be repeated if the patient does not become breathless and there are no clinical signs of pulmonary oedema.

If the blood pressure remains low despite 500 ml of fluid
• **Put in a Swan-Ganz catheter:** in right ventricular (RV) infarction, the right atrial pressure will be high (12–20 mmHg) and equal to or greater than the wedge pressure or PA diastolic pressure.
• **Give more fluid if necessary** to raise the wedge pressure/PA diastolic pressure to around 15 mmHg.
• **Start dobutamine** if the blood pressure remains low despite an adequate left ventricular (LV) filling pressure.

Pulmonary oedema present
• Start an **inotrope** (Table 12.5).

■ **Table 12.5.** Inotropic therapy in myocardial infarction

Systolic BP 80–100 mmHg	• **Dobutamine** 5–20 µg/kg per min (p. 294). This both increases cardiac output and blood pressure and reduces left atrial pressure
Systolic BP < 80 mmHg	• **Dopamine** 15–20 µg/kg per min (p. 293). At this dose dopamine has a vasoconstrictor effect
If this fails	• **Start noradrenaline** at 2 µg/min (p. 293), increasing the dose as required • **Reduce dopamine** to 2.5 µg/kg per min (renal vasodilator dose)

• **When the patient is stable with an adequate blood pressure, insert a Swan–Ganz catheter.** Measurement of the PA diastolic pressure or wedge pressure allows you to titrate the doses of inotrope and vasodilator to achieve the optimum haemodynamic result.

If Swan–Ganz catheterization is not feasible, you must rely on the clinical signs and the chest X-ray to estimate left atrial pressure (Table 12.6).
• **Providing the systolic BP has increased to at least 100 mmHg, start a nitrate infusion,** initially at low dose (isosorbide dinitrate 2 mg/hour). Adjust the doses of inotrope and nitrate, aiming for a PA

■ **Table 12.6. Myocardial infarction: prediction of left atrial pressure from the chest X-ray**

Appearances	Likely left atrial pressure (mmHg)
Normal lungs	<15
Distension of upper lobe veins	15–20
Interstitial pulmonary oedema	20–25
Alveolar pulmonary oedema	>25

NB Changes in the chest X-ray may lag several hours behind haemodynamic changes

diastolic/wedge pressure of 15–20 mmHg with a systolic BP of >100 mmHg.

• Diuretics are ineffective in patients with cardiogenic shock, but can be used once the cardiac output has increased (as shown by improvement in the patient's mental state and skin perfusion).

Arrhythmias and heart block

1 **Sinus bradycardia** is common after inferior MI but only needs treatment (p. 22) if causing hypotension, low cardiac output or ventricular escape rhythms.

2 **Second degree and complete heart block.**

   • **Inferior infarction:** pacing only needed if the patient has hypotension or low cardiac output, unresponsive to atropine.

   • **Anterior infarction:** pacing always indicated. Prophylactic pacing is indicated for conduction abnormalities which carry a high risk of progression to complete heart block in anterior infarction (Table 12.7).

3 **Tachyarrhythmias** are managed along standard lines, bearing in mind the following points:

   • hypokalaemia, hypoxia, acidosis and anxiety predispose to arrhythmias and should be corrected. In patients with significant arrhythmias, plasma potassium should be kept 4.5–5 mmol/l;

   • **accelerated idioventricular rhythm** (regular broad complex rhythm at a rate <120/min) does not need treatment;

   • **broad complex tachycardia (rate >120/min) after infarction is usually VT** rather than SVT with aberrant conduction (pp. 10–11). The

■ **Table 12.7. Indications for prophylactic pacing in anterior infarction**

- New right bundle branch block with either left axis (S wave > R in lead II) or right axis deviation (S wave > R in lead I) or new left bundle branch block
- Alternating left/right bundle branch block
- Second degree heart block (Mobitz II)

safest treatment is synchronized DC shock. **Verapamil can cause severe hypotension (and death) if given for VT.**

Further chest pain

A mild bruised sensation is common for 24–36 hours after infarction.

- **Infarct extension** (prolonged chest pain with fresh ST elevation) should be treated with further thrombolytic therapy unless contraindicated (p. 295). Use alteplase (plasminogen activator) if streptokinase or anistreplase have recently been given.
- **Unstable angina** (angina on minimal exertion or at rest) may occur after infarction and usually signifies severe coronary artery disease. Management is given in Chapter 13.
- **Pericarditis** is a common cause of new chest pain and usually occurs 2–3 days after infarction. The diagnosis is based on the patient's description of the pain (pleuritic or postural). A pericardial friction rub is not always heard. Treat with soluble aspirin 600 mg 6-hourly p.o. or indomethacin 25–50 mg 8-hourly p.o. until the pain has gone. Pericarditis is a relative contraindication to full anticoagulation (but not low-dose heparin s.c) because of the risk of haemopericardium.

New systolic murmur

1 This may be due to:
- misdiagnosis of a pericardial rub;
- mild mitral regurgitation due to ischaemic papillary muscle dysfunction;
- ventricular septal defect (Appendix 12.2);
- papillary muscle rupture (Appendix 12.3).

2 **Ventricular septal defect or papillary muscle rupture must be excluded (by echo-Doppler or Swan–Ganz catheterization):**
- if the murmur is loud (Grade III/VI or more) or accompanied by a thrill;

- if associated with pulmonary oedema, hypotension or low cardiac output.

Fever

Fever (up to 38°C) and a neutrophil leukocytosis (up to 12–15 $\times$ 10^9/l) is a common response to infarction, usually with a peak at 3–4 days, but check for:

- thrombophlebitis at cannula sites;
- signs of deep vein thrombosis;
- infection related to a Swan–Ganz catheter or pacing wire;
- pericarditis;
- urinary tract infection;
- pneumonia.

Appendices

12.1. Enzyme changes after myocardial infarction

Enzyme	Rises (hours)	Peaks	Return to normal (days)
CK	4–8	12–24 hours	3–4
CK-MB	4–8	12–20 hours	2–3
AST	8–12	18–36 hours	3–4
LDH	8–12	3–6 days	8–14

NB
- Peak enzyme levels are usually higher and reached earlier after thrombolysis with reperfusion
- Raised CK-MB levels may occur in the following: myocarditis, cardiac trauma, hypothermia, subarachnoid haemorrhage, renal failure

AST, aspartate transaminase (glutamic oxaloacetic transaminase); CK, creatine kinase; CK-MB, MB isoenzyme of creatine kinase; LDH, lactic dehydrogenase.

Based on
Lee TH, Goldman L. Serum enzyme assays in the diagnosis of acute myocardial infarction. Recommendations based on a quantitative analysis. *Ann Intern Med* 1986;**105**:221–33.

12.2. Ventricular septal defect

Incidence
One percent of infarcts. Usually occurs 5–10 days after infarction, more commonly after anterior infarction (defect in apical septum) than inferior (defect in basal septum).

Diagnosis
• **Clinical:** sudden haemodynamic deterioration, with pulmonary oedema and often cardiogenic shock. Pansystolic murmur, typically maximal at lower left sternal edge and often accompanied by a thrill.
• **Echocardiography:** the VSD may be seen. Systolic flow from LV to RV detectable by Doppler.
• **Swan–Ganz catheterization:** shows a step-up in oxygen saturation from right atrium to RV and PA (for calculation of the size of the shunt, see p. 292). The wedge pressure is high.

Action
Pulmonary oedema and hypotension should be managed as described above. Early surgical repair is recommended and you should discuss the case with your regional Cardiac Unit once the diagnosis has been established.

12.3. Papillary muscle rupture

Incidence
One percent of infarcts. Usually occurs 2–10 days after infarction, more commonly after inferior infarction (with rupture of posteromedial papillary muscle) than anterior (anterolateral papillary muscle).

Diagnosis
• **Clinical:** sudden haemodynamic deterioration, with pulmonary oedema and often cardiogenic shock. Pansystolic murmur, typically maximal at the apex.
• **Echocardiography:** may show a flail mitral leaflet. Severe mitral regurgitation detected by Doppler.

• **Swan–Ganz catheterization:** principally of use to exclude VSD. The wedge pressure is high with a large v wave.

Action
As for VSD.

12.4. Right ventricular infarction

Incidence
Five to 10% of inferior infarcts.

Diagnosis
• **Clinical: the clue to the diagnosis is a raised JVP** (which often rises further on inspiration) **with clear lungs.** Pulsus paradoxus (p. 118) and a right ventricular third sound may also be present.
• **ECG:** ST segment elevation in a lead placed over the right fifth intercostal space in the midclavicular line (RV4) may be detected in the first few hours after RV infarction.
• **Echocardiography:** the right ventricle is dilated, with akinesis/dyskinesis of the free wall.
• **Swan–Ganz catheterization:** the right atrial pressure is high (12–20 mmHg) and equal to or greater than the wedge pressure/PA diastolic pressure.

Action
Management of hypotension and low cardiac output due to RV infarction is discussed on pp. 94–95. If asymptomatic, no treatment is needed: **do not give a diuretic simply because the JVP is raised.**

13 Unstable Angina

Defined as angina at rest or on minimal exertion, without ECG or enzyme evidence of myocardial infarction.

Priorities

1 If angina is present at rest, record an ECG and meanwhile give sublingual glyceryl trinitrate. Start a nitrate infusion (Table 13.1).

■ **Table 13.1.** Isosorbide dinitrate infusion in unstable angina

• Add isosorbide dinitrate ('Isoket') 20 ml of 1mg/ml solution to 80 ml dextrose 5% in a burette (1 mg/5 ml)
• Run in fast until the pain starts to diminish then reduce the infusion rate to 2 mg/hour (10 ml/hour)
• If angina recurs, run in fast then maintain at 4 mg/hour. The infusion rate can be further increased to a maximum of 10 mg/hour, providing systolic BP is >110 mmHg

2 Transfer the patient to the Coronary Care Unit. Investigation is given in Table 13.2 and the treatment regimen in Table 13.3.

Further management

If angina does not recur
1 After 2 days, tail off the i.v. nitrate infusion. Change the beta-blocker to one which allows once-daily dosage.
2 Mobilize the patient: if angina does not occur, perform an exercise stress test before discharge.
3 Discuss further management with a cardiologist before discharging the patient:

■ **Table 13.2. Investigation in unstable angina**

- **ECG** on admission, daily for 3 days and if pain recurs
- **Chest X-ray**
- **Cardiac enzymes** on admission, daily for 2 days and if pain recurs
- **Urea, sodium and potassium**
- **Blood glucose** by stick test
- **Full blood count** (to exclude anaemia)

■ **Table 13.3. Initial treatment regimen in unstable angina**

- **Bed rest**
- **Nitrate,** orally (e.g. isosorbide mononitrate 20–40 mg 12-hourly) and by i.v. infusion if angina at rest
- **Beta-blocker* or calcium antagonist†**
- **Aspirin** 300 mg daily
- Diazepam 5 mg 8-hourly if anxious

*A beta-blocker with a short plasma half-life (e.g.propranolol, metoprolol) should be used initially so that its haemodynamic effects can be more rapidly reversed if necessary. Ajust the dose to achieve a resting heart rate around 50/min.

† If a beta-blocker is contraindicated, give a calcium antagonist instead. Diltiazem is preferable as it tends to slow the heart rate; nifedipine may occasionally worsen angina.

- if the patient is aged <50 years;
- if angina occurs on mobilization;
- if the exercise test is abnormal (chest pain or ST depression >1 mm; a fall in systolic BP >10 mmHg relative to the previous stage).

If angina recurs at rest

1 Increase the nitrate infusion.

2 Prescribe both a beta-blocker and a calcium antagonist. Maintain a heart rate around 50 beats/min provided the systolic BP is >100 mmHg.

3 Start a heparin infusion at 1 000u/hour.

4 Discuss further management with a cardiologist.

14 Aortic Dissection

Consider the diagnosis in any patient with **severe chest or upper abdominal pain of abrupt onset,** especially if:

• there are **associated neurological symptoms** — syncope, transient ischaemic attack, stroke or paraplegia;

• the patient is at increased risk of dissection because of **hypertension** or **Marfan's syndrome.**

Priorities

1 Relieve pain with diamorphine 5 mg i.v. (in the small or elderly, 2.5 mg) with further doses every 15 minutes as required. Complete your clinical assessment (Table 14.1).

■ **Table 14.1. Examination in suspected aortic dissection**

• **Blood pressure in both arms** (the difference in systolic pressure is normally <15 mmHg)
• **Peripheral pulses** — ?absence ?asymmetry
• **Early diastolic murmur of aortic regurgitation?** (Have the patient lean forward and hold his breath in expiration)
• **Limb power, tendon reflexes and plantar responses**

---

2 Obtain an ECG and PA chest X-ray (and lateral film if the patient's condition allows, to differentiate aortic unfolding from widening).

• The ECG is principally of use in assessing the likelihood of acute myocardial infarction.

• Aortic dissection can rarely involve the right coronary artery and cause inferior infarction. If this combination is suspected, thrombolytic therapy must not be given.

3 The working diagnosis is aortic dissection if:

• one or more major pulses is absent or asymmetric; *or*

• there is aortic regurgitation; *and*

- **the chest X-ray shows a widened mediastinum.** Other radiological signs of dissection are separation of inner and outer edges of aortic calcification by >1 cm and a small left pleural effusion.

Further management

1 Transfer the patient to the Intensive Care Unit. Put in an **arterial line** and a **urinary catheter**. Anuria (due to involvement of both renal arteries) will influence the decision to operate.
2 Start hypotensive therapy (Table 14.2). Aim to reduce systolic BP to 100–120 mmHg, providing the urine output remains >30 ml/hour.

■ **Table 14.2.** Hypotensive therapy for acute aortic dissection

1 Labetalol infusion
- Make up a solution of 1 mg/ml by diluting the contents of two ampoules (200 mg) to 200 ml with normal saline or dextrose 5%
- Start the infusion at 15 ml/hour and increase it every 15 min as necessary

2 Nitroprusside plus propranolol
- **Nitroprusside infusion**
  a Make up a solution of 100 µg/ml by adding 50 mg to 500 ml dextrose 5%
  b Start the infusion at 6 ml/hour (10 µg/min) and increase it by steps of 10 µg/min every 5 min as necessary
- **Propranolol:** Give 0.1 mg/kg i.v. every 4–6 hours

3 Trimetaphan infusion: this should be used if there are contraindications to beta-blockade such as airways obstruction or congestive heart failure
- Make up a solution of 10 mg/ml by diluting the contents of two ampoules (500 mg) to 50 ml with normal saline or dextrose 5%
- Start the infusion at 6 ml/hour (1 mg/min) and increase the infusion rate every 15 min as necessary

DeBakey
classification

I   II   III

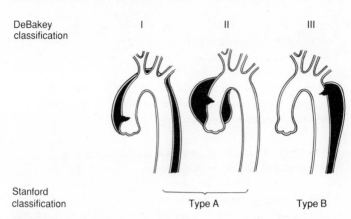

Stanford
classification

Type A   Type B

Fig. 14.1. Classification of aortic dissection.

3 Contact the regional Cardiac Unit to discuss further investigation and management. In general, dissections involving the ascending thoracic aorta are managed surgically; others are managed medically in the first instance (Fig. 14.1).

15   Severe Hypertension

- Defined by a diastolic BP >120 mmHg.
- **Emergency i.v. therapy is rarely required and is potentially dangerous.** Abrupt reduction of blood pressure may cause stroke, myocardial infarction or renal failure.

Priorities

1 **Check the blood pressure yourself.**
  - Examine the fundi and look for evidence of an underlying cause (Appendix 15.1).
  - Urgent investigation is given in Table 15.1.
2 **Are there indications for emergency treatment?**
  - Left ventricular failure with alveolar pulmonary oedema.
  - Hypertensive encephalopathy (p. 108).
  - Acute aortic dissection.

If so:

3 Transfer the patient to the ITU.
4 Put in an arterial line to allow continuous monitoring of the blood pressure and a urinary catheter to monitor urine output.
5 Give **frusemide** 40–80 mg i.v. if there is left ventricular failure or encephalopathy.
6 Start i.v. antihypertensive therapy (Table 15.2).

Further management

1 **Admit the patient if there is:**
  - papilloedema, retinal haemorrhages or exudates;
  - renal failure;
  - interstitial pulmonary oedema;
  - the diastolic pressure is >130 mmHg.
2 Start oral therapy (Table 15.3). Recheck the blood pressure

■ **Table 15.1.** Urgent investigation in the patient with severe hypertension

- **Urea and electrolytes**
- **Urinalysis** (plus urine microscopy if abnormal)
- **Chest X-ray**
- **ECG**

■ **Table 15.2.** Intravenous therapy for hypertensive emergencies. Aim to reduce diastolic BP to 100–110 mmHg within 1 hour. Options are:

1 Labetalol — the treatment of choice if phaeochromocytoma is suspected; avoid in left ventricular failure
- Make up a solution of 1 mg/ml by diluting the contents of two ampoules (200 mg) to 200 ml with normal saline or dextrose 5%. Start the infusion at 15 ml/hour and increase it every 15 min

2 Nitroprusside
- Make up a solution of 100 μg/ml by adding 50 mg to 500 ml dextrose 5%. Start the infusion at 6 ml/hour (10 μg/min) and increase it by steps of 10 μg/min every 5 min

3 Diazoxide
- Give a 'mini-bolus' of 50–100 mg every 5–10 min

■ **Table 15.3.** Initial oral therapy for severe hypertension: aim to reduce diastolic BP to around 110 mmHg over the first 24 hours

Interstitial pulmonary oedema	• Frusemide 20 mg (higher doses will be necessary in patients with impaired renal function): *plus* • Nifedipine 10–20 mg 8-hourly
Phaeochromocytoma suspected	• Labetalol 100–200 mg 12-hourly
Beta-blockers contraindicated	• Nifedipine 10–20 mg 8-hourly • Clonidine 100–200 μg 8-hourly • Hydralazine 25–50 mg 8-hourly
Other patients	• Atenolol 50–100 mg once daily • Any of the above

NB Avoid ACE inhibitors as initial treatment because of unpredictable first-dose hypotension

every 30 minutes. If the diastolic BP is unchanged after 4 hours, repeat the dose or add another drug.

3 Discuss urgently with a renal physician if there is:

- evidence of acute glomerulonephritis (>2 + proteinuria and/or cell casts in the urine);
- acute renal failure.

Problems

1 Hypertensive encephalopathy, subarachnoid haemorrhage or stroke?

- These may be difficult to distinguish clinically. Hypertensive encephalopathy is favoured by:

    a gradual onset of symptoms (Table 15.4);

    b focal neurological signs absent, or appearing late.

- If there is diagnostic doubt, a CT scan should be obtained to exclude cerebral or subarachnoid haemorrhage before starting i.v. therapy (Table 15.2).

■ **Table 15.4.** Clinical features of hypertensive encephalopathy

Early features	• Headache
	• Nausea and vomiting
	• Confusional state
	• Retinal haemorrhages, exudates or papilloedema
Late features	• Focal neurological signs
	• Fits
	• Coma

2 Recent stroke.

- Rapid lowering of the blood pressure may worsen the neurological deficit.
- Treat if diastolic BP >120 mmHg after 48 hours (Table 15.3).
- Long-term antihypertensive treatment is indicated if diastolic BP is >100 mmHg after 3 months.

Appendix

15.1. Causes of secondary hypertension

Cause	Clues
Drugs	Corticosteroids, carbenoxolone, oral contraceptives
Coarctation of the aorta	Radio-femoral delay
Renal artery stenosis	Abdominal bruit
Renal disease	Palpable kidneys, raised urea and creatinine, abnormal urinalysis or microscopy
Phaeochromocytoma	Paroxysmal headache, sweating, and palpitation
Primary hyperaldosteronism	Hypokalaemia
Cushing's syndrome	Truncal obesity, thin skin with purple abdominal striae, proximal myopathy

16 Pulmonary Oedema

Causes:
- **high pulmonary capillary pressure** from cardiac disease or fluid overload (overtransfusion, renal failure);
- **increased pulmonary capillary permeability** — the adult respiratory distress syndrome (ARDS) or 'shock lung'.

Priorities

1 Give oxygen 50%.
2 Check the blood pressure and pulse and listen to the heart and lungs.
   If there is any diagnostic doubt, obtain a chest X-ray before starting drug treatment. Inspiratory crackles are not always present; wheeze is common and may lead to the misdiagnosis of asthma.
3 Attach an ECG monitor and treat arrhythmias.
4 Put in a peripheral i.v. cannula and give the following drugs:
   - **diamorphine** 2.5–5.0 mg by slow i.v. injection;
   - **frusemide** 40–80 mg i.v.
   - **glyceryl trinitrate spray** two puffs sublingually (if systolic BP >90 mmHg).
   If there is wheeze, give:
   - **nebulized salbutamol** or **aminophylline** 250 mg (5 mg/kg) i.v. over 10 minutes (stop the injection if this causes frequent ventricular extrasystoles).
5 If pulmonary oedema is due to overtransfusion, venesect using a large bore cannula or a blood donation set.
6 Investigations required urgently are given in Table 16.1.
7 Has the patient got ARDS rather than cardiogenic pulmonary oedema (Table 16.2)?
   The management of ARDS is outlined in Appendix 15.1
8 Has the patient got renal failure? In patients with a blood urea >20 mmol/l, conventional doses of frusemide are often ineffective.

■ **Table 16.1.** Urgent investigation in pulmonary oedema

- **ECG** (?arrhythmia; ?evidence of infarction or other cardiac disease, e.g. left ventricular hypertrophy, left bundle branch block)
- **Chest X-ray** (to confirm the clinical diagnosis and exclude other causes of breathlessness — effusion, pneumothorax, pneumonia)
- **Arterial blood gases** (if not improving within 30 min)
- **Urea and electrolytes**
- **Full blood count**
- **Echocardiogram** (if valvular disease or VSD suspected)

■ **Table 16.2.** When to suspect ARDS rather than cardiogenic pulmonary oedema

- The patient is at risk of ARDS: sepsis, major trauma, major surgery, acute pancreatitis and opiate poisoning are the most important predisposing factors
- Normal ECG
- The chest X-ray shows diffuse bilateral shadowing (often sparing the costophrenic angles), but without cardiomegaly or distension of upper lobe pulmonary veins

- Try a frusemide infusion (p. 190)
- If this fails, dialysis will be needed. In extreme circumstances, venesect 500 ml while this is being arranged.

Further management of cardiogenic pulmonary oedema

If the patient is hypotensive or still breathless after 30 minutes

Drug therapy depends on the blood pressure
1 **Systolic BP >100 mmHg:**
  - give another dose of frusemide 40–80 mg i.v.;
  - start a **nitrate infusion** (p. 101): if the patient remains breathless, increase the infusion rate every 15–30 minutes providing systolic BP is >110 mmHg.

2 Systolic BP 80–100 mmHg:
- start a **dobutamine infusion** at a dose of 5 μg/kg per min
(p. 294): increase the dose by 2–3 μg/kg per min every 15–30
minutes until systolic BP is 110 mmHg or a maximum dose of 20
μg/kg per min has been reached;
- a **nitrate infusion** can be added if systolic BP is maintained at
>100 mmHg.

3 Systolic BP < 80 mmHg (cardiogenic shock):
- start a **dopamine infusion** at 10 μg/kg per min (p. 293). Increase
the dose by 5 μg/kg per min every 15 minutes until systolic BP is
>100 mmHg: if systolic BP remains <90 mmHg despite dopamine
20 μg/kg per min, use **noradrenaline** instead (p. 293).

Check arterial gases and pH
- Increase the inspired oxygen concentration if necessary to
maintain Pao_2 around 10 kPa.
- Discuss ventilation with an anaesthetist if Pao_2 is <8 kPa
despite 60% oxygen, or Pao_2 is rising.
- If arterial pH is less than 7.20, infuse 50 mmol of sodium
bicarbonate (50 ml of 8.4% solution) over 15 minutes (severe
metabolic acidosis has a negative inotropic effect and facilitates
ventricular arrhythmias).

Put in a urinary catheter if systolic BP is < 90 mmHg or if no urine is passed after 1 hour
- The urine output is a good guide to the cardiac output and
should ideally be >30 ml/hour (>0.5 ml/kg per hour).
- If urine output is <30 ml/hour, start a dopamine infusion at 2.5
μg/kg per min (p. 293).

Put in a Swan-Ganz catheter if indicated (Table 16.3)
- Adjust the doses of inotrope and nitrate, aiming for a PA
diastolic/wedge pressure of 15–20 mmHg with a systolic BP>100
mmHg.

■ **Table 16.3.** Indications for Swan–Ganz catheterization in the patient with pulmonary oedema

- **Suspected ARDS**
- **Exclusion of VSD** in the patient with pulmonary oedema and a systolic murmur after myocardial infarction (p. 99)
- **Associated hypotension** requiring treatment with an inotrope

Decide what has caused or precipitated the attack (Tables 16.4, 16.5)

- Discuss further management with a cardiologist if you suspect valvular disease or a VSD (for which urgent surgery may be needed).
- Stop drugs with a negative inotropic effect (p. 25 for reversal of beta-blockade).

■ **Table 16.4.** Causes of cardiogenic pulmonary oedema 'out of the blue'

- Painless myocardial infarction
- Acute myocarditis
- Acute aortic regurgitation (aortic dissection, bacterial endocarditis, chest trauma)
- Acute mitral regurgitation (ruptured chordae or papillary muscle; p. 99)
- Acute VSD (after myocardial infarction; p 99)
- Severe aortic stenosis
- Severe mitral stenosis
- Left atrial myxoma

■ **Table 16.5.** Precipitants of pulmonary oedema in patients with previously stable valvular or left ventricular disease

- Myocardial infarction
- Arrhythmia (the onset of atrial fibrillation is a common precipitant of pulmonary oedema in patients with mitral or aortic stenosis)
- Drugs with a negative inotropic effect (e.g. betablockers)
- Poor compliance with diuretic therapy
- Drugs causing fluid retention (e.g. NSAIDs, steroids)
- Excessive i.v. fluid perioperatively

Appendix

16.1. Management of the adult respiratory distress syndrome

1 Put in a Swan–Ganz catheter. The differentiation of ARDS from cardiogenic pulmonary oedema is confirmed if the PA wedge pressure is <20 mmHg.

2 Discuss further management with an anaesthetist. The key elements are as follows.

Maintenance of oxygenation

keep Pao_2 9–11 kPa by adjusting the inspired oxygen concentration (FIO_2). Ventilation will be needed if Pao_2 is <8 kPa despite FIO_2 60%.

Monitoring of PA wedge pressure

This should be kept 10–15 mmHg at end-expiration.
Ventilation with positive end-expiratory pressure (PEEP) increases PA wedge pressure but usually results in a net decrease in LV filling pressure (as pleural pressure is often increased by a greater amount).

Correction of hypotension

If systolic BP is <90 mmHg, give colloid
i.v. to increase PA wedge pressure to around 15 mmHg. If hypotension persists, start an inotrope (Table 3.5, p. 31).

Sepsis

Sepsis may either cause or complicate ARDS: once blood cultures have been taken, start antibiotic therapy according to the likely source (Table 10.2, p. 67).

Steroids

There is no firm evidence that high dose corticosteroid affects the course of established ARDS and it should not be given.

17 Pericarditis

Consider the diagnosis in any patient with:
• pleuritic or postural chest pain especially following a flu-like prodrome or myocardial infarction;
• a pericardial friction rub;
• unexplained enlargement of the cardiac shadow on the chest X-ray.

Priorities

1 Relieve severe pain with **diamorphine** 2.5–5 mg i.v. over 3–5 minutes with an anti-emetic.
2 Look for evidence (Table 17.1) of:
   • **cardiac tamponade** (high JVP, pulsus paradoxus >20 mmHg, enlarged cardiac shadow);
   • **myocarditis** (interstitial pulmonary oedema);
   • **myocardial infarction** (ECG appearances).
3 **Is there an underlying cause requiring specific therapy?**
(Table 17.2.)

■ **Table 17.1. Urgent investigation in suspected pericarditis**

• **Chest X-ray** — enlarged cardiac shadow, ?interstitial oedema, ?consolidation
• **ECG** (Table 4.5, p. 37)
• **Cardiac enzyme series** (for later analysis; p. 98)
• **Full blood count**
• **Urea, sodium and potassium**
• **Echocardiogram** (if cardiac tamponade suspected or cardiac shadow enlarged — ?effusion or myocarditis)
• **Viral serology** (for later analysis)
• **Blood culture** (if suspected bacterial infection)

■ **Table 17.2.** Causes of pericarditis

- 'Idiopathic'
- Infectious diseases (viral, bacterial, fungal and tuberculous)
- Acute myocardial infarction
- Collagen disease, e.g. systemic lupus erthythematosus (SLE)
- Uraemia
- Pericardial surgery, trauma or irradiation
- Dressler's syndrome and postpericardiotomy syndrome
- Drugs — procainamide, hydralazine
- Neoplastic diseases (most commonly carcinoma of the bronchus or breast)
- Myxoedema

Further management

1 The diagnosis is confirmed by a pericardial friction rub and/or characteristic ST segment changes (Table 4.5, p. 37)

- The changes on the initial ECG may be impossible to distinguish from those of acute myocardial infarction. If there is diagnostic doubt, thrombolytic therapy must not be given.

2 Immediate pericardiocentesis is only indicated to relieve **cardiac tamponade** (Chapter 18).

3 If **bacterial pericarditis** is suspected:

- start antibiotic therapy after taking blood cultures:
  a flucloxacillin 1 g 6-hourly i.v.; *plus*
  b gentamicin i.v. (p. 71).
- obtain an echocardiogram to look for an effusion or evidence of endocarditis;
- perform pericardiocentesis if there is an effusion large enough to be drained safely (e.g. echo-free space >2 cm) (Chapter 51). Send fluid for cell count, Gram stain and culture. Consider tuberculous or fungal infection if the effusion is purulent but no organisms are seen on Gram stain;
- Discuss further management with a cardiologist.

4 If there is chest pain, start an **anti-inflammatory agent** (e.g. indomethacin 25–50 mg 8-hourly p.o).

5 Steroids are not indicated routinely and should only be considered for:

- recurrent pericarditis with a presumed autoimmune aetiology, e.g. Dressler's syndrome;
- underlying collagen disease if there is evidence of systemic activity. Discuss with a rheumatologist first.

18   Cardiac Tamponade

Consider cardiac tamponade in any patient with **hypotension** or **breathlessness** associated with:
- a raised JVP;
- pulsus paradoxus (Table 18.1).

■ **Table 18.1. Pulsus paradoxus**

1 A fall in systolic BP >10 mmHg on inspiration. May occur in cardiac tamponade, acute severe asthma and right ventricular failure
2 Check for pulsus paradoxus as follows:
  - Inflate the blood pressure cuff above systolic BP
  - Slowly deflate the cuff, watching the chest, and note the pressure at which sounds are first heard in expiration
  - Continue deflating the cuff and note the pressure at which sounds are first heard throughout expiration and inspiration

Priorities

1 Give oxygen, attach an ECG monitor and put in a peripheral venous cannula.
2 **Obtain an ECG and chest X-ray** to exclude other causes of hypotension/breathlessness (Table 18.2).
3 **Obtain an echocardiogram** to confirm the presence of a pericardial effusion and to exclude biventricular failure.
4 Perform **pericardiocentesis** immediately if a significant effusion is present (echo separation >1.5 cm) (Chapter 51). Obtain advice first in the following circumstances:
  - signs of tamponade but small effusion (echo separation <1.5 cm);
  - effusion with dilated left ventricle (pericardiocentesis may lead to further ventricular dilation).
5 If pericardiocentesis cannot be performed immediately, treat with i.v. colloid or blood and dopamine or noradrenaline (Tables 57.3, 57.4, p. 293) until the systolic BP is >90 mmHg.

■ **Table 18.2.** Causes of
hypotension with a
raised jugular venous
pressure

- Cardiac tamponade
- Severe biventricular failure
- Right ventricular infarction
- Pulmonary embolism
- Tension pneumothorax

Further management

This is directed at the underlying causes (Appendix 18.1).

- Patients with malignant effusion will usually require further
intervention to prevent recurrent tamponade, e.g. radiotherapy or
creation of a pericardial window.
- Antibiotic therapy for bacterial pericarditis is given on p. 116.

Appendix

18.1. Non-traumatic causes of cardiac tamponade

Cause	Percentage ($n = 56$)
Malignant disease (most commonly carcinoma of the bronchus or breast)	32
Idiopathic pericarditis	14
Uraemia	9
Acute myocardial infarction (receiving heparin)	9
Diagnostic procedures with cardiac perforation	7.5
Bacterial pericarditis	7.5
Tuberculous pericarditis	5
Radiation	4
Myxoedema	4
Aortic dissection	4
Postpericardiotomy syndrome	2
SLE	2
Cardiomyopathy (receiving anticoagulants)	2

Reference

Guberman BA, Fowler NO, Engel PJ, Gueron M, Allen JM. Cardiac tamponade in medical patients. *Circulation* 1981;**64**:633–40.

19 Deep Vein Thrombosis

• Deep vein thrombosis (DVT) cannot reliably be confirmed or excluded on clinical grounds. Venography is the most widely available diagnostic test.

• Heparin should not be started before other causes of leg swelling have been considered (Table 19.1).

■ **Table 19.1. Causes of leg swelling**

Venous/lymphatic	• Deep vein thrombosis
	• Superficial thrombophlebitis
	• Inferior vena cava obstruction (e.g. by tumour)
	• Varicose veins
	• Post-phlebitic syndrome
	• Vein harvesting for coronary bypass grafting
	• Congenital lymphoedema
	• Dependent oedema (e.g. in paralysed limb)
Musculoskeletal	• Calf haematoma
	• Ruptured Baker's cyst
	• Muscle tear
Skin	• Cellulitis
Systemic	• Congestive heart failure
	• Liver failure
	• Renal failure
	• Nephrotic syndrome
	• Hypoalbuminaemia
	• Chronic respiratory failure
	• Pregnancy
Drugs	• Nifedipine
	• Diltiazem

Management of the swollen leg

1 Is there an infective or systemic cause of leg swelling mimicking DVT?

- Cellulitis is recognized by tenderness, erythema and induration of the skin, with fever.
- Oedema in congestive heart failure, or renal or liver disease is usually bilateral, but may initially be unilateral, or asymmetric.

2 Is a musculoskeletal cause possible?

- Onset of pain and swelling after trauma; *or*
- Localized swelling or tenderness.

Discuss further management with an orthopaedic surgeon. Consider calf ultrasound or knee arthrography as first-line investigations instead of venography.

3 Is DVT likely?

- Risk factors are present (Table 19.2); *or*
- Evidence of pulmonary embolism (Chapter 20).

A heparin infusion should be started before venography.

■ **Table 19.2.** Factors predisposing to deep vein thrombosis

- Recent surgery particularly abdominal or pelvic
- Malignant disease
- Immobility (including long car or plane journey)
- Previous DVT or pulmonary embolism
- Recent child-birth
- Severe obesity
- Use of high oestrogen contraceptive pill
- Family history of DVT

Treatment of proven DVT

Standard treatment

1 Bed rest with elevation of the leg.

2 Analgesia.

3 Give heparin by i.v. infusion (p. 296).

4 Start warfarin on the 3rd day and stop heparin on the 5th day provided the prothrombin ratio is around two (p. 297).

5 The duration of warfarin therapy is controversial. The following are guidelines:

- three months for first DVT without extension above the groin;
- six months for first DVT extending above the groin or with proven pulmonary embolism;
- indefinite if recurrent thrombo-embolism.

Problems

1 **Suspected DVT, but the venogram was negative.**
   - Consider other causes of leg swelling (Table 19.1).
   - Idiopathic asymmetric leg swelling is a recognized syndrome and carries a benign prognosis. No treatment is necessary.
2 **Should every DVT be treated by anticoagulation?**
   - Thrombosis in the popliteal or more proximal veins of the leg should always be treated with anticoagulation (unless contraindicated).
   - Whether DVT confined to the venous sinuses of the calf requires anticoagulation is controversial, particularly in the older patient.

20 Pulmonary Embolism

Consider the diagnosis in any patient with:

- acute breathlessness;
- pleuritic chest pain;
- haemoptysis;
- hypotension;
- syncope.

If the patient is at risk of deep vein thrombosis (Table 19.2, p. 121) and you cannot make a confident alternative diagnosis, treat the patient for pulmonary embolism until proven otherwise.

Priorities

1 **Give oxygen and check arterial gases.** Hypoxia is invariable with large pulmonary emboli but normal gases do not exclude a small embolus.

2 **Obtain an ECG and chest X-ray.** These are principally of value in excluding alternative diagnoses (e.g. myocardial infarction, pneumonia, pneumothorax).

- The ECG will usually show only sinus tachycardia, or minor ST/T abnormalities.
- The chest X-ray may show an elevated hemi-diaphragm, a small pleural effusion or focal shadowing (the classic wedge-shaped shadow is rare).
- **A normal ECG and chest X-ray do not exclude the diagnosis.**

3 **Give 5000–10 000 units of heparin by i.v. bolus (100 u/kg).**

4 **If the patient is hypotensive (systolic BP <90 mmHg):**

- **connect an ECG monitor:** atrial fibrillation or flutter may occur with large pulmonary emboli and should be treated with intravenous digoxin (Table 2.7, p. 19);
- **start an infusion of colloid** (e.g. Haemaccel) : run in fluid rapidly until systolic BP is >100 mmHg. This will increase right ventricular filling and hence cardiac output. If the patient remains hypotensive after 500 ml of colloid has been given;

- **start dobutamine** with a dose of 5 µg/kg per min and increase it by 5 µg steps up to 20 µg/kg per min until systolic BP is >100 mmHg (Table 57.5, p. 294). If the systolic BP remains <90 mmHg, noradrenaline should be given (Table 57.3, p. 293);
- **decide whether thrombolytic therapy should be given:**
  a persistent hypotension after treatment for 30–60 minutes;
  b no contraindication to streptokinase (Table 57.6, p. 295).
  Streptokinase accelerates the lysis of thrombus and may improve survival in this group of patients. Because it can cause fatal bleeding, **the diagnosis must be confirmed by pulmonary angiography before streptokinase is given.** Continue heparin by infusion whilst waiting for angiography to be done.

5 If the patient is not hypotensive, or if thrombolytic therapy is contraindicated, continue heparin by infusion (p. 296).

Further management

1 Confirm the diagnosis. Further investigation to confirm or exclude pulmonary embolism is essential. A scheme for this is shown in Fig. 20.1.

2 Heparin infusion (p. 296). This should be continued for 5 days. The amount of heparin needed to maintain satisfactory anticoagulation can fluctuate and the kaolin-cephalin clotting time (KCCT) should be checked daily. Adjust the dose to keep the KCCT 1.5–2.5 times control.

3 Warfarin (p. 297). This should be started after 3 days (when the diagnosis has been confirmed) and overlapped with heparin infusion for 2 days. The prothrombin ratio should be kept 2.0–3.0 times control (3.0–4.5 in patients with recurrent thrombo-embolism). Warfarin should be given for 3–6 months unless the patient is at risk of recurrent thrombo-embolism, in which case it should be continued indefinitely.

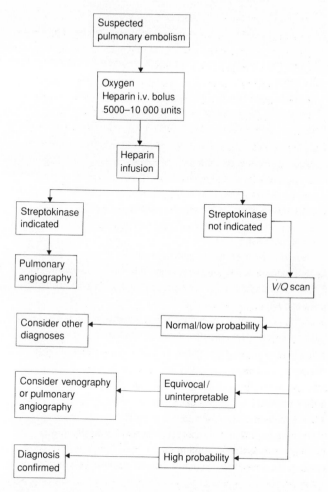

Fig. 20.1. Summary of management of suspected pulmonary embolism.

21   Acute Asthma

- Consider the diagnosis in any patient with **acute breathlessness and wheeze.**
- Always measure peak flow and arterial blood gases.
- The severity of an attack is easily underestimated.

Priorities

If respiratory arrest appears imminent
- exhausted patient making ineffective respiratory efforts;
- 'silent' chest;
- systolic BP <90 mmHg with cold skin.

1 Give oxygen 100% and adrenaline 0.5–1 mg i.v., s.c. or i.m.

2 Call an anaesthetist in case urgent intubation and ventilation are needed.

3 Continue treatment as below. Some patients will improve rapidly but ventilation will be needed if the patient becomes increasingly exhausted or Paco$_2$ remains >7 kPa or Pao$_2$ <7 kPa on 60% oxygen.

Other patients

1 Give oxygen and nebulized salbutamol 1 ml of nebulizer solution (5 mg) diluted with 2 ml normal saline or sterile water.

2 Give hydrocortisone 200 mg i.v.

3 Recheck peak flow, measure arterial blood gases and arrange a chest X-ray.

4 Consider **aminophylline** if the patient is still breathless.
- Do not give if the patient has been taking oral theophylline or aminophylline or has been given aminophylline i.v. by the GP.
- Give aminophylline 250–500 mg (5 mg/kg) by slow i.v. injection over 10–15 minutes.

5 Assess the severity of the attack from the clinical signs (Table

21.1) and arterial blood gases (Table 21.2). This will guide further therapy. Increase the inspired oxygen concentration if Pao_2 is <10 kPa.

■ **Table 21.1. Acute asthma: signs of a severe attack**

• Unable to speak without pauses
• Respiratory rate >30/min
• Pulse rate >120/min
• Systolic BP <100 mmHg
• Pulsus paradoxus >20 mmHg
• Peak expiratory flow rate <150 l/min or the patient is too breathless to use the meter

■ **Table 21.2. Arterial blood gases in acute asthma**

	Pao_2* (kPa)	$Paco_2$	pH
Mild	> 10	< 4	> 7.45
Moderate	8–10	< 4	> 7.45
Severe	< 8	4.5–6	7.35–7.45
Exhaustion	< 7	> 6	< 7.35

* Pao_2 must be related to the inspired oxygen concentration. The values given are with the patient breathing air.

Further management

1 Confirm the diagnosis by:
  • positive features in the history (Table 21.3);
  • the exclusion of other causes of breathlessness and wheeze (Table 21.4);
  • chest X-ray:
    a clear lung fields;
    b overexpansion of the lungs, shown by squared-off apices and flattened diaphragms (the anterior sixth rib should normally cross the midpoint of the diaphragm).

■ **Table 21.3. Features supporting a diagnosis of asthma**

- Previous similar episodes of breathlessness or wheeze responding to bronchodilator therapy
- Diurnal and seasonal variation in symptoms
- Wheeze provoked by exercise or allergen exposure
- Eczema or hayfever
- Family history of asthma
- 'Chestiness' or 'wheezy bronchitis' in childhood

■ **Table 21.4. Causes of acute breathlessness and wheeze**

- Acute asthma
- Acute infective exacerbation of chronic airflow limitation
- Pulmonary oedema
- Pulmonary embolism
- Anaphylactic reaction
- Upper airways obstruction

2 Upper airways obstruction (Table 21.5) should always be considered in patients with no history of previous similar attacks. If you suspect this, discuss management with an ENT surgeon or chest physician.

3 Patients with a severe attack should be admitted to ITU in case ventilation is required. An **arterial line** is useful as frequent arterial blood samples will be needed.

4 Guidelines for treatment are given in Table 21.6. Reassess the patient after 2 hours and if there has been no improvement, intensify the treatment.

■ **Table 21.5. Upper airways obstruction**

Causes	• Inhalation of foreign body
	• Tumours of larynx and trachea (preceding hoarseness)
	• Angioedema (associated urticaria)
	• Acute epiglottitis
Clues to the diagnosis	• Stridor (inspiratory wheeze)
	• No response to bronchodilator
	• Raised $Paco_2$

■ **Table 21.6.** Summary of treatment in asthma

Treatment	Grade of attack		
	Mild	Moderate	Severe
Oral prednisolone	+	+	+
Nebulized salbutamol	+	+	+
Continuous oxygen		+	+
Nebulized ipratropium		+	+
Hydrocortisone i.v.		+	+
Aminophylline i.v.			+
Intravenous fluids (with K$^+$)			+

Steroid therapy

Bronchial inflammation and oedema are more important factors in acute airflow limitation than increased smooth muscle tone.

• Start hydrocortisone 200 mg 8-hourly i.v. in moderate or severe attacks.

• Convert to oral prednisolone 30–60 mg daily after 48 hours if improving.

• In mild attacks, give oral prednisolone 30–60 mg as a single morning dose.

• Start inhaled steroid before discharge (e.g. 'Becloforte' two puffs 12-hourly).

• Stop prednisolone after 10–14 days (taper if the patient has previously been receiving oral steroid.)

Continuous oxygen

• Start with 35–50% humidified oxygen via a controlled delivery mask.

• Increase if necessary to keep arterial Po_2 around 10 kPa (75 mmHg).

Bronchodilator therapy

• Give nebulized salbutamol 2.5–5 mg (0.5–1 ml of nebulizer solution) 4–6 hourly.

• In moderate or severe attacks, add ipratropium 250–500 μg

(1–2 ml of nebulizer solution) 4–6 hourly. The two can be given together or alternately every 2–3 hours.

• Salbutamol may be given by i.v. infusion (Table 21.7) instead of by nebulizer: this may be helpful if the patient will not keep a mask on.

• An aminophylline infusion (Table 21.7) should be given in severe attacks.

■ **Table 21.7.** Bronchodilator infusions in acute severe asthma

Salbutamol	• Add 5 mg (5 ml of 1 mg/ml solution) to 500 ml normal saline or 5% dextrose (giving a salbutamol concentration of 10 µg/ml) • Start at 1 ml/min, increasing up to 3 ml/min if necessary
Aminophylline	• **Loading dose:** give 250–500 mg (5 mg/kg) i.v. over 10–15 min (omit if previous treatment with theophylline or aminophylline) • **Maintenance dose:** 0.5 mg/kg per hour by i.v. infusion. If you cannot check levels, halve the dose in patients with congestive heart failure or liver disease **For an average sized adult, add 250 mg to 1 litre of saline or dextrose 5% and infuse over 8 hours** • **Nausea and vomiting** are common toxic effects • The **therapeutic range** for theophylline is 10–20 mg/l

Other points

1 Further monitoring.
   • **Peak flow rate** should be measured every 6 hours (before and after bronchodilator therapy).
   • **Arterial gases** should be rechecked:
   a if Paco$_2$ was above 5 kPa on admission (recheck 20–30 minutes after institution of treatment);
   b if the peak flow is not improving;
   c if the patient's clinical condition worsens.

2 Antibiotics.
   • Give where there is evidence of respiratory infection — fever,

purulent (green) sputum or focal shadowing on the chest X-ray.
- The choice of antibiotics is as for pneumonia (Table 23.2, p.138).
- Yellow sputum may be due to eosinophils and a raised white cell count to steroids.

3 Physiotherapy. Start only if there is evidence of respiratory infection.

4 Plasma potassium. Salbutamol and steroids may result in significant hypokalaemia. Check electrolytes the day after admission and give potassium supplements if potassium is less than 3.5 mmol/l.

Problems

Admit or discharge?

1 The severity of an attack can easily be underestimated.

2 **Only discharge the asthmatic if:**
- symptoms were due to the omission of usual bronchodilator therapy; *and*
- bronchospasm was promptly relieved by nebulized salbutamol (confirmed by measurement of peak flow); *and*
- no persisting cause of bronchospasm (e.g. infection).

3 **If in doubt, admit.**

Failure to improve

Consider:

1 **Wrong diagnosis:** other causes of acute breathlessness and wheeze are given in Table 21.4.

2 **Untreated respiratory infection.**

3 **Pneumothorax.**

4 **Inadequate therapy:**
- switch to maximal therapy;
- give salbutamol by infusion (Table 21.7) if the patient is too restless to use the nebulizer;
- increase steroid therapy to hydrocortisone 200 mg 4-hourly i.v.

22 Acute Exacerbation of Chronic Airflow Limitation

Consider in any patient with chronic airflow limitation (chronic bronchitis, emphysema or asthma) who develops:

- increased breathlessness;
- confusional state or drowsiness (due to worsening respiratory failure).

Priorities

1 Give oxygen 24% (preferably humidified) via a controlled delivery mask (e.g. Ventimask).

2 Give salbutamol 5 mg (1 ml of nebulizer solution) and ipratropium 500 µg (2 ml of nebulizer solution) diluted in 2 ml normal saline or sterile water via a nebulizer.

3 Investigations required urgently are given in Table 22.1.

■ **Table 22.1. Urgent investigation in acute exacerbation of chronic airflow limitation**

- **Chest X-ray**
- **ECG**
- **Peak expiratory flow rate** before and after bronchodilators (Table 58, p. 300)
- **Arterial blood gases**
- **Blood culture**
- **Sputum for Gram stain**

4 The working diagnosis of an **infective exacerbation** (the commonest cause) is based on an **increase in sputum volume or the development of purulent sputum**.

- Other causes of deterioration in respiratory function must be excluded (Table 22.2).
- Any pneumothorax unless very small must be drained (Chapter 53).

■ **Table 22.2. Chronic airflow limitation: causes of deterioration in respiratory function**

- Infective exacerbation
- Pneumonia (new shadowing on chest X-ray)
- Pneumothorax (differentiate from bulla; p. 144)
- Pulmonary embolism (pleuritic chest pain with clear lung fields; Chapter 20)
- Sedative drugs
- Sputum plugging (e.g. as a result of dehydration)
- Pulmonary oedema (Chapter 16)

Further management of infective exacerbation

1 Recheck arterial gases 20 minutes after starting oxygen 24%.
Management of oxygen therapy is summarized in Fig. 22.1, and a regimen for doxapram infusion is shown in Table 22.3.

2 Start the following drugs:

- **salbutamol** 2.5–5.0 mg 6-hourly by nebulizer;
- **ipratropium** 250–500 µg 6-hourly by nebulizer;

■ **Table 22.3. Doxapram infusion in respiratory failure with CO_2 retention**

- **Dosage: 1.5–4 mg/min, according to the response** (a 500 ml bottle contains 2 mg/ml in 5% dextrose)
- **Recheck arterial gases after 30 min**

NB May interact with aminophylline to cause agitation

| Time period (min) | Infusion rate | | |
	mg/min	ml/min	Drops/min*
0–15	4.0	2.0	40
15–30	3.0	1.5	30
30–60	2.0	1.0	20
60+	1.5	0.75	15

* With standard burette (20 drops/ml). Multiply ×3 if paediatric burette (60 drops/ml).

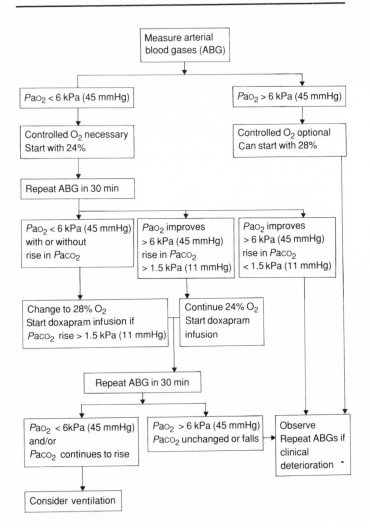

Fig. 22.1. Summary of management of oxygen therapy in acute exacerbation of chronic airflow limitation. Redrawn from Gribbin HR. *Respiratory Diseases in Practice* 1987;**Feb**:16–25.

- **prednisolone** 30–60 mg orally as a single daily dose (or hydrocortisone 200 mg 8-hourly i.v. if severely drowsy or vomiting);
- **aminophylline** 250 mg in 500 ml fluid (alternately normal saline and 5% dextrose) over 8 hours i.v.;
- **antibiotics** as for pneumonia (Table 23.2, p. 138).

3 Unless the patient is too drowsy to cooperate, request **physiotherapy** urgently to obtain a sputum specimen and to dislodge sputum plugs.

4 Treat atrial fibrillation/flutter with digoxin (Table 2.7, p. 19).

5 Treat coexistent hypoxic heart failure with diuretics.
- The diagnosis is made from:
  a raised JVP;
  b cardiomegaly;
  c ECG evidence of right ventricular hypertrophy (P pulmonale, right axis deviation, dominant R wave in V1).
- Ankle swelling is common as a result of tissue hypoxia and is not a reliable sign of heart failure. It responds to oxygen therapy.

Problems

Ventilation

- Indicated for respiratory failure unresponsive to doxapram.
- Relatively contraindicated if previous exercise capacity was severely limited (Table 22.4).
- In patients with worsening respiratory failure, a management policy should be decided in advance by chest physician and anaesthetist.

Failure to improve

1 Possibilities are:
- inadequate therapy;
- other causes of respiratory failure in chronic airflow limitation (Table 22.1).

■ **Table 22.4. Functional assessment in chronic airflow limitation**

- Distance walked on the flat
- How many stairs without stopping?
- Frequency of acute exacerbations
- Ever ventilated?
- Previous lung function tests and arterial blood gases
- Concurrent illness

2 Recheck arterial gases and obtain a chest X-ray (check for a pneumothorax).

3 Further treatment options are:

- increase the frequency of nebulized salbutamol and ipratropium (e.g. alternatively every 2 hours); *or*
- salbutamol by i.v. infusion (5–30 µg/min; see Table 57.3, p. 293);
- hydrocortisone 200 mg 8-hourly i.v. in place of prednisolone orally;
- occasionally acetylcysteine (2–5 ml of 20% solution 6-hourly by nebulizer) may loosen mucus plugs.

23 Pneumonia

Consider the diagnosis in any patient with:

- **acute dyspnoea and fever;**
- **septicaemia;**
- **acute confusional state.**

Examination of the chest may be normal and a chest X-ray should always be obtained.

Priorities

1 Give oxygen.
2 Check the blood pressure: if systolic BP is <90 mmHg, put in a peripheral i.v. line and give colloid 500 ml over 15–30 minutes. See p. 68 for further management of septic shock.
3 Investigation of the patient with suspected pneumonia is given in **Table 23.1.**
4 Start antibiotic therapy as soon as blood has been taken for culture. Your initial choice of antibiotics depends on the clinical setting (Table 23.2).
5 Transfer the patient to the Intensive Care Unit if:

- respiratory rate >30/min or exhaustion;
- Pao_2 <8 kPa (60 mmHg) despite 35% oxygen;

■ **Table 23.1. Urgent investigation of the patient with suspected pneumonia**

- **Chest X-ray** (Appendix 23.1)
- **Arterial blood gases**
- **Full blood count**
- **Blood culture**
- **Urea and electrolytes**
- **Sputum for Gram stain**
- **Pleural fluid** (if present) **for Gram stain** (aspirate with a 21 gauge (green) needle)

■ **Table 23.2. 'Blind' antibiotic therapy for pneumonia**

Mild pneumonia

Community acquired	• **Amoxycillin** 500 mg 8-hourly p.o.; *or* • **Erythromycin** 500 mg 6-hourly p.o. if penicillin allergy, influenza epidemic or features to suggest 'atypical' pneumonia (Appendix 23.2)

Severe pneumonia

Community acquired	• **Amoxycillin** 500 mg 8-hourly i.v.; *plus*
	• **Erythromycin** 500 mg 6-hourly i.v. (best given by a long line or central line to avoid thrombophlebitis); *plus*
	• **Flucloxacillin** 500 mg 6-hourly i.v. if staphylococcal pneumonia is suspected
	   a Influenza epidemic
	   b Chest X-ray shows cavitation or pneumothorax
	   c Gram stain of sputum shows Gram-positive cocci in clusters

Hospital acquired ('nosocomial')	• **Third generation cephalosporin;** *or* • **Aminoglycoside plus anti-pseudomonal penicillin** (e.g. gentamicin plus azlocillin) if *Pseudomonas* infection possible (neutropenic/on ventilator)
Inhalation pneumonia*	• **Benzylpenicillin plus metronidazole** if community acquired • **Third generation cephalosporin** if hospital acquired

* At risk: recent general anaesthetic; cardiopulmonary resuscitation; stroke with impaired gag/cough reflexes.

- $Paco_2$ >6 kPa (45 mmHg);
- systolic BP <90 mmHg despite i.v. fluids.

Put in an arterial line, central venous line and urinary catheter. Discuss the need for ventilation with an anaesthetist.

Further management

Supportive treatment consists of the following.

1 Oxygen: should be continued until Pao_2 is >8 kPa (60 mmHg) with the patient breathing air (or >10 kPa (75 mmHg) on 28% oxygen).

2 Attention to fluid balance: losses are increased due to fever and tachypnoea.

- Patients with severe pneumonia should receive i.v. fluids (2–3 l/day) with a daily check of urea and electrolytes.
- If the patient is oliguric or blood urea is high (>15 mmol/l), measure CVP to guide fluid replacement.

3 Analgesia for pleuritic chest pain: use paracetamol or an NSAID such as indomethacin.

4 Physiotherapy if patients are producing sputum but have difficulty in expectorating it.

Sputum retention is a common problem in patients with chronic airflow limitation or bronchiectasis and for these patients physiotherapy should be started on admission.

5 Bronchodilator therapy with inhaled salbutamol and/or ipratropium (p. 133) if there is wheeze.

6 Fibreoptic bronchoscopy should be performed in patients with suspected inhalation pneumonia to remove particulate matter.

Problems

The patient is no better despite antibiotic therapy for 48 hours

- Does current antibiotic therapy cover the likely pathogens?
- Repeat the chest X-ray — are there any new findings such as cavitation or pleural effusion? If pleural fluid is now present, this should be aspirated and sent for Gram stain and culture.
- Consider pulmonary tuberculosis: send sputum for Ziehl–Nielsen

staining. If no sputum is being produced, it can be induced by inhalation of saline (p. 141). Perform a Mantoux test (intermediate strength — 10 units (0.1 ml of one in 1000)).

- Consider AIDS-associated penumonia if the patient belongs to a group at high risk.
- Consider non-infective causes of chest X-ray shadowing such as pulmonary infarction or pulmonary oedema.
- Discuss the case with a chest physician. Invasive diagnostic procedures (e.g. broncho-alveolar lavage, transbronchial biopsy) may be indicated.

The post-operative patient — pneumonia or pulmonary embolism?

Acute dyspnoea and fever are features of both. Pneumonia is favoured by:

- initial fever >39°C;
- white cell count >15 $\times$ 10^9/l;
- purulent sputum.

If you remain uncertain, treat for both conditions until a ventilation/perfusion scan can be performed.

Pneumonia in the patient with known or suspected AIDS

(Table 23.3)

- If the patient has **purulent sputum with focal shadowing on the chest X-ray**, a bacterial pathogen is likely: start antibiotic therapy

■ Table 23.3. Causes of pneumonia in the patient with AIDS

Common	• *Pneumocystis carinii*
	• Cytomegalovirus
Less common	• *Legionella pneumophila*
	• *Pneumococcus*
	• *Histoplasma capsulatum*
	• *Cryptococcus neoformans*
	• *Mycobacterium avium* complex

according to Table 23.2. Send sputum for Gram and Ziehl–Nielsen staining.

• If the patient has a **non-productive cough with diffuse shadowing on the chest X-ray**, *Pneumocystis carinii* pneumonia is likely, although other pathogens are possible. Discuss management with a chest physician. There are two approaches to diagnosis:

   a invasive: bronchoscopy with broncho-alveolar lavage and transbronchial biopsy (check platelet count and prothrombin time first);

   b non-invasive: sputum is induced by inhalation of nebulized 3% saline for 5–20 minutes (after gargling with water to reduce contamination by oral debris) and examined for cysts or trophozoites of *Pneumocystis*. Stains based on monoclonal antibodies are under development.

• See **Appendix 23.3** for the treatment of *Pneumocystis carinii* pneumonia.

Appendices

23.1. Interpretation of the chest X-ray in suspected pneumonia

The **distribution of shadowing** is a poor guide to the causative organism. Other features to look for are:

• **pleural effusion** — if present, aspirate a sample and send for Gram stain and culture;

• **cavitation** — particularly associated with *Staphylococcus aureus* infection but may also occur with Gram-negative and anaerobic infections;

• **pneumothorax** — which may occur in *S. aureus* pneumonia and also pulmonary tuberculosis.

23.2. Typical features of pneumococcal, *Mycoplasma* and *Legionella* pneumonias

	Pneumococcal	*Mycoplasma*	*Legionella*
Onset	Acute	Subacute	Subacute
Initial symptoms	Rigor Pleuritic pain	Cough	Cough Headache
Temperature (°C)	39–40	<39	39–40
Chest signs	Bronchial breathing common Pleural rub common	Focal crackles common Bronchial breathing uncommon Radiological involvement greater than signs	
WBC count (× 10⁹/l)	>15	<15	<15
Differential WBC count	Neutrophilia	Normal	Neutrophilia
Useful clues	*Herpes labialis*	Young adults Epidemic	Hyponatraemia Confusion Gastrointestinal symptoms (abdominal pain, vomiting, watery diarrhoea) Epidemic

WBC, white blood cell.

23.3. Treatment of a first episode of *Pneumocystis carinii* pneumonia

No allergy to co-trimoxazole

• Give **trimethoprim** 20 mg/kg **and sulphamethoxazole**
100 mg/kg orally or i.v. (diluted 1 : 25 in normal saline or dextrose 5%) in
3–4 divided doses/day for up to 21 days.

• Give **folinic acid** 15 mg/day if the white cell count is $<1.5 \times 10^9/l$ or
platelet count is $<50 \times 10^9/l$ before or during treatment.

• **Adverse effects:** nausea (if given orally), rash, neutropenia,
thrombocytopenia, hepatotoxicity.

No clinical improvement after 5 days, or co-trimoxazole allergy

• Give **pentamidine 4 mg/kg** by i.v. infusion over 1 hour (in 250 ml of
dextrose 5%) daily for 14–21days.

• **Adverse effects:** hypotension, sterile abscesses at i.m. injection sites,
hypoglycaemia, nephrotoxicity, neutropenia, hepatotoxicity.

NB Seek expert advice as drug regimens are changing. An alternative
treatment of mild to moderate pneumonia is inhaled pentamidine 600 mg
in 6 ml sterile water (via a suitable nebulizer) once daily for 21 days.

24 Pneumothorax

Consider the diagnosis with:
- **sudden breathlessness or chest pain,** particularly following invasive procedures, e.g. subclavian vein puncture, lung biopsy, chest aspiration;
- **acute exacerbations of asthma or chronic airflow limitation.** Pneumothorax may be painless and contribute to respiratory failure;
- **hypoxia or an increase in inflation pressure in mechanically ventilated patients.** Asymmetry of chest expansion is a useful clue.

Priorities

If the patient has signs of a pneumothorax and is hypotensive (systolic BP <90 mmHg), suspect a tension pneumothorax:
- insert the largest cannula to hand into the second intercostal space in the midclavicular line on the side with absent or reduced breath sounds;
- whilst the chest drainage set is being prepared, an underwater seal can be improvised using an i.v. fluid extension line attached to the needle hub and its distal end placed under water in a bowl.

Further management

1 Obtain a chest X-ray. The classical signs of hyperresonance and reduced or absent breath sounds unilaterally may not be found with a small pneumothorax.

2 Is it a pneumothorax or a lung bulla?
You may rupture the lung if you mistake an emphysematous bulla for a pneumothorax. Points in favour of a bulla are:
- adhesions between the lung and the parietal pleura;
- a scallop-shaped edge to the cavity;

- faint markings over the lucency caused by the lung enfolding the bulla;
- the presence of other bullae.

3 Check arterial blood gases in patients with pre-existing respiratory disease.

Management options

Young, fit patient with small pneumothorax
- **Observation alone** (since spontaneous resolution often occurs): admit overnight and repeat the chest X-ray the following day. If the pneumothorax has not increased in size, discharge the patient and arrange a further chest X-ray in 1 week.
- **Needle aspiration** (p. 273).

Other patients in whom chest drainage is needed
- Large pneumothorax (maximum width of pneumothorax >50% maximum width of hemithorax).
- Coexistent respiratory disease even if the pneumothorax is small.
- Significant symptoms.
- Failure of needle aspiration.
- Haemopneumothorax.

The technique of insertion of a chest drain is described in Chapter 53.

Situations where surgical advice should be sought
- Failure of the lung to re-expand after insertion of a chest drain.
- Recurrent pneumothoraces on the same side.
- Bilateral pneumothoraces.

Problems

Pneumothorax suspected, but chest X-ray appears normal
See Table 24.1.

■ **Table 24.1.** Apparently normal chest X-ray in suspected pneumothorax

1 If there is no obvious lung margin, recheck
  • The lung apices
  • The right border of the heart
2 In the supine patient look for
  • Unusually sharp appearance of the cardiac border or diaphragm
  • A vertical line parallel to the chest wall (caused by retraction of the middle lobe)
  • A diagonal line from the heart to the costophrenic angle.

25 Hyperventilation

- Hyperventilation ($Paco_2 < 4.3$ kPa (32 mmHg)) is a respiratory response to organic lung disease, hypoxia, metabolic acidosis or pain. For causes of coma with hyperventilation; see Table 6.3, p. 46.
- In patients without significant organic disease it may present acutely with panic and carpopedal spasm, or with recurrent breathlessness, chest pain or dizziness.

Management

Panic and carpopedal spasm

1 Take the pulse and blood pressure and listen to the chest.
2 If the patient is unable to control their breathing (Table 25.4), place a paper bag lightly over the mouth to induce CO_2 rebreathing. (If applied too firmly it may exacerbate hyperventilation).
3 If this fails, give diazepam (e.g. Diazemuls) in 2 mg aliquots i.v. until sedation occurs. If this is required, the patient must either be admitted or accompanied home (after observation).
4 Further assessment it described below.

Hyperventilation as the cause of recurrent symptoms (Table 25.1)

1 Suspect in the patient with an irregular, thoracic, sighing respiratory pattern. Symptoms which point strongly to the diagnosis (and which may not be volunteered) are:
  - air-hunger and breathlessness at rest or when talking or eating;
  - chest pain of variable character, site, precipitation and duration.
2 Investigations to exclude organic disease are given in Table 25.2.
  - Mild airflow limitation is a common cause of hyperventilation.
  - Metabolic acidosis, preradiological pneumonia and pulmonary embolism may all cause hyperventilation.

■ **Table 25.1.** Symptoms which may be associated with hyperventilation in the absence of organic disease

Breathlessness	• At rest especially sitting, after bending or immediately after lying down
	• With trivial exertion, one or two steps, or 50 m on the flat
	• Talking or eating
	• Situational, e.g. in confined spaces
	• With emotion
	• Feeling of having to take gulps of air
	• Associated sighing or throat clearing
Chest pain	• At rest or on minimal exertion
	• Relieved by exertion
	• Left submammary or axillary
	• Continuous ache or jabs
	• Variable character, site and duration
Others	• Dizziness
	• Digital paraesthaesiae
	• Fatigue
	• Anxiety

■ **Table 25.2.** Investigation in suspected hyperventilation

Chest X-ray	• Check for a small pneumothorax, signs of infection, overexpansion of the lung fields (the anterior part of the 6th rib normally crosses the midpoint of the diaphragm)
ECG	• Hyperventilation may induce T wave changes and even ST depression. Ischaemic heart disease must be excluded first if these occur
Arterial blood gases	• Pco_2 is normally >4.3 kPa (32 mmHg)
Peak expiratory flow rate	• Table 58.1, p. 300
Blood glucose	• By stick test

3 Perform a hyperventilation provocation test (Table 25.3).

4 Immediate treatment consists of:

- reassurance and explanation, which are often sufficient to defuse an alarming symptom. A positive provocation test is useful in demonstrating the underlying mechanism;
- simple breathing exercises (Table 25.4).

■ **Table 25.3. Hyperventilation provocation test**

- Ask the patient to take deep breaths at 30–40 breaths/min for up to 3 min
- Ask which symptoms were reproduced. Was the sensation similar or an exact reproduction?
- The test is positive if the index symptoms were reproduced exactly

■ **Table 25.4. Breathing exercises in the treatment of hyperventilation**

- Place one hand on the chest and the other on the abdomen
- Recognize diaphragmatic breathing when the top hand remains still and the lower hand moves out during inspiration
- Breath slowly (8–10 breaths/min) to a regular rhythm — slowly in — 2, 3 — slowly out — 2, 3 —, etc.
- Resist taking gasps

Hyperventilation-induced chest pain

1 Any prolonged pain, however atypical the distribution, should be treated as ischaemic until proved otherwise.

2 A confident diagnosis of hyperventilation-induced pain can be made if:

- there are long-standing associated symptoms suggestive of hyperventilation (Table 25.1); *and*
- there are no signs of organic disease; *and*
- the ECG is normal; *and*
- the hyperventilation provocation test is positive.

26 Stroke

The working diagnosis of stroke is based on the sudden or rapid onset of a focal neurological deficit.

Priorities

1 If the patient is unconscious, initial resuscitation is as for coma from any cause (Chapter 6). Coma after stroke almost always results from cerebral haemorrhage and the prognosis is poor.

2 Check the blood glucose by stick test. If <5 mmol/l, give 50 ml of 50% dextrose i.v.

3 Is there evidence of an illness masquerading as stroke (Table 26.1)? Features in the clinical assessment which should arouse suspicion are:

- progression of symptoms over days or weeks (mass lesion, although this may also occur in 'stuttering' infarction (p. 153);
- extracranial malignancy (cerebral metastasis);
- head injury (intracranial haematoma);
- fever and neck stiffness (meningitis, encephalitis);
- fluctuating neurological signs (chronic subdural haematoma).

4 Is there evidence of a potentially treatable cause of stroke (Table 26.2)?

■ **Table 26.1. Diseases which may masquerade as stroke**

- Hypoglycaemia
- Todd's paresis following a seizure
- Meningitis (Chapter 28)
- Encephalitis
- Brain abscess
- Brain tumour
- Chronic subdural haematoma (Appendix 26.1)
- Extradural haematoma (following trauma)
- Hypertensive encephalopathy (Table 15.4, p. 108)

■ **Table 26.2. Potentially treatable causes of stroke**

- Hyperosmolar hyperglycaemia (HONK) (Chapter 37)
- Ruptured saccular aneurysm or AV malformation (Chapter 27)
- Cerebellar haematoma (Appendix 26.2)
- Embolism from the heart
- Aortic dissection and other extracranial arterial disease (Chapter 14)
- Vaso-occlusive crisis of sickle cell disease (Chapter 46)
- Arteritis (e.g. cranial arteritis, SLE)

■ **Table 26.3. Urgent investgation of the patient with stroke**

- **Blood glucose**
- **Full blood count**
- **Sickle solubility test** if appropriate (p. 235)
- **Urea, sodium and potassium**
- **ECG** (?recent MI)
- **Chest X-ray** (?neoplasm)
- **CT scan** if:
  a suspected intracranial infection
  b recent head injury
  c suspected cerebellar stroke (Appendix 26.2)
  d consider if no history obtainable

5 **Investigations needed urgently:** Table 26.3.
6 **Specific therapy to increase cerebral perfusion or protect the brain from ischaemic damage?** No therapies (corticosteroids, glycerol, naftidrofuryl, calcium antagonists, haemodilution) have been shown to improve outcome in large controlled trials.

Further management

1 **General supportive measures.**
- If the gag reflex is weak, give only water initially.
- Start an i.v. infusion (usually 2 litres in 24 hours) or insert a nasogastric tube if the patient cannot drink by 12–24 hours.
- Start physiotherapy within 1–2 days to prevent contractures and

encourage recovery of function. Start speech therapy for dysphasia.
- Give a stool softener to prevent constipation and faecal impaction.
- Urinary incontinence is common but often temporary: exclude faecal impaction and urinary tract infection. A urinary catheter (or penile sheath) should be used to prevent skin maceration.

2 **Further investigation:** Table 26.4.

3 **Decide if the stroke is likely to be ischaemic (80% cases) or haemorrhagic** (Table 26.5). This determines therapy for secondary prevention.

■ **Table 26.4.** Further investigation of the patient with stroke

- ESR (?arteritis, endocarditis, myeloma)
- **Serum cholesterol** in patients aged <50 years
- **Syphilis serology**
- **CT scan:**
  a if suspected mass lesion
  b to exclude haemorrhage before starting anticoagulant/antiplatelet therapy
  c if the diagnosis is unclear
  d in patients aged <50 years
- **Echocardiography if:**
  a cardiomegaly
  b suspected endocarditis
  c diastolic murmur
  d systolic murmur with other signs of significant valvular disease
  e atrial fibrillation in patients aged <60 years (also exclude thyrotoxicosis)

Secondary prevention

Ischaemic stroke

- The most important modifiable risk factors are cigarette smoking and hypertension (phase V diastolic BP >100 mmHg).
- Aspirin 150–300 mg daily reduces the risk of recurrence. Ideally,

■ **Table 26.5. Stroke: ischaemic or haemorrhagic?**

Points in favour of ischaemic stroke (embolus or thrombosis)	• Stuttering onset • Rapid resolution (within 24 hours) • Previous transient ischaemia attack (TIA) (including amaurosis fugax) • Carotid bruit
Points in favour of haemorrhage	• Headache or vomiting at onset • Sudden onset with progression • Reduced conscious level • Neck stiffness

CT scan should be done before starting aspirin to exclude haemorrhage.

Presumed cardiac embolic source
• Anticoagulation (Table 26.6) is indicated except in patients with endocarditis or other absolute contraindications.
• CT scan must be considered first to exclude haemorrhage.
• Anticoagulation may cause haemorrhage into an infarcted area and should not be started for 72 hours if the stroke is large (e.g. affecting more than one limb for longer than 24 hours).

Problems

'Stuttering stroke'
• 'Stuttering' or progressing stroke, in which the neurological deficit increases in a stepwise fashion over hours or days after its onset, is usually due to thrombosis of the carotid or basilar arteries (but may be due to recurrent embolism from an atheromatous plaque in the carotid artery, or a cardiac source).
• Heparin is probably of benefit in reducing the risk of progression (infusion as in Table 26.6, but preceded by a bolus of 1000 units). However, CT scan must be done first to exclude haemorrhage.
• Discuss further management with a neurologist.

■ **Table 26.6. Anticoagulation after embolic stroke**

- Start a heparin infusion of 1000 u/hour
- Adjust the dose to achieve a kaolin cephalin clotting time of 1.5–2.0 ×
control
- Continue heparin for 7–10 days
- Start warfarin on day 5.

Based on
Grotta JC. Current medical and surgical therapy for cerebrovascular
disease. *N Engl J Med* 1987;**317**:1505–16.

Hypertension
- Acute treatment is not indicated unless there is evidence of
hypertensive encephalopathy (Table 15.4, p. 108) or **aortic dissection**
(Chapter 14), because of the risk of reducing cerebral blood flow.
- In other hypertensive patients, treatment should not be started
until 3 months after the stroke.

Atrial fibrillation but no structural heart disease
- A significant number of strokes in patients with atrial fibrillation are due
to haemorrhage rather than infarction. CT scanning must therefore be
done first if anticoagulant therapy is considered.
- The risk : benefit ratio of long-term warfarin anticoagulation in
these patients is still unclear.

Appendices

26.1. Chronic subdural haematoma

Risk factors (which may often be absent)
- Previous head injury (within 1 year).
- Alcohol abuse.
- Anticoagulant therapy.

Clinical features

- Headache.
- Reduced conscious level relatively common and sometimes fluctuating.
- Hemiparesis
- Visual field defect and hemisensory loss are rare.
- Papilloedema in one-third of patients.

If suspected

- Obtain skull X-rays which may show depression or lateral displacement of calcified pineal (or, rarely, a fracture), but are normal in 50% with proven chronic subdural haematoma.
- Discuss further management with a neurosurgeon.
- Computed tomography (CT) scan is the definitive investigation.

26.2. Cerebellar stroke

At risk

- Age >50 years (male > female).
- Previous hypertension.

Clinical features

- Headache (usually occipital).
- Dizziness, vertigo, nausea and vomiting.
- Nystagmus and gaze paresis.
- Truncal ataxia (may be unable to stand).
- Limb ataxia (less common).

If suspected

- Discuss further management with a neurologist.
- Computed tomography (CT) scan is the definitive investigation.

27 Subarachnoid Haemorrhage

Consider the diagnosis in any patient with:

- **severe headache of sudden onset;**
- **coma.**

Priorities

If the patient is comatose
See Chapter 6.

If the patient is not comatose
1 Give pethidine (1 mg/kg) i.m. (plus an anti-emetic, e.g. metoclopramide 10 mg i.m.) to relieve the headache.
2 The clinical features will usually allow you to distinguish subarachnoid haemorrhage from other causes of headache (Table 27.1).
3 If the diagnosis is suspected, it should be confirmed or excluded by CT scan or examination of the CSF (Table 27.2).
4 If subarachnoid haemorrhage is confirmed, discuss further management with a neurosurgeon. Rupture of a berry aneurysm is the commonest cause **(Appendix 27.1)** and surgical obliteration of the aneurysm prevents rebleeding. The optimum timing of surgery is controversial.

■ **Table 27.1.** Clinical features of subarachnoid haemorrhage

- Severe headache of sudden onset — may be associated with transient loss of consciousness
- Nausea, vomiting and photophobia
- Depressed level of consciousness
- Neck stiffness — may be absent in the first few hours after a bleed
- Subhyaloid haemorrhages (retinal haemorrhages with curved lower and straight upper borders) — pathognomonic but uncommon
- Focal neurological signs if intracerebral extension
- Low-grade fever

■ **Table 27.2.** Urgent investigation in suspected subarachnoid haemorrhage

• **CT scan**	• Blood in subarachnoid spaces
	• May show intracerebral haematoma
• **Lumbar puncture**	• Raised opening pressure
	• Uniformly blood-stained CSF
	• Xanthochromia of the supernatant (from 2 hours to 3 weeks after the bleed)

NB Lumbar puncture
• **Should not be performed in patients with focal neurological signs or reduced conscious level** who may have an intracerebral haematoma
• **Should be performed if the CT scan is normal in patients with a suggestive history** (as minor bleeds may not be detected on CT)

Further management (before aneurysm surgery)

• **Bedrest**, preferably in a darkened side-room.
• **Analgesia** as required (e.g. codeine phosphate 30–60 mg 4-hourly p.o.). Start a stool softener to prevent constipation.
• **Nimodipine** 60 mg 4-hourly p.o. reduces cerebral infarction and improves outcome after subarachnoid haemorrhage. Other therapies are not of proven benefit. **Beta-blockers** are not indicated except to treat sustained severe hypertension.

Problems

Hypertension
• First ensure that adequate analgesia has been given.
• If sustained and severe (systolic BP >200 mmHg, diastolic BP >110 mmHg) cautious treatment should be given, e.g. nifedipine 10 mg 8-hourly p.o. or metoprolol 50 mg 12-hourly p.o. Otherwise, antihypertensive treatment is not indicated and may be harmful.

Neurological deterioration (Table 27.3)

• Check plasma sodium and urea: hyponatraemia can occur due to inappropriate antidiuretic hormone (ADH) secretion (Chapter 39).

• Obtain a CT scan (Table 27.3).

■ **Table 27.3. Causes of neurological deterioration after subarachnoid haemorrhage**

• Recurrent haemorrhage — peak incidence in the first 2 weeks
• Vasopasm causing cerebral ischaemia or infarction — peak incidence at 5–9 days
• Cerebral oedema
• Communicating hydrocephalus — occurs in 5–10% of cases from 1–8 weeks after the haemorrhage
• Hyponatraemia due to inappropriate ADH secretion

Appendix

27.1. Causes of subarachnoid haemorrhage

Common

• Rupture of saccular ('berry') aneurysm of circle of Willis (circa 50% of cases).

• Primary cerebral, cerebellar or brainstem haemorrhage with rupture of the haematoma into the subarachnoid space (circa 25%).

Uncommon

• Bleeding from arteriovenous malformation.

• Bleeding tendency.

• Bleeding from intracranial tumours, notably metastatic melanoma.

Based on

Richardson A. Subarachnoid haemorrhage. *Br Med J* 1969;4:89–92.

28 Bacterial Meningitis

• Consider the diagnosis in any febrile patient with headache, neck stiffness or a reduced level of consciousness (Table 28.1).

• **If an intracranial mass lesion** (brain abscess or subdural empyema) (Table 28.2) **is suspected, computed tomography must be done before lumbar puncture.**

■ **Table 28.1.** Neurological features of bacterial meningitis

---

• **Meningeal irritation:** headache, neck stiffness, vomiting, photophobia
• **Reduced level of consciousness**
• **Seizures**
• **Cranial nerve palsies***

---

* **Long tract signs** (e.g. hemiparesis, extensor plantar response) suggest brain abscess or subdural empyema.

Priorities

If the patient is comatose
See Chapter 6.

If the patient has septic shock (systolic BP <90 mmHg)
• Put in an i.v. line and give colloid 500 ml over 15–30 minutes.
• Take blood cultures and start antibiotic therapy immediately (Table 28.3).
• If you suspect meningococcal septicaemia (young adult with purpuric rash), give hydrocortisone 300 mg i.v. in case hypotension is due to bilateral adrenal haemorrhage (Waterhouse-Friderichsen syndrome).
• See Chapter 10 for further management of septic shock.

If an intracranial mass lesion is suspected (Table 28.2)
• Take blood cultures and start antibiotic therapy (Table 28.3).
• Arrange CT scan.

■ **Table 28.2.** Features suggesting an intracranial mass lesion in the patient with meningitis

- Source of infection outside the CNS (e.g. middle ear or paranasal sinuses)
- Preceding morning headache or vomiting
- Papilloedema
- Focal neurological signs

In other patients

1 A lumbar puncture should be done without delay (Chapter 54).

2 Record the opening pressure.

3 Send CSF for:

- cell count;
- protein concentration;
- glucose (fluoride tube);
- Gram stain (plus Ziehl–Nielson and India ink if immuno-compromised; Appendices 28.2 and 28.3).

4 If the CSF is cloudy (pyogenic bacterial meningitis):

- start antibiotic therapy immediately **(Table 28.3)**;
- intrathecal antibiotics are unnecessary and potentially dangerous.

5 If the CSF is bloodstained (traumatic tap or subarachnoid haemorrhage):

- collect three consecutive tubes and check the red cell count in

■ **Table 28.3.** 'Blind' antibiotic therapy for suspected bacterial meningitis in adults

	First choice	Second choice
Normal host defences	Benzylpenicillin 1.8 g 3-hourly i.v.	Chloramphenicol 1 g 6-hourly i.v.
Immunocompromised or age >70 years	Ampicillin 2 g 4-hourly i.v. *plus* Cefotaxime 2 g 4-hourly i.v.	Chloramphenicol 1 g 6-hourly i.v.

the first and third (p. 310);
- check for xanthrochromia in the supernatant;
- see Chapter 27 for further management of subarachnoid haemorrhage.

6 Other urgent investigations in suspected meningitis are given in Table 28.4.

■ **Table 28.4. Urgent investigation in suspected meningitis**

- **Lumbar puncture** if not contraindicated
- **Blood culture**
- **Full blood count**
- **Blood glucose** (for comparison with CSF glucose)
- **Chest X-ray**
- **Skull X-ray if** suspected sinus infection (nasal discharge, sinus tenderness)

Further management

Organisms seen on Gram stain
- Modify or start antibiotic therapy (Table 28.5). Seek expert advice.
- The cell count will usually be high with a polymorphonuclear leucocytosis but may be low in overwhelming infection.

■ **Table 28.5. Gram stain of the CSF in pyogenic bacterial meningitis**

Appearance	Probable organism	Antibiotic first choice*
Gram + ve cocci	Pneumococcus	Benzylpenicillin
	Staphylococcus aureus	Flucloxacillin *plus* rifampicin
Gram – ve cocci	Meningococcus	Benzylpenicillin
Gram + ve rods	*Listeria monocytogenes*	Ampicillin *plus* gentamicin
Gram – ve rods	*Haemophilus influenzae*	Chloramphenicol
	Enteric bacteria	Cefotaxime

* Dosage as in Table 28.3. For *Staph. aureus* meningitis, give flucloxacillin 2 g 4-hourly i.v. *plus* rifampicin 600 mg 12-hourly p.o. (or vancomycin if penicillin allergy). See p. 71 for gentamicin dosages.

No organisms seen on Gram stain

Management is directed by the clinical picture and CSF formula (Table 28.6).

■ **Table 28.6.** CSF formulae in meningitis

	Pyogenic	Viral	Tuberculous	Cryptococcal
Cell count/mm^3	>1000	<500	<500	<150
Predominant cell type	Polymorphs	Lymphos	Lymphos	Lymphos
Protein concentration (g/l)	>1.5	0.5–1	1–5	0.5–1
CSF: blood glucose	<50%	>50%	<50%	<50%

NB
- **The values given are typical, but many exceptions occur**
- **Antibiotic therapy substantially changes the CSF formula in pyogenic bacterial meningitis,** leading to a fall in cell count, increased proportion of lymphocytes and fall in protein level. However, the low CSF glucose level usually persists

1 Normal cell count: meningitis excluded. Consider other infectious diseases which may give rise to meningism (e.g. tonsillitis, viral hepatitis).

2 High polymorph count: this is typical of pyogenic bacterial meningitis but may occur early in the course of viral meningitis.
- **If the patient has a reduced conscious level and/or CSF glucose is low, start antibiotic therapy.**
- If the patient is alert, the CSF glucose is normal and there are no other features to suggest bacterial infection, hold off antibiotic therapy and repeat the lumbar puncture in 12 hours. By this time an increasing proportion of the cells will be lymphocytes in viral meningitis.

3 High lymphocyte count: this may be seen in many diseases (Table 28.7).

■ **Table 28.7.** Causes of meningitis with a high CSF lymphocyte count

- Viral infection
- Partially treated pyogenic bacterial infection
- Other bacterial infections — tuberculosis, leptospirosis, brucellosis, syphilis
- Fungal (cryptococcal) infection
- Parameningeal infection — brain abscess or subdural empyema
- Neoplastic infiltration

- Distinguishing between viral and partially treated pyogenic bacterial meningitis can be difficult. **If in doubt, start antibiotic therapy, awaiting the results of culture of blood and CSF.**
- If tuberculous or cryptococcal meningitis are possible on clinical grounds (Appendices 28.1 and 28.2) or on the results of CSF examination, ask for a Ziehl-Nielson stain and India ink preparation.

Meningococcal meningitis
Treatment of contacts: rifampicin should be given to family members and other close contacts (adults: 600 mg twice daily for 2 days; children 1–12 years: 10 mg/kg twice daily for 2 days; infants 3–12 months: 5 mg/kg twice daily for 2 days; infants <3 months: not recommended).

Appendices

28.1. Tuberculous meningitis

1 **At risk:**
- immigrants from India, Pakistan and Africa, with recent contact with TB;
- patients with previous pulmonary TB;
- alcoholics;
- i.v. drug abusers;
- immunocompromised.

2 **Suggestive clinical features:**
- subacute onset;

- cranial nerve palsies;
- retinal tubercles (pathognomonic but rarely seen);
- hyponatraemia.

3 The chest X-ray is often normal.

4 The CSF usually shows a high lymphocyte count with a high protein concentration (Table 28.6). Acid-fast bacilli may not be seen on Ziehl–Nielson stain.

5 CT scan commonly shows hydrocephalus (and may also show cerebral infarction due to arteritis or tuberculoma).

6 Treatment: combination chemotherapy with isoniazid, rifampicin, pyrazinamide and streptomycin.

7 Seek expert advice if the diagnosis is confirmed.

28.2. Cryptococcal meningitis

1 At risk: immunocompromised (organ transplant, lymphoma, steroid therapy, AIDS).

2 Suggestive clinical features:

- insidious onset;
- neck stiffness absent or mild;
- papular or nodular skin lesions.

3 The CSF usually shows a high lymphocyte count with a raised protein concentration (Table 28.6). Cryptococci may be seen on Gram stain as large Gram-positive cocci. India ink preparation is positive in 60%.

4 The diagnosis may also be confirmed by CSF culture or serological tests for cryptococcal antigen on CSF or blood.

5 Treatment: amphotericin B 0.3 mg/kg per day i.v. plus flucytosine 150 mg/kg per day orally or i.v. both in four divided doses.

6 Seek expert advice if the diagnosis is confirmed.

Reference

Dismukes WE, Cloud G, Gallis HA *et al.* Treatment of cryptococcal meningitis with combination amphotericin B and flucytosine for four as compared with six weeks. *N Engl J Med* 1987;**317**:334–41.

29 Spinal Cord Compression

Consider the diagnosis in any patient with:

- thoracic spine pain;
- weakness of the legs;
- sphincter failure.

Early diagnosis and treatment are crucial to preserving cord function.

Priorities

1 **The working diagnosis of cord compression is based on the clinical features (Table 29.1).** The signs may be mild in the early stages.

■ Table 29.1. Clinical features of spinal cord compression

- Spinal or radicular pain
- Leg 'stiffness' or clumsy gait
- Urinary hesistancy or frequency (painless retention is a late sign)
- Bilateral upper motor neuron signs in the legs
- Impaired sensation — check for a sensory level
- Reduced anal tone

2 **Look for a cause: cord compression is usually due to extradural disease (Table 29.2), of which malignancy is the most common.**

3 **Obtain X-rays of the spine (Table 29.3):** these may show supporting evidence, but **if normal do not exclude cord compression.**

4 **Discuss further management with a neurosurgeon.**

Treatment is either surgical decompression or radiotherapy (if malignancy has previously been diagnosed by histology).

■ **Table 29.2.** Causes of extradural spinal cord compression

Cause	Comment
Malignancy	Most commonly carcinoma of breast or bronchus, myeloma, lymphoma
Abscess	Severe back pain with local tenderness Systemic illness with fever
Haematoma	Warfarin anticoagulation
Prolapse of cervical or thoracic intervertebral disc	
Trauma	
Atlanto-axial subluxation	Long-standing rheumatoid arthritis

■ **Table 29.3.** Urgent investigation in suspected spinal cord compression

- **Anteroposterior (AP) and lateral X-rays of the spine** (look for loss of pedicles, vertebral body destruction, spondylolisthesis, soft tissue mass)
- **Chest X-ray** (primary or secondary carcinoma, tuberculosis)
- **Full blood count**

Problems

The patient with known malignancy who has back pain but no abnormal signs.

- With a focal abnormality on spinal X-ray: arrange myelography or computed tomography.
- With normal spinal X-ray: arrange bone scintigraphy. If this shows increased uptake at the site of the pain, myelography or computed tomography should be performed.

30 Guillain–Barré Syndrome (Acute Idiopathic Polyneuropathy)

Consider the diagnosis in any patient with:

- paraesthesiae in the fingers and toes;
- weakness of the arms and legs.

Respiratory failure (which may rapidly progress to respiratory arrest) and autonomic instability are the major complications.

Priorities

1 Make the diagnosis from the clinical signs (Table 30.1): generalized arreflexia is the clue. Other causes of acute polyneuropathy are rare and can be excluded on clinical grounds or by later investigation (Appendix 30.1).

2 Measure the vital capacity with a spirometer. Predicted normal values are given in Table 58.3, p. 301. As a rule of thumb, vital capacity (ml) is 25 × height (cm) in men and 20 × height (cm) in women.

- If no spirometer is available, the breath-holding time in full inspiration provides a guide to the vital capacity (normal >30 seconds).

- Arterial blood gases can remain normal despite a severely reduced vital capacity.

3 Transfer to ITU:

- patients whose vital capacity is <80% predicted;
- patients who are unable to walk.

Ventilation may be necessary: see Problems (p. 168). These

■ Table 30.1. Neurological signs in Guillain–Barré syndrome

- Limb weakness proximal > distal
- Arreflexia
- Bilateral facial weakness is common
- Mild distal sensory impairment

patients are also at risk of cardiovascular complications so monitor the ECG and blood pressure.

Further management

1 **Confirm the diagnosis by CSF examination** which typically shows:
- **raised protein** (>1 g/l);
- **normal cell count or mild lymphocytic pleocytosis** (usually <20 lymphocytes/mm^3).

CSF protein may be normal in the early phase but rises later — repeat lumbar puncture after 24 hours if there is diagnostic doubt.

2 **Measure vital capacity (4-hourly to daily, depending on initial value)** until the weakness has reached a plateau.

3 **Supportive management consists of:**
- bed rest;
- physiotherapy to prevent contractures;
- ventilation for respiratory failure (**Problems**);
- feeding by nasogastric tube (or parenteral nutrition) if lower cranial nerve involvement interferes with swallowing;
- heparin 5000 units s.c. 12-hourly if unable to walk;
- aspirin or paracetamol for myalgia/arthralgia;
- stool softener to prevent constipation;
- fluid restriction if hyponatraemia occurs (due to inappropriate ADH secretion).

4 **Plasma exchange** should be considered in patients seen within 2 weeks of the onset of weakness who need or are likely to need ventilation: discuss this with a neurologist. **Steroids** and **immunosuppressive therapy** are not beneficial.

Problems

Respiratory failure
- Patients whose vital capacity falls below 80% predicted should be transferred to the ITU with facilities for endotracheal intubation to hand. Measure vital capacity 4-hourly.

- The decision to ventilate the patient should be taken jointly with an anaesthetist. As a general rule, ventilation is required if the vital capacity falls below 25–30% predicted.

Arrhythmias

- Transient arrhythmias (supraventricular tachycardia or bradycardia) without haemodynamic compromise require no treatment.
- Severe prolonged bradycardias may occur and are treated with temporary pacing.

Abnormalities of blood pressure

- Sustained severe hypertension (diastolic BP >120 mmHg) should be treated with labetalol by infusion (p. 104).
- If hypotension does not respond to i.v. fluids (guided by measurement of CVP), treat with dopamine or noradrenaline infusion (Tables 57.3, 57.4, p. 293).

Appendices

30.1. Causes of acute polyneuropathy

Cause	Clues	Diagnostic tests
Guillain–Barré syndrome	• Table 30.1 • Infection in previous month (**Appendix 30.2**)	• CSF: raised protein, normal cell count
Acute intermittent porphyria	• Abdominal pain • Vomiting • Drug exposure	• Urinary porphobilinogen
Toxin exposure	• Occupational history	• Toxicology
Polyarteritis nodosa	• Stepwise progression	• ESR • Muscle biopsy • Angiography
Diphtheria	• Children • No immunization • Palate involved first	

30.2. Infectious diseases which may precede Guillain-Barré syndrome

- Hepatitis A and B
- *Mycoplasma pneumoniae*
- Cytomegalovirus
- Epstein–Barr virus
- *Campylobacter jejuni*
- HIV

31 Major Epilepsy

Convulsive status epilepticus

• Defined as repeated generalized convulsive seizures without recovery of normal alertness between seizures.
• Prompt treatment is needed to reduce cerebral damage.

Priorities

1 Give oxygen.
2 Put in an i.v. cannula. Check blood glucose (stick test immediately) and give:
   • **diazepam i.v.** 5 mg over 30 seconds followed by 2 mg/min up to 20 mg or until seizures stop;
   • **dextrose 25 g i.v. (50 ml of dextrose 50% solution).**
3 Unless the patient is known to be taking phenytoin with good compliance, give: **phenytoin i.v. 50 mg/min to a total dose of 18 mg/kg — in the average adult, give 1 g over 20 minutes** (may cause hypotension if given too quickly).

Further management

1 If you suspect malnourishment or chronic alcohol abuse, give: **thiamine 100 mg i.v.** (e.g. Parentrovite IVHP which contains 250 mg thiamine).
2 If seizures continue despite diazepam and phenytoin:
   • **confirm that plasma sodium is normal:** if <120 mmol/l, it should be corrected with hypertonic saline (Table 39.2, p. 211);
   • **check arterial blood gases and pH;**
   • if **hypocalcaemia** is possible (recent thyroid or parathyroid surgery): give calcium gluconate 1 g i.v. (10 ml of 10% solution) over 5 minutes;
   • **give further anticonvulsant therapy:**

a diazepam i.v. infusion: put 100 mg in 500 ml dextrose 5% and run in at 40 ml/hour; *or*

b phenobarbitone i.v. 100 mg/min to a total dose of 20 mg/kg or until seizures stop; *or*

c paraldehyde i.m. 5 ml into each buttock.

3 If seizures still continue:
- you must discuss management with a neurologist;
- consider general anaesthesia with neuromuscular blockade.

4 Once seizures have been controlled: look for the cause (Appendix 31.1). Investigation is given in Table 31.1.

■ **Table 31.1. Investigation after control of status epilepticus or a first seizure**

- Blood glucose
- Urea and electrolytes
- Full blood count
- Arterial blood gases and pH
- Blood culture if febrile
- Chest X-ray
- **Lumbar puncture if suspected bacterial meningitis** (Chapter 28).
- **CT scan** if:
  a focal neurological signs
  b papilloedema
  c head injury

The patient seen after a single generalized convulsive seizure

First seizure

1 Is there evidence for a **structural cause**?
- Focal seizure, as shown by an aura or motor activity (sustained deviation of the head or eyes or unilateral jerking of the limbs), with secondary generalization.
- Residual focal signs.

2 Could the seizure be a **toxic effect of drugs** (Appendix 31.1) or due to **alcohol withdrawal**?

3 Does the patient have an **infectious or metabolic disease**
requiring urgent treatment, e.g. bacterial meningitis, acute renal
failure? Investigation is given in Table 31.1.

4 Idiopathic epilepsy is the likely diagnosis in young patients
without evidence of an underlying illness.

- Discharge if fully recovered.
- Advise the patient not to drive.
- Outpatient follow-up by a neurologist should be arranged.
- Whether anticonvulsant therapy should be started after a first fit
  is controversial: find out the policy in your area.

Known idiopathic epilepsy

1 If the current history deviates from the usual pattern of seizures,
consider:

- intercurrent infection;
- alcohol abuse;
- poor compliance with therapy.

2 Take blood for anticonvulsant levels.

3 If fully recovered and with no evidence of intercurrent illness, the
patient can be discharged.

4 Arrange early outpatient neurological follow-up if seizures have
been occurring frequently.

Appendix

31.1. Causes of epilepsy

Intracranial infection	• Meningitis
	• Encephalitis
	• Brain abscess
	• Subdural empyema
	• Cerebral malaria
Vascular disease	• Subarachnoid haemorrhage
	• Cerebral infarction
	• Cerebral haemorrhage
	• Hypertensive encephalopathy

31.1 (Continued)

Intracranial neoplasm

Head injury

Idiopathic epilepsy

Metabolic	• Hyponatraemia
	• Hypoglycaemia
	• Hypocalcaemia
	• Severe renal failure
	• Haemodialysis
	• Liver failure
	• Anoxia (e.g. cardiac arrest)
	• Alcohol withdrawal
Drugs (as a toxic effect)	• Amphetamines
	• Lignocaine
	• Benzypenicillin
	• Theophylline
	• Lithium
	• Salicylate
	• Dextropropoxyphene
	• Tricyclic antidepressants

32 Acute Upper Gastrointestinal Haemorrhage

- Usually presents with **haematemesis** or **melaena.**
- Should also be considered in any patient with:

  a syncope especially with associated anaemia or dyspeptic symptoms;

  b unexplained acute hypotension.

- **Joint medical and surgical management** is essential because the commonest cause, peptic ulceration, may require urgent surgery (Appendix 32.1).

Priorities

1 Put in a large bore i.v. cannula (e.g. yellow or grey Venflon). **Take 20 ml of blood for urgent investigations** (Table 32.1).

■ **Table 32.1.** Urgent investigation in upper gastrointestinal (GI) haemorrhage

- **Full blood count**
- **Cross-match at least 4 units of whole blood** (specify rapid cross-match)
- **Prothrombin time** (if liver disease is suspected)
- **Urea and electrolytes**

2 Estimate the volume of blood lost from the history and signs: pulse rate, systolic BP and skin temperature (Table 32.2).

Hypovolaemic shock (systolic BP < 90 mmHg with cold extremities)

- Give oxygen and attach to an ECG monitor.
- Rapidly transfuse colloid until the systolic BP is 100 mmHg.
- Start transfusing blood as soon as it is available via a second i.v. cannula.

If, despite 1000 ml of colloid, the systolic BP is still <90 mmHg use grouped but not cross-matched blood. (Save a sample of the transfused blood for a retrospective cross-match.)

- **Put in a CVP line,** when the blood pressure is stable, and adjust the infusion rate to maintain the CVP around + 5 cm H_2O.
- **Put in a urinary catheter** to monitor urine output.
- **Discuss further management with the surgical team.**

No shock

- In those with evidence of significant blood loss (Table 32.2), start an infusion of colloid, and transfuse blood when it is available.
- In patients over 60 years or with suspected variceal bleeding, put in a CVP line.

■ **Table 32.2. Upper GI haemorrhage: evidence of significant blood loss without shock**

- History of syncope in association with bleeding
- Persisting tachycardia (pulse rate >100/min)
- Cool extremities
- Postural fall in systolic BP of >20 mmHg

- If there are no signs of hypovolaemia, either heparinize the venous cannula or start a slow infusion of normal saline to keep it patent.

Further management

Blood transfusion
This should be given until a normal blood volume has been restored as shown by:
- pulse rate <100/min;
- systolic BP >110 mmHg;
- warm extremities;
- urine output >30 ml/hour (0.5 ml/kg per hour).

If the initial haemoglobin was <10 g/dl (indicating either prolonged acute or previous chronic loss), continue transfusion until the haemoglobin is around 12 g/dl. As a rough guide, each unit of blood restores about 1 g/dl to the haemoglobin count.

Check the haemoglobin daily for the first 3 days and again before discharge. If the final haemoglobin is less than 12 g/dl, give ferrous sulphate 200 mg 12-hourly for 1 month.

Allowed to eat or nil by mouth?

- **Patients shocked on admission or with evidence of significant blood loss** should not eat until endoscopy has been performed, in case urgent surgery is needed.
- **Patients without signs of hypovolaemia** can eat (but should remain nil by mouth for 6 hours before endoscopy).

H$_2$-antagonists

Start an H$_2$-antagonist **(Table 32.3)**. There is some evidence that they can reduce the incidence of rebleeding in peptic ulceration.

■ Table 32.3. Dosages of H$_2$-antagonists

	Oral	Intravenous
Cimetidine	800 mg at night	200 mg 6-hourly
Ranitidine	300 mg at night	50 mg 8-hourly

Endoscopy

Emergency endoscopy is needed for:

- **shock on admission (but not before adequate resuscitation);**
- **continued bleeding or rebleeding;**
- **signs of chronic liver disease or known varices.**

In such patients it may be more practical to perform endoscopy in the operating theatre with the patient prepared for surgery.

Other patients should if possible be endoscoped within 24 hours of admission.

Management after endoscopy

Peptic ulcer

• Bleeding from a peptic ulcer usually stops spontaneously. The mortality is highest in patients over 60 years who continue to bleed or rebleed, and may be reduced by early surgery (Table 32.4).

■ **Table 32.4. Indications for early surgery in patients with bleeding from peptic ulcer**

• Continued bleeding (requiring >4 units of blood after initial restoration of blood volume)
• Significant rebleeding (with fall in blood pressure)
• Endoscopy shows active bleeding from the ulcer or stigmata of recent bleeding (adherent clot, visible vessel)

• In those unfit for surgery, endoscopic treatment (ulcer sclerosis, heater probe, laser) may be used.
• An H_2-antagonist should be given for 6 weeks.
• Repeat endoscopy at 6 weeks (with biopsy) is indicated for all gastric ulcers.

Bleeding oesophageal varices

1 Start vasopressin and nitrate infusions. Both lower portal pressure. Nitrates offset the coronary vasospasm that vasopressin may produce (Table 32.5).

   • **Vasopressin must be given via a central vein** to avoid the risk of skin necrosis from extravasation.
   • **Somatostatin** is an effective alternative to vasopressin, but is expensive and should not yet be used 'first line'.

2 Correct clotting abnormalities. If the prothrombin time is >1.5 × control, give:

   • **vitamin K 10 mg i.v.** (not i.m.);
   • **2 units fresh frozen plasma.**

   If the platelet count is <50 × 10^{12}/l, give platelet concentrate.

■ **Table 32.5.** Vasopressin and nitrate for bleeding oesophageal varices

Vasopressin infusion	• Add 120 units (6 × 1 ml ampoules 20 u/ml) to 250 ml dextrose 5% • Infuse 50 ml (24 units) over 15 min and then 50 ml/hour (0.4 u/min) for 12 hours
Nitrate infusion	• **Nitroglycerin** ('Tridil'): start at 200 µg/min, increasing this to 400 µg/min provided systolic BP is >90 mmHg • **Isosorbide dinitrate** ('Isoket'): start at 2 mg/hour, increasing this by 2 mg/hour every 30 min to a maximum dose of 10 mg/hour provided systolic BP is >90 mmHg

3 If bleeding continues:
  • **Insert a Sengstaken–Blakemore tube** (Section 3). Contact the regional Liver Unit to discuss further management: **injection sclerotherapy** can significantly reduce the incidence of rebleeding.
  • Recheck the platelet count if >4 units of blood have been transfused.

4 Other measures:
  • **i.v. H$_2$-antagonist or sucralfate** 1 g 6-hourly (orally or via gastric channel of Sengstaken–Blakemore tube) to prevent stress ulceration.
  • **lactulose** 30 ml initially 6-hourly to prevent encephalopathy (Table 33.4, p. 185).

Erosive gastritis

There are two groups of patients:

1 Previously well patients in whom erosive gastritis is related to aspirin, non-steroidal anti-inflammatory drugs (NSAIDs) or alcohol. Bleeding usually stops quickly and no specific treatment is needed.

2 Critically ill patients with stress ulceration, in whom the mortality is high. Treatment consists of:

- **Sucralfate 1–2 g 6-hourly orally/via nasogastric tube**
(there is evidence that i.v. H_2-antagonists and antacids predispose to pneumonia).
- **Correction of clotting abnormalities** (p. 178).
- As a last resort, if bleeding is catastrophic, surgery with partial gastric resection can be performed but carries a high mortality.

Mallory–Weiss tear
Bleeding usually stops spontaneously and rebleeding is rare. If bleeding continues, the options are:
- Surgery with oversewing of the bleeding point.
- Tamponade using a Sengstaken–Blakemore tube.
- 'Interventional' radiology: either selective infusion of vasopressin into the left gastric artery, or embolization.

Oesophagitis/oesophageal ulcer
- Treat with H_2-antagonist for 6 weeks.

Problems

Suspected upper GI haemorrhage with 'negative' endoscopy
In a significant proportion of patients, a first endoscopy does not reveal a source of bleeding.
- Discuss repeating the endoscopy especially if blood or food obscured the views obtained.
- Patients who presented with melaena only should be investigated for a small bowel or proximal colonic source of bleeding if no upper GI source is found. A normal blood urea suggests a colonic cause of melaena.

Appendix

32.1. Causes of acute upper GI haemorrhage

Cause	Percentage (n = 526)
Gastric ulcer	25 %
Duodenal ulcer	23 %
Oesophagitis/ulcer	6 %
Mallory–Weiss tear	6 %
Gastritis/erosions	5 %
Varices	2 %
Others	6 %
No cause found	27 %

Reference

Dronfield MW, Langman MJS, Atkinson M *et al.* Outcome of endoscopy and barium radiography for acute upper gastrointestinal bleeding: controlled trial in 1037 patients. *Br Med J* 1982;**284**:545–8.

33 Acute Hepatic Encephalopathy

Decompensated chronic liver disease and fulminant hepatic failure

Make a working diagnosis in the patient with:

- a reduced conscious level; *and*
- unexplained prolongation of the prothrombin time; *or*
- known liver disease; *or*
- signs of liver disease; *and*
- no other cause of coma (Chapter 6).

Priorities

1 **Resuscitate as for any cause of coma**, but in particular:
- **Check the blood glucose by stick test.** If <5 mmol/l, give 50 ml of 50% dextrose i.v. Recheck after 5 minutes; hypoglycaemia may be prolonged and refractory.
- **If there is Grade 2 coma with vomiting or Grade 3–4 coma (Table 33.1), arrange intubation and ventilation** (NB avoid sedation and use pancuronium for muscle relaxation).

2 **If systolic BP is <80 mmHg and the JVP is low:** give 500 ml colloid i.v. over 15–30 minutes.

■ **Table 33.1.** Grading of hepatic encephalopathy

Grade 1	Mildly drowsy with impaired concentration and psychomotor function
Grade 2	Confused, but able to answer questions
Grade 3	Very drowsy and able to respond only to simple commands; incoherent and agitated.
Grade 4	Unrousable **4a** Responsive to painful stimuli **4b** Unresponsive

3 Start an i.v. infusion of 10% dextrose in all cases (because of the high risk of hypoglycaemia). Use a large peripheral vein as it can use cause thrombophlebitis.

4 Investigations needed urgently are given in Table 33.2.

5 Decide if there is fulminant hepatic failure or decompensated chronic liver disease. Fulminant hepatic failure is associated with severe cerebral oedema, whilst chronic liver disease is not and this difference affects further management.

• Fulminant hepatic failure is rare and usually caused by paracetamol overdose or viral hepatitis (Appendix 33.1).

• In the UK, the diagnosis of fulminant hepatic failure is made if encephalopathy appears within 8 weeks of the onset of initial symptoms.

6 Put in a CVP line if encephalopathy is Grade 2 or more or if systolic BP is <90 mmHg. Measurement of PA wedge pressure helps guide further management of patients with fulminant hepatic failure as pulmonary oedema (cardiogenic or ARDS) is a common complication.

• **If papilloedema is present or fulminant hepatic failure is suspected maintain the patient at 45°** (as lying the patient flat may lead to coning).

■ **Table 33.2.** Urgent investigation in suspected liver failure

• **Prothrombin time**
• **Full blood count** including platelets
• **Urea*, creatinine, sodium and potassium**
• **Liver function tests** (for later analysis)
• **Markers of viral hepatitis** (HBsAg and IgM anti-HBc; IgM anti-HAV) (for later analysis)
• **Paracetamol level** (if no evidence of chronic liver disease)
• **Arterial blood gases and pH** (preferably via an arterial line to avoid multiple punctures)
• **Blood culture**
• **Urine microscopy and culture**
• **Ascitic fluid microscopy and culture** (p. 185)
• **Chest X-ray**

* Urea may be low because of reduced hepatic synthesis; if markedly elevated with a normal creatinine, suspect upper GI haemorrhage.

- Treat clotting defects with platelet concentrates or fresh frozen plasma before central vein cannulation.
- Put in an arterial line and urinary catheter.

7 **Further management of hypotension** is described in Chapter 3.

8 **Discuss with the regional Liver Unit the transfer of:**
- all patients with suspected fulminant hepatic failure;
- patients with decompensated chronic liver disease causing encephalopathy more severe than Grade 2.

Further management

Fulminant hepatic failure (before transfer)

1 If Grade 3 or 4 coma, to reduce cerebral oedema:
- give mannitol 20% 100 ml i.v. over 20 minutes, provided urine output is >30 ml/hour and PA wedge pressure is <15 mmHg;
- hyperventilate to an arterial $P\text{CO}_2$ of 3.3–4.0 kPa (25–30 mmHg).

2 Check blood glucose by stick test every hour and give further dextrose 50% if <5 mmol/l.

3 Steroids are contraindicated. Give ranitidine and vitamin K (Table 33.4). Gut purgation is unhelpful and may be harmful.

Decompensated chronic liver disease

1 Check for precipitants (Table 33.3).

2 If there is ascites, remove 10 ml of fluid for microscopy and culture.

■ **Table 33.3. Precipitants of decompensated chronic liver disease**

- Acute gastrointestinal haemorrhage
- Intercurrent infection especially bacterial peritonitis
- Alcoholic binge
- Surgery
- Sedatives
- Hypokalaemia, hypoglycaemia
- Constipation

- Bacterial peritonitis is common and may not be accompanied by abdominal tenderness.
- Assume it is present if ascitic fluid shows >250 WBC/mm³ of which >75% are polymorphs.
- Treat with a combination of amoxycillin, gentamicin (Appendix 10.1, p. 71) and metronidazole.

3 Start antibiotic therapy with a third generation cephalosporin for suspected septicaemia if there is fever and the WBC count is >11 × 10⁹/l, even if no evidence of focal infection.

4 Start a liver failure regimen (Table 33.4).

■ **Table 33.4.** Liver failure regimen in decompensated chronic liver disease

1 Reduce the intestinal nitrogenous load
- Stop dietary protein
- Start lactulose 30 ml every 3 hours until diarrhoea begins then reduce to 30 ml 12-hourly
- Magnesium sulphate enemata 80 ml of a 50% solution twice daily (useful even in the absence of gastrointestinal bleeding)
- Neomycin may be helpful, although its contribution is controversial

2 Reduce the risk of gastric stress ulceration
- Ranitidine 300 mg p.o. at night (50 mg 8-hourly i.v.), or sucralfate 1 g 6-hourly p.o.

3 Maintain blood glucose >5 mmol/l
- Continue 10% dextrose by i.v. infusion. Titrate the rate against the CVP or PA wedge pressure
- Check blood glucose routinely every 1–2 hours and immediately if a deterioration in conscious level occurs

4 Other aspects of fluid balance
- Avoid normal saline even if plasma sodium is low
- Add potassium to maintain a plasma level >3.5 mmol/l

5 Drugs
- Give vitamin K 10 mg p.o. or i.v. (not i.m.) and folic acid 10 mg p.o. once daily
- Avoid sedatives and opiates
- Other drugs that are contraindicated are listed on p. 317

Appendix

33.1. Causes of fulminant hepatic failure

1 In the UK, paracetamol poisoning or viral hepatitis (usually non-A/non-B) are the commonest causes.

2 In continental Europe, NSAIDs and viral hepatitis are the commonest causes.

3 Other causes are:
- acute fatty liver of pregnancy;
- Weil's disease;
- poisoning with *Amanita phalloides*;
- halothane;
- viral haemorrhagic fevers.

34 Acute Renal Failure

The diagnosis is made from:
- a rapidly rising plasma urea or creatinine;
- a urine output of <400 ml per day or <30 ml/hour for three consecutive hours: this is not an invariable feature and 'non-oliguric' renal failure may occur.

'Pre-renal' causes are the commonest (Appendix 34.1) and must always be excluded.

Priorities

The oliguric patient with suspected acute renal failure (ARF)
1 Investigations required are given in Table 34.1.
2 Assess the patient's fluid status.
  - Look at fluid and weight charts.
  - Are there signs of volume-depletion (JVP not visible, postural hypotension) or overload (JVP raised, peripheral oedema, basal lung crackles)?
  - Is there pulmonary oedema on the chest X-ray?
  - Put in a central line to measure the CVP.
3 If the arterial pH is <7.0, give sodium bicarbonate 50 mmol (50 ml of 8.4% solution) i.v. over 15 minutes.

■ Table 34.1. Urgent investigation in suspected acute renal failure

- Plasma potassium, urea and creatinine
- Urine stick testing, biochemistry (Table 34.3), microscopy (Table 34.6) and culture
- Blood glucose (by stick test)
- Arterial blood gases and pH
- Chest X-ray
- ECG (if plasma potassium >6 mmol/l)

■ **Table 34.2.** Urgent treatment of hyperkalaemia (plasma potassium >6.5 mmol/l)

1 If the ECG has abnormalities associated with hyperkalaemia (widening of the QRS complex, loss of the P wave, peaking of the T wave or a sine wave pattern)
- **Give 10 ml of calcium chloride 10% i.v. over 5 min:** this can be repeated every 5 min up to a total dose of 40 ml
- **Give sodium bicarbonate 50 mmol (50 ml of 8.4% solution) i.v. over 15 min**
- **Give 25 g of dextrose (50 ml of dextrose 50%) with 10 units of soluble insulin i.v. over 15–30 min:** this will usually reduce plasma potassium for several hours

2 If the ECG is normal, give dextrose/insulin alone

3 Further treatment is needed: start calcium resonium and discuss with your Renal Unit; urgent dialysis may be indicated

4 Is the plasma potassium high?
- If it is 5.5–6.5 mmol/l, start calcium resonium (15 mg 8-hourly p.o.).
- If it is >6.5 mmol/l, treat as in Table 34.2.

5 If the patient does not have pulmonary oedema and the CVP is <10 cmH₂O (relative to the mid-axillary line), give a fluid challenge (Fig. 34.1).

6 If systolic BP is <90 mmHg despite a CVP of 5–10 cmH₂O see Chapter 3.

7 Insert a bladder catheter (with scrupulous sterile technique) and collect a specimen of urine for stick testing, microscopy, biochemistry and culture (Table 34.3).

Further management

Suspected pre-renal failure but no response to fluid challenge

1 Give frusemide and low-dose dopamine **(Table 34.4).** These may prevent progression to acute tubular necrosis or

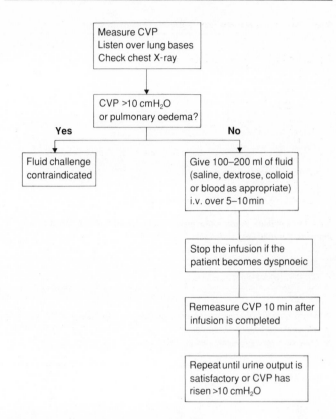

Fig. 34.1. Fluid challenge in oliguric renal failure.

convert oliguric to non-oliguric renal failure, making management of fluid balance easier.

Omit frusemide if aminoglycosides have been used.

2 If oliguria persists, or urea and creatinine continue to rise, it is likely that ischaemic acute tubular necrosis has occurred. The management is now that of established renal failure (p. 192).

■ **Table 34.3.** Urine biochemistry in oliguric renal failure

	Pre-renal	Oliguric ATN
Urine osmolality (mosmol/kg)	>500	<350
Urine sodium (mmol/l)	< 20	> 40
Urine: plasma osmolality	> 1.5	< 1.2
Urine: plasma urea	> 8	< 2
Urine: plasma creatinine	> 40	< 20
Fractional excretion of sodium (%) (calculated as urine/plasma sodium divided by urine/plasma creatinine × 100)	< 1	> 3

NB **These indices assume previously normal renal function and may not apply in the following situations:**

1 **Diuretic therapy** — which increases urinary sodium excretion
2 **After contrast media**
3 **Chronic renal failure**
4 **The elderly** — in whom tubular function and concentrating ability may be reduced
5 **Acute glomerulonephritis and acute interstitial nephritis** — which may give a low fractional sodium excretion
6 **Diabetic hyperglycaemic states**
7 **Hepatorenal syndrome**

ATN, acute tubular necrosis.

■ **Table 34.4.** Frusemide and dopamine for suspected pre-renal failure unresponsive to fluid challenge

Frusemide	• Do not give if aminoglycosides have been used
	• Give 250 mg i.v. over 1 hour
	• If the urine output remains less than 40 ml/hour over the next hour, give a further 500 mg i.v. over 2 hours
	• If the urine output increases, further doses can be given as required up to a maximum daily dose of 2 g or a continuous infusion can be started
Dopamine	• Give 2.5 µg/kg per min (Table 57.4, p. 293) via a central vein

Renal failure 'out of the blue'

1 Causes are given in Appendices 34.1, 34.2 and investigations required in Table 34.5.

■ **Table 34.5.** Investigation in acute renal failure 'out of the blue'

- **Full blood count and film** (normocytic anaemia suggests chronic renal failure)
- **Plasma sodium, potassium, urea, creatinine, calcium and glucose**
- **Creatine kinase** if rhabdomyolysis suspected (urine stick test positive for blood, but no RBC on microscopy)
- **Blood culture**
- **Clotting screen** if the patient has purpura or jaundice, or the blood film shows haemolysis or a low platelet count (suspected DIC)
- **Urine microscopy and stick testing for protein and blood**
- **Urine sodium, urea and osmolality (with plasma osmolality)**
- **ECG**
- **Chest X-ray**
- **Abdominal ultrasound** to exclude ureteric obstruction and assess renal size (small kidneys suggest chronic renal failure)

2 **Consider a post-renal cause.**
- Are there symptoms of bladder outflow obstruction and was there a large residual volume?
- Perform a rectal (and vaginal) examination to exclude a pelvic tumour causing ureteric obstruction.
- Obtain abdominal ultrasound.

Discuss further management with a urologist if bladder outflow or ureteric obstruction is found.

3 **Is there evidence of intrinsic renal disease?**
- Has the patient received any potentially nephrotoxic drugs (Appendix 34.2)?
- Check urine by stick test and microscopy (Table 34.6).
- A renal biopsy may need to be done to establish the diagnosis if pre- and post-renal causes and infection have been excluded: discuss this with a nephrologist.

■ **Table 34.6.** Urinalysis and urine microscopy in acute renal failure*

Red cells, red cell casts, proteinuria (2+ or more)	• Acute glomerulonephritis • Acute vasculitis
Stick test positive for blood, but no red cells on microscopy	• Rhabdomyolysis
Tubular cell casts, granular casts, tubular cells	• Acute tubular necrosis (ATN)
Normal or near-normal	• Pre-renal causes • Urinary tract obstruction • Some causes of ATN (more commonly in nephrotoxic or non-oliguric ATN) • Hypercalcaemia • Tubular obstruction • Renal atheroembolism

* In patients with a bladder catheter, red and white cells in the urine may be due to the catheter itself.

Established acute renal failure

Indications for urgent dialysis
• **Hyperkalaemia:** plasma potassium >5.5 mmol/l despite restricted intake and calcium resonium.
• **Pulmonary oedema.**
• **Severe metabolic acidosis.**
   Renal replacement therapy is best started early (e.g. when urea is around 40 mmol/l and creatinine around 600 μmol/l). **Peritoneal dialysis** (if transfer to a Renal Unit for haemodialysis or haemofiltration is not possible) is described in Chapter 55.

Management before dialysis is required
1 **Fluid balance.**
   • Restrict the daily fluid intake to 500 ml plus the previous day's measured losses (urine, nasogastric drainage, etc.), allowing more if the patient is febrile.
   • The patient's fluid status should be assessed daily (including daily weighing) and the next day's fluids adjusted appropriately.

2 Diet.
- Energy content >2000 kcal (8400 kJ)/day.
- Protein content 20–40 g/day.
- Sodium and potassium <50 mmol/day.

3 Potassium.
- If plasma potassium rises above 5 mmol/l despite dietary restriction, start calcium resonium which may be given orally (15 g three or four times daily) or by retention enema (30 g).

4 Infection.
- Patients with ARF are prone to serious infection especially pneumonia and urinary tract infection.
- Urinary catheters and vascular lines should be removed wherever possible.
- If the patient develops a fever, search for a focus of infection, take blood cultures and start antibiotic therapy to cover both Gram-positive and -negative organisms (e.g. amoxycillin 500 mg 8-hourly i.v. plus flucloxacillin 500 mg 6-hourly i.v., or a third-generation cephalosporin).

5 Drugs. Make sure all drug dosages are adjusted appropriately (see Table 60.1, p. 314).

How to keep on good terms with your Renal Unit

- **Contact them early** about patients with acute renal failure — preferably before plasma creatinine is over 400 μmol/l.
- **Preserve forearm veins** as these may be required for dialysis. Intravenous infusions should be given into central veins.
- **Check hepatitis B surface antigen before transfer.**

Appendices

34.1. Causes of acute renal failure

	Examples
Pre-renal ARF	
Hypotension	• Cardiogenic shock, septicaemia
True volume depletion	
• Gastrointestinal losses	• Vomiting, diarrhoea, haemorrhage
• Renal losses	• Diuretics, hyperglycaemic states
• Skin losses	• Burns
Third-space sequestration	• Intestinal obstruction, pancreatitis, peritonitis
Oedematous states	• Congestive heart failure, cirrhosis, nephrotic syndrome
Selective renal ischaemia	• Hepatorenal syndrome, bilateral renal artery stenosis
Post-renal ARF	
Urethral obstruction	• Prostatic enlargement
Ureteric obstruction	• Carcinoma of the bladder, prostate, cervix or large bowel
	• Calculi, papillary necrosis
	• Surgical accident
Intrinsic renal disease	
Glomerular	• Primary or part of a systemic disease
Vascular	• Vasculitis
	• Coagulopathy, e.g. haemolytic uraemic syndrome
Tubular	• Acute tubular necrosis due to ischaemia or nephrotoxins
	• Tubular obstruction in myeloma or acute uric acid nephropathy
Interstitial	• Drug-related acute interstitial nephritis
	• Acute bacterial pyelonephritis

Based on

Rose BD. **Pathophysiology of Renal Disease.** New York: McGraw-Hill 1981; 56.

34.2. Drugs which may cause or contribute to acute renal failure

1 **Impairment of renal perfusion:**
  • diuretics;
  • NSAIDs (interference with intrarenal blood flow);
  • angiotensin-converting enzyme inhibitors (especially in patients with bilateral renal artery stenosis);

2 **Nephrotoxic acute tubular necrosis:**
  • aminoglycosides;
  • sulphonamides;
  • rifampicin;
  • paracetamol poisoning;
  • contrast media (especially in patients with volume depletion or pre-existing renal impairment due to diabetes or myeloma).

3 **Acute interstitial nephritis:**
  • many antibiotics;
  • diuretics;
  • cimetidine.

35 Overview of Diabetic Emergencies

1 Urine should be tested for glucose in all hospital patients.

2 Blood glucose must be checked in ill diabetics and any patient with:

- reduced conscious level/confusion;
- fits;
- septicaemia;
- liver failure;
- hypothermia;
- acute neurological deficit;
- i.v. feeding.

Management

Glycosuria on routine testing

- Check the blood glucose either fasting or 2 hours after a meal.
- Diabetes is diagnosed by a fasting venous plasma level >8 mmol/l or a level 2 hours after a meal of >11 mol/l.

Hypoglycaemia

1 If the patient is drowsy or fitting (this may sometimes occur with mild hypoglycaemia if diabetic control has been poor):

- **give 50 ml of 50% dextrose i.v. or glucagon 1 mg i.v./i.m./s.c.;**
- recheck the glucose by stick test after 5 minutes and again after 30 minutes.

2 In non-diabetics consider the causes in Table 35.1.

3 If hypoglycaemia recurs or is likely to recur (e.g. liver disease, sepsis, sulphonylurea excess):

- start 10% dextrose at 1000 ml over 12 hours via a central or large antecubital vein;
- adjust the rate to keep the blood glucose level at 5–10 mmol/l;

■ **Table 35.1. Causes of hypoglycaemia**

Common	• Excess insulin
	• Sulphonylureas — rare with tolbutamide or glipizide, but common with chlorpropamide and glibenclamide
	• Alcoholic binge
	• Severe liver disease
	• Sepsis
Other	• Insulinoma
	• Hypopituitarism
	• Hypoadrenalism
	• Salicylate poisoning

• after excess sulphonylurea therapy, maintain the glucose infusion for 24 hours then tail off, but check blood glucose by stick test routinely for 3 days.

4 If hypoglycaemia is only partially responsive to 10% dextrose infusion:
  • give 20% or 30% dextrose via a central vein;
  • if the cause is intentional insulin overdose, consider local excision of the injection site.

Blood glucose >11 mmol/l

1 Check the urine or plasma for ketones. If 2 + or greater, measure arterial pH.
2 Assess the conscious level and state of hydration.
3 The patient can now be placed in one of three groups (Table 35.2).

■ **Table 35.2. Categorization of patients with blood glucose >11 mmol/l**

	Glucose (mmol/l)	Dehydration	Ketones	pHa	Drowsiness
DKA	>15	+ +	+ + +	< 7.2	+ +
HONK	>30	+ + + +	+	> 7.2	+ + +
Diabetes*	>11	−/+	− to + +	7.4	−

* Either poorly controlled or newly diagnosed.

Further management
- **Diabetic ketoacidosis** (DKA); Chapter 36.
- **Hyperosmolar non-ketotic hyperglycaemia** (HONK); Chapter 37.

Diabetes
- Confirm the blood glucose stick test by laboratory measurement.
- Perioperative management; Chapter 38.

Poorly controlled diabetes
- Insulin-dependent diabetes: modify the insulin regimen (Table 36.6, p. 204), or treat with insulin infusion if there is a significant intercurrent illness (e.g. sepsis, myocardial infarction).
- Non-insulin dependent diabetes: if there is significant intercurrent illness, treat with insulin.

Newly diagnosed diabetes
- Treatment depends on the **clinical state, ketone level** and **blood glucose** (Table 35.3).

■ **Table 35.3.** Treatment of newly diagnosed diabetes (blood glucose ≥11 mmol/l)

Clinical state	Ketones	Glucose	Treatment
Intercurrent illness	+ to ++*	>15	Insulin
	+	11–15	Recheck glucose and ketones in 2 hours
Well	−/+	>20	Oral hypoglycaemic
	−/+	11–20	Diet alone
	++*	>11	Insulin

* The patient has mild DKA caught early before major fluid loss has occurred. Insulin can be given as an i.v. infusion (Table 36.2, p. 200) or as a three times daily s.c. regimen.

36 Diabetic Ketoacidosis

Consider ketoacidosis in:
- any ill diabetic, particularly if they are vomiting or tachypnoeic;
- any drowsy or comatose patient.

Priorities

1 Check the blood glucose by stick test. A value of less than 10 mmol/l excludes the diagnosis. It will usually be over 20 mmol/l. Other investigations required urgently are given in Table 36.1.

2 If ketones are low (trace or 1+), suspect hyperosmolar nonketotic coma. Treatment is similar, but there are important differences (Chapter 37).

3 Oxygen should be given if the arterial oxygen is less than 80 mmHg (10.5 kPa).

4 Start fluid replacement via a peripheral i.v. line.
- If the systolic BP is <90 mmHg, give colloid 500 ml over 15–30 minutes.
- If the systolic BP is >90 mmHg give normal saline, 1 litre over 15–30 minutes.

■ **Table 36.1. Urgent investigation in suspected diabetic ketoacidosis**

- **Blood glucose** (stick test and laboratory measurement)
- **Ketones** (stick test of plasma or urine with Ketostix)
- **Sodium, potassium and urea**
- **Blood culture** (by separate venepuncture)
- **Arterial blood for gases and pH**
- **Full blood count** (white counts of up to 20×10^9 may occur from acidosis, rather than infection)
- **MSU or CSU for microscopy and culture**
- **Chest X-ray** (?pneumonia)
- **ECG** (infarction may complicate or precipitate DKA)

■ **Table 36.2.** Insulin infusion in diabetic ketoacidosis

1 Add 50 units of soluble insulin to 50 ml normal saline
2 Discard 10 ml via the tubing (some of this insulin will be adsorbed onto the plastic)
3 Start the infusion at a rate of 6 u/hour: do not delay treatment if a pump cannot be found; the infusion can be given via a burette
4 Check blood glucose initially every 2 hours, and adjust the infusion rate as below

Blood glucose* (mmol/l)	Insulin rate (u/hour)	i.v. fluid
>15	6	Normal saline
10–15	3	Dextrose
5–10	1	Dextrose
<5	0.5	Dextrose

* Slight modification of the ranges may be needed according to the stick test used (e.g. relevant BM-Test gradations are 4.5, 9 and 17 mmol/l; for Glucostix, 4, 10 and 14 mmol/l).

5 Insert a nasogastric tube if the patient is too drowsy to answer questions. Inhalation of vomit is a potentially fatal complication.
6 Give insulin 10 units i.v. whilst a pump is being prepared (Table 36.2).

Further management

1 Fluid replacement.
  • **Put in a CVP line.** If the ECG suggests recent infarction, fluid replacement is best guided by measurement of the wedge pressure.
  • **A standard regimen is given in Table 36.3.** Reduce the infusion rate if the CVP rises above 10 cmH$_2$O. The rate must take into account urinary losses which will remain high until the blood glucose is below the renal threshold — usually around 10 mmol/l.

■ **Table 36.3.** Fluid replacement in diabetic ketoacidosis

Start with normal saline	• 1 litre over 15–30 min (no added potassium until plasma level known) • 1 litre over 1 hour (+ KCl according to Table 36.4) • 1 litre over 2 hours (+ KCl) • 1 litre 8-hourly (+ KCl) until the fluid deficit has been corrected (as shown by warm extremities with a normal pulse and BP)
When the glucose is <15 mmol/l change to dextrose	• Use 10% dextrose if significant metabolic correction is still needed (acidotic, ketones more than 1+) • Otherwise use 5% dextrose • Give concurrent normal saline if still hypovolaemic

NB Hyponatraemia may occur in DKA due to osmotic shift of water. **Hypertonic saline must not be given**

2 Potassium replacement.
   • Give none in the first litre of normal saline whilst awaiting the plasma level.
   • On average, 20 mmol are added to each litre of fluid, but titrate according to the plasma level (Table 36.4).
3 Bicarbonate. This should only be given if the acidosis is very severe (arterial pH <7.1):
   • pH less than 7.0: give 50 ml of 8.4% sodium bicarbonate with 26 mmol potassium over 30 minutes;

■ **Table 36.4.** Potassium replacement in diabetic ketoacidosis

Plasma potassium (mmol/l)	Potassium added (mmol/l)
<3	40
3–4	30
4–5	20
>5	Give none

- pH 7.0–7.1: give 25 ml of 8.4% sodium bicarbonate with 13 mmol potassium;
- Recheck arterial pH after each dose.

4 Antibiotic therapy. Bacterial infection is a common precipitant and complication of ketoacidosis and may not cause fever.

- Look for a focus of infection. 'Hidden' areas are the feet and perineum (a rectal examination is obligatory).
- A case can be made for giving antibiotic therapy to all patients. In the absence of an obvious focus, give: **amoxycillin 500 mg 8-hourly i.v. plus flucloxacillin 500 mg 6-hourly i.v.**
- If there is infection of the feet or perineum add: **metronidazole 1 g 8-hourly p.r.** and obtain a surgical opinion.
- Changes can be made once the results of bacteriology are available.

5 Give heparin 5000 units 8-hourly s.c. until the patient is well enough to walk.

6 Put in a urinary catheter if no urine has been passed after 4 hours, but not otherwise.

Monitoring progress

A schedule is given in Table 36.5.

■ **Table 36.5. Monitoring progress in the first 24 hours**

Check hourly	• **Conscious level** (e.g. Glasgow Coma Scale; Appendix 6.1, p. 49) until fully conscious • **BP and pulse rate** until stable and then 4-hourly • **CVP** until the infusion rate is 1 litre 8-hourly or less • **Blood glucose stick test** • **Urine output**
Check 2-hourly	• **Blood glucose laboratory measurement** until <20 mmol/l then check 4-hourly • **Plasma potassium** until the infusion rate is 1litre 8-hourly or less • **Arterial pH** until >7.3 and then monitor ketogenesis from the urine ketone level

Problems

No fall in blood glucose after 2 hours
- Check that the i.v. lines are running.
- Double the insulin infusion rate.
- Recheck after a further 2 hours and double the insulin infusion rate again if necessary.

When to stop the insulin infusion
- Continue until ketones disappear from the urine (usually at 24–48 hours).
- The patient may then take food with soluble insulin given subcutaneously.
- Continue the infusion for 1 hour after the first subcutaneous dose.

Changeover to S.C. insulin
- Start with short-acting insulin three times daily.
- Base the total daily dose on double the total dose of insulin given over the last 12 hours.
- Check the blood glucose 2- to 4-hourly and give top-up insulin injections if it rises above 15 mmol/l.
- When insulin requirements are stable, change to a twice-daily insulin regimen (e.g. Table 36.6).

Intramuscular insulin regimen
- Give 20 units of soluble insulin i.m. stat (instead of the initial i.v. bolus).
- Continue with 8–10 units i.m. every hour.
- When the blood glucose is 10–15 mmol/l, reduce to 6 units every 2 hours until the patient is eating and subcutaneous insulin is started.
- If the blood glucose has not fallen and the arterial pH not risen after 4 hours, change to a continuous intravenous infusion using a burette or pump.

■ **Table 36.6. Establishing a twice-daily insulin regimen**

1 Estimate total daily insulin dose from recent requirements
2 Give two-thirds total daily dose before breakfast and one-third before supper, each dose made up half of short-acting (soluble) insulin and half of intermediate-acting (isophane or zinc suspension) insulin
3 Check blood glucose before breakfast, mid-morning, mid-afternoon and before bedtime, aiming for levels between 4–7 mmol/l
4 Adjust insulin doses as required

Unsatisfactory blood glucose	Adjust
Before breakfast	Evening intermediate-acting
Mid-morning	Morning short-acting
Mid-afternoon	Morning intermediate-acting
Before bedtime	Evening short-acting

37 Hyperosmolar Non-ketotic Hyperglycaemia

1 Consider the diagnosis in the patient with hyperglycaemia where dehydration and drowsiness are severe.

2 HONK is differentiated from DKA by:

- blood glucose >30 mmol/l, but only trace or 1+ ketones in plasma or urine;
- plasma osmolality >350 mosmol/kg (normal range 280–300 mosmol / kg).

This can be measured directly or calculated from the formula:

Osmolality = 2(Na + K) + Urea + Glucose

Management

This is the same as for DKA with the following exceptions.

- **Half-normal saline** is used for fluid replacement if the plasma sodium is >145 mmol/l.

- **Insulin sensitivity is greater** in the absence of severe acidosis (Table 37.1).

- **The risk of thromboembolism is high.** Unless contraindicated (e.g. recent stroke), start a heparin infusion at 1000 u. hourly.

- **Total body potassium is lower** and the plasma level more variable as treatment begins. Check the level 30 minutes after starting insulin and then 2-hourly.

- Most patients can subsequently be maintained on **oral hypoglycaemic agents.** These should be substituted if the daily insulin requirement falls to around 20 units (e.g. glibenclamide initially 5 mg once daily).

■ Table 37.1. Insulin infusion in hyperosmolar non-ketotic hyperglycaemia

Blood glucose*	Insulin rate (u/hour)
>20	3
13–20	2
5–13	1
<5	0.5

* If the blood glucose has not fallen by 10 mmol/l after 2 hours, double the infusion rate.

38 Perioperative Management of Diabetes

Minor surgery is defined as surgery without entry of a body cavity or transection of a major limb bone.

Insulin-dependent diabetes

If the patient can be put first on a morning list
1 Omit intermediate or long-acting insulin the night before.
2 Omit the usual morning insulin.
3 Check blood glucose before and after surgery and 4 hours later.
4 On return from theatre give carbohydrate and 50–75% of the usual total morning insulin dose as short-acting insulin.
5 Give the usual evening insulin before supper.

Mini-pump method (suitable whatever time surgery is scheduled)
1 Omit intermediate or long-acting insulin the night before.
2 Start an i.v. infusion of soluble insulin at 8 a.m. on the day of surgery. Prepare a pump containing 25 units of soluble insulin in 50 ml of saline (0.5 u/ml) and give 0.5 u/hour.
3 Check blood glucose before and after surgery and 4 hours later. Increase the infusion rate if >15 mmol/l (Table 38.1).
4 Give the usual evening insulin before supper and take down the pump.

'GIK' (glucose-insulin-potassium) regimen (suitable whatever time surgery is scheduled; no pump required)
1 Omit intermediate or long-acting insulin the night before.
2 Check blood glucose on the morning of surgery.

■ **Table 38.1. Continuous insulin infusion using a pump**

• Add 50 units of soluble insulin to 50 ml of saline in the syringe. Flush 10 ml of solution through the line before connecting to the patient
• Check blood glucose and start the infusion at the appropriate rate

Blood glucose* (mmol/l)	Insulin infusion rate[†] (u/hour)
<5	0.5
5–15	2
15–20	4
>20	6

* Check blood glucose at least hourly during surgery and 2-hourly post-operatively. Adjust the infusion rate as required, aiming to keep blood glucose between 5–10 mmol/l.
† In patients with insulin resistance (e.g. because of inotrope infusion), higher infusion rates may be needed.

■ **Table 38.2 Insulin addition to dextrose**

Blood glucose (mmol/l)	Insulin addition (u/l)
<4	8
4–7	16
7–12	24
12–15	32

3 Add soluble insulin to a 1 litre bag of dextrose 5% with potassium 20 mmol/l, according to the blood glucose (Table 38.2).
4 Infuse at 100 ml/hour.
5 Check blood glucose before and after surgery and 4 hours later.
6 Give the usual evening insulin before supper and take down the infusion.

Non-insulin-dependent diabetes
Blood glucose should be checked pre-operatively. Management depends on level of control.
1 If control is good (random blood glucose <12 mmol/l)
  • omit oral hypoglycaemics on the day of surgery;

- avoid i.v. dextrose peri-operatively;
- check blood glucose after surgery and 4 hours later.

2 If control is poor:
- convert to soluble insulin 10 units s.c. three times daily before surgery;
- manage as for insulin-dependent diabetes on the day of surgery.

Major surgery

This is defined as surgery involving entry of a body cavity or transection of a major limb bone.

Insulin-dependent diabetes

Admit 48 hours before operation to establish good control. Give the usual total daily dose of insulin as three divided doses of soluble insulin before meals.

On the day of operation
- At 8 a.m., start an i.v. infusion of dextrose 5% at 100 ml/hour, with added potassium as required, and i.v. insulin via a pump (Table 38.1).

After surgery
1 Check blood glucose 2-hourly until stable and then 6-hourly.
2 When the patient can eat and no longer requires i.v. fluids, give soluble insulin s.c. before breakfast and stop the pump.
3 Start with a three times daily soluble insulin regimen giving an additional dose before bedtime if blood glucose >15 mmol/l.
4 After 24–48 hours, convert back to the patient's usual regimen.

Non-insulin-dependent diabetes

Admit 48 hours before operation to establish good control. Check blood glucose on admission. Management depends on level of control.

1 If control is good (random blood glucose <12 mmol/l):
 • stop biguanides (metformin) and long-acting sulphonylureas (notably chlorpropamide);
 • convert to short-acting sulphonylurea (e.g. tolbutamide).

2 If control is poor: convert to soluble insulin 10 units s.c. three times daily before meals.

On the day of operation
 • Omit oral hypoglycaemic or s.c. insulin.
 • Manage as for insulin-dependent diabetes.

During and after surgery
Manage as for insulin-dependent diabetes until i.v. infusions are down and the patient is eating, when oral hypoglycaemics can be restarted.

39 Hyponatraemia

- Consider hyponatraemia in any patient with **seizures or reduced conscious level.**
- **Hyponatraemia is common in ill patients but only requires urgent treatment if causing severe neurological effects,** when plasma sodium concentration will be <120 mmol/l.

Hyponatraemia with severe neurological effects

Priorities

1 If the patient is comatose, start resuscitation along standard lines (Chapter 6). Seizures should be treated with diazepam (see p. 171).

2 Check blood glucose by stick test. Hyponatraemia may occur in severe hyperglycaemia due to osmotic shift of water from the intracellular space. Plasma osmolality is normal or high, and **treatment with hypertonic saline is inappropriate and may be fatal.**

3 Send blood for urgent urea and electrolytes. If a patient with an i.v. infusion has an unexpectedly low plasma sodium concentration, check first that the blood sample was not taken from a downstream vein.

4 Assess the patient's fluid status from the fluid charts, blood pressure, JVP and the presence or absence of peripheral and pulmonary oedema. Check previous (biochemical) results: is renal function normal?

5 If significant hyponatraemia is confirmed (plasma sodium <120 mmol/l, give hypertonic saline (Table 39.1).

- If hypertonic saline is not immediately available, sodium bicarbonate can be given over the first hour.
- Give frusemide 40 mg i.v. unless the patient is volume depleted

■ **Table 39.1.** Saline infusion for hyponatraemia with severe neurological effects

- Give 70 mmol sodium/hour as hypertonic saline
- Check plasma sodium hourly and adjust the dose aiming to raise plasma sodium by 2 mmol/l per hour
- Stop the saline infusion when plasma sodium is 125 mmol/l

Fluid	Sodium concentration (mmol/l)	Volume (ml) containing 70 mmol Na$^+$
3% saline	515	140
5% saline	856	80
8.4% sodium bicarbonate	1000	70

(with low blood pressure and venous pressure). The diuresis will help raise plasma sodium concentration.

- **When plasma sodium has risen to 125 mmol/l, stop the infusion of hypertonic saline.**
- Plasma sodium should then be allowed to return slowly to normal by restricting water intake to 800 ml/day.
- Rapid correction of plasma sodium to normal or supranormal levels may result in central pontine myelinolysis.

Problems

Severe hyponatraemia in the patient with renal failure

Contact the Renal Unit. Treatment with hypertonic saline may precipitate pulmonary oedema. Once seizures have been controlled, dialysis should be used to restore plasma sodium to normal.

The comatose patient: when should hyponatraemia be treated?

- Treatment with hypertonic saline should not be given unless plasma sodium is <120 mmol/l.
- If plasma sodium is 120–130 mmol/l, other causes of coma

should be suspected, e.g. subarachnoid haemorrhage or meningitis, liver failure, acute renal failure and diabetic emergencies.

Hyponatraemia without severe neurological effects

1 If the patient has no symptoms attributable to hyponatraemia or is only mildly symptomatic (e.g. headache, nausea, lethargy), hypertonic saline should not be given.

2 Hyponatraemia is seen in a large number of diseases, usually late in their course when the diagnosis is obvious. However, it may be a diagnostic clue to several conditions (Table 39.2).

■ **Table 39.2. Diseases in which hyponatraemia may be a diagnostic clue**

- *Legionella* pneumonia
- Addison's disease (hypoadrenalism)
- Hypothyroidism
- Diuretic or purgative abuse
- Acute intermittent porphyria (SIADH)
- Oat cell carcinoma of bronchus (SIADH)
- Drug related SIADH (e.g. chlorpropamide, carbamazepine, narcotics, chlorpromazine)

SIADH, syndrome of inappropriate ADH secretion.

3 SIADH is overdiagnosed. The diagnosis should only be made if all the following are present:

- plasma sodium concentration <130 mmol/l; plasma osmolality <275 mosmol/kg; urine sodium concentration >20 mmol/l; urine osmolality > plasma osmolality;
- no oedema or signs of hypovolaemia (check for postural hypotension);
- normal renal, thyroid and adrenal function (checked by the short tetracosactrin (Synacthen) test);
- the patient is not taking diuretics.

Management

This depends principally on the patient's fluid status.

Volume depleted

• Give normal saline i.v. (with potassium supplements if required) until the volume deficit has been corrected.

• In asymptomatic patients in whom hyponatraemia is due to diuretic therapy, withdrawal of the diuretic and a normal diet is usually sufficient.

Oedematous

• The combination of hyponatraemia and oedema can occur in congestive heart failure, liver failure, renal failure (acute or chronic) and the nephrotic syndrome.

• Correction of the hyponatraemia (if indicated) requires treatment of the underlying disease.

• Management is difficult and expert advice should be sought.

Normovolaemic (SIADH)

• Restrict fluid intake to 800 ml/day.

• In patients with oat cell carcinoma of the bronchus, demeclocycline can be combined with water restriction.

40 Hypercalcaemia

• **Usually seen in patients known to have a malignancy involving bone** (most often carcinoma of the breast or bronchus, myeloma or lymphoma) but may also occur without obvious bone metastases.

• **Common precipitants** are dehydration, immobilization and treatment with thiazides.

• **May give rise to many non-specific symptoms** (anorexia, nausea, vomiting, constipation, thirst, polyuria, weakness, malaise, confusional state), **particularly when plasma calcium is >3.0 mmol/l.**

Priorities

If plasma calcium is >3.0 mmol/l and the patient is symptomatic, the first-line treatment is rehydration.

1 Assess the degree of volume depletion. Are there complicating factors (congestive heart failure, advanced renal failure) which make i.v. saline therapy hazardous? If so, dialysis may be indicated.

2 In patients with mild symptoms, oral rehydration (a fluid intake of at least 2–3 l/day) may be sufficient.

3 Patients with more severe symptoms should receive i.v. saline. Options are:

• i.v. saline 3–4 litres over 24 hours via a peripheral vein;

• forced saline diuresis (Table 40.1): this is potentially hazardous and should only be used when rapid reduction in plasma calcium is required (e.g. because the patient is comatose or has major cardiac arrhythmias).

Further management

If plasma calcium remains >3.0 mmol/l despite rehydration, drug therapy is indicated.

■ **Table 40.1.** Forced saline diuresis for severe hypercalcaemia

- Put in a **urinary catheter** to monitor urine output
- Put in a **central venous line** to monitor CVP
- Give **normal saline** 1 litre over 3–4 hours i.v.
- If the CVP rises above 10 cmH$_2$O (relative to mid-axillary line), give **frusemide** 40 mg i.v. and slow the infusion rate.
- **Check plasma potassium and calcium 4-hourly.** Give potassium i.v. as required

- **The combination of calcitonin 100–200 units 12-hourly s.c. and prednisolone 10–20 mg 8-hourly p.o.** is effective (at least in the short term) and safe.
- **Mithramycin, diphosphonates** and **phosphate** should not be given except on expert advice. Intravenous phosphate is particularly hazardous.
- **Specific treatment** will be needed to prevent a recurrence of hypercalcaemia (e.g. chemotherapy for malignancies, surgery for primary hyperparathyroidism).

41   Acute Adrenal Insufficiency

Consider the diagnosis in any patient with **unexplained hypotension or mild hyponatraemia and:**

- **corticosteroid therapy (prednisolone >7.5 mg daily;** or
- **pigmentation** (buccal mucosa, scars, palmer creases); or
- **preceding anorexia, nausea, vomiting and weight loss.**

Treatment requires **correction of fluid depletion as well as steroid replacement therapy.**

Priorities

1 If the patient is unconscious, initial resuscitation is as for any cause of coma (Chapter 6).

2 If systolic BP is **<90 mmHg**, give colloid 500 ml i.v. over 15–30 minutes.

3 Check blood glucose by stick test: if <3.5 mmol/l, give 50 ml of 50% dextrose i.v. Other investigations are given in Table 41.1.

4 Check for causes of decompensation, of which **infection** is the commonest. **Start antibiotic therapy for suspected septicaemia** (Table 10.2, p. 67):

■ **Table 41.1. Urgent investigation in suspected acute hypoadrenalism**

- **Urea, sodium and potassium**
- **Full blood count**
- **Plasma cortisol** (10 ml blood in a heparinized tube, for later analysis)
- **Blood glucose**
- **Blood culture**
- **Chest X-ray**
- **ECG**

Typical biochemical findings in acute adrenal insufficiency:	**a** raised urea
	b low sodium (120–130 mmol/l)
	c raised potassium (5–7 mmol/l)
	d low glucose

- if the white count is $>20 \times 10^9/l$; *or*
- if there is fever or temperature $<36°C$.

Further management

1 **Fluid replacement.**
- **If systolic BP remains** <90 mmHg after 500 ml colloid, put in a central line and infuse normal saline to keep the CVP 5–10 cmH$_2$O. See Chapter 3 for further management of hypotension.
- **If systolic BP is** >90 **mmHg**, give normal saline 1 litre every 6–8 hours until the fluid deficit has been corrected, as judged by clinical improvement and the absence of postural hypotension.
- **Hyperkalaemia** is common in acute hypoadrenalism and potassium should not be added if plasma K$^+$ is >5 mmol/l.

2 **Steroid replacement therapy.**
- **Give hydrocortisone (sodium succinate):**
  a 100 mg i.v. stat;
  b then 200 mg by i.v. infusion over the first 24 hours;
  c then 100 mg i.v. daily until vomiting has stopped.
- **Maintenance therapy is with cortisol** 30 mg p.o. daily which can be given in divided doses (20 mg mane and 10 mg nocte) **and fludrocortisone** 0.05–0.1 mg p.o. daily.

3 **To confirm the diagnosis** in equivocal cases (where the initial cortisol level is borderline) and to differentiate primary from secondary hypoadrenalism, use the **short tetracosactrin (Synacthen) test.**

This should be done when the patient has recovered, as hydrocortisone (but not fludrocortisone) must be stopped for 24 hours before the test. Causes of acute adrenal insufficiency are given in Appendix 41.1.

Problems

The patient on long-term corticosteroid therapy or receiving replacement therapy for hypoadrenalism: when should the dose be increased?

- **Mild infection**; double the usual dose.
- **Minor surgery**; 100 mg hydrocortisone sodium succinate i.m. 6-hourly for 24 hours starting with the premedication then return to usual dose.
- **Severe infection or major surgery**; hydrocortisone i.m. as for minor surgery but continue for 72 hours or until taking oral fluids. After this give the same dose orally (and restart fludrocortisone) and gradually taper over 2 weeks to the usual maintenance dose.

Appendices

41.1 Causes of acute adrenal insufficiency

Acute stress in patients with chronic adrenal dysfunction due to:
- Corticosteroid therapy.
- Autoimmune adrenalitis.
- Tuberculosis.
- Other rare causes, e.g. bilateral adrenal metastases.

Bilateral adrenal haemorrhage due to:
- Septicaemia (Waterhouse–Friderichsen syndrome).
- Anticoagulant therapy (heparin or warfarin).

41.2 Steroid doses with equivalent glucocorticoid effect*

Steriod	Dose (mg)
Cortisone acetate	25
Hydrocortisone (cortisol)	20
Prednisolone	5
Methyl prednisolone	4
Dexamethasone	0.75

* The normal glucocorticoid output of the adrenals is equivalent to 20–40 mg of hydrocortisone daily; with stress this may increase to the equivalent of 300 mg hydrocortisone daily.

42   Thyrotoxic Crisis

The commonest presentations are:
- agitation or mania;
- cardiac failure usually with fast atrial fibrillation;
- worsening angina pectoris (may occur with relatively mild thyrotoxicosis if there is severe coronary disease).

Suspect the diagnosis where these are associated with:
- an acutely ill patient known to have partially treated thyrotoxicosis;
- exophthalmos or goitre (**NB** these may frequently be absent);
- patient aged <50 years with unexplained fever.

The mortality of untreated thyrotoxic crisis is high. **If the diagnosis is suspected, antithyroid treatment must be started before biochemical confirmation.**

Priorities

1 Give oxygen and attach an ECG monitor. Investigations needed urgently are listed in Table 42.1.

2 Priority management of hypotension or pulmonary oedema is as for any other cause except that supraventricular tachycardias are unlikely to respond to DC countershock.

■ **Table 42.1.** Urgent investigation in suspected thyrotoxic crisis

- **Thyroid function** (TSH, free T_3 and free T_4*)
- **Urea, sodium and potassium**
- **Full blood count**
- **Blood glucose**
- **Culture of blood and urine**
- **ECG**
- **Chest X-ray**

* If severely ill, increased production of reverse tri-iodothyronine may lead to near normal thyroxine levels.
T_3, tri-iodothyronine; T_4, thyroxine; TSH, thyroid-stimulating hormone.

3 Give a beta-blocker intravenously (e.g. propranolol 0.5–1 mg) if:

- **there is** *no* **heart failure (normal chest X-ray);** *and*
- **there is angina at rest;** *or*
- **the ventricular rate is** >150/min; *or*
- **there is severe agitation.**

If there is no haemodynamic deterioration after the first dose, give further doses every 15 minutes until the ventricular rate is about 100/min.

4 If there is atrial fibrillation or flutter start digoxin (Table 42.2).

5 If there is severe agitation, give chlorpromazine 100–200 mg i.m. (NB should not be given if the patient is hypotensive).

■ **Table 42.2.** Digoxin therapy in thyrotoxicosis

- There is relative digoxin resistance (increased renal excretion and reduced action on AV conduction) so high doses must be given
- **Loading dose**: 0.5 mg i.v. over 30 min followed by 0.25 mg i.v. over 30 min every 2 hours until the ventricular rate is <100/min or up to a total dose of 1.5 mg
- **Maintenance dose**: 0.25–0.5 mg daily p.o.

Further management

1 If no precipitant is obvious (trauma, surgery, metabolic derangement) look for signs of infection.

- Give broad-spectrum antibiotics (e.g. amoxicillin 500 mg 8-hourly i.v. plus flucloxacillin 500 mg 6-hourly i.v.) even in the absence of a focus of infection if the white count is >20 × 10^9/l.
- Fever and mild leucocytosis are common in the absence of infection.

2 Start antithyroid therapy (Table 42.3).

- Start either propylthiouracil or carbimazole (which act principally by inhibiting thyroxine synthesis).
- Use propylthiouracil if severely ill as it has a faster onset of action.

■ **Table 42.3.** Antithyroid therapy in thyrotoxic crisis

Carbimazole	• Initially 20–40 mg orally 6-hourly • After 1 week reduce to 20 mg 8-hourly
Propylthiouracil	• Initially 150–300 mg orally 6-hourly • After 24 hours reduce to 100–200 mg 6-hourly
Iodine	**NB Do not start within 4 hours of carbimazole or propylthiouracil** • Give either Lugol's iodine 60 ml 8-hourly orally or sodium iodide 0.5–1.0 g by i.v. infusion every 12 hours • Iodine can be tailed off after 2 days if propylthiouracil is used or after 1 week with carbimazole

• After 4 hours, start iodine (which inhibits secretion of thyroxine).
• If iodine is started before antithyroid drugs, excess thyroxine may be produced leading to an exacerbation of the crisis.

3 Oral propranolol can be used to block the peripheral effects of thyroid hormones **if there is no pulmonary oedema or hypotension.** If there is any doubt, it should not be used.

• Give 40 mg initially. A further dose can be given after 1 hour if the BP has not fallen and there is no breathlessness.
• Maintain on propranolol 40–160 mg 6-hourly. Aim to reduce the heart rate to below 100/min.

4 Anticoagulate if in atrial fibrillation.

• Start a heparin infusion 1000 u/hour.
• Start warfarin after 3 days and continue for 3 months after reversion to sinus rhythm.

5 General measures.

• **Intravenous fluid therapy.**
• **Fever** will be reduced by propranolol and chlorpromazine. Other measures are fanning, tepid sponging and paracetamol (as aspirin displaces throxine from thyroid binding globulin).
• There is no evidence supporting the use of glucocorticoid steroids to reduce the peripheral conversion of T_4 to T_3.

6 Exchange transfusion or peritoneal/haemodialysis may be considered in a patient who fails to improve within 24–48 hours. Discuss with an endocrinologist.

43 Hypothermia (including Myxoedema Coma)

- Hypothermia is defined as a core temperature <35°C.
- Coma occurs if the core temperature falls below 27°C.
- Measure rectal temperature with a low reading thermometer in any patient admitted with a reduced level of consciousness who has been exposed to the cold.
- At high risk are the elderly (in whom hypothermia is often the consequence of acute illness) and vagrants (due to the combination of alcohol and cold exposure).

Priorities

1 **If unconscious, start resuscitation as for coma from any cause (Chapter 6).**
2 Give oxygen, connect to an ECG monitor and put in a peripheral i.v. line.

- **Ventricular fibrillation** may occur at core temperatures below 28–30°C. DC countershock may not be effective until the temperature is >30°C. Continue cardiopulmonary resuscitation for longer than usual (as hypothermia protects the brain from ischaemic injury).
- Do not put in a central line until core temperature is >30°C because of the risk of precipitating VF.
- Sinus bradycardia does not need treatment: temporary pacing is only indicated for complete heart block.

3 **Check blood glucose.** Treat hypoglycaemia. Raised blood glucose (10–20 mmol/l) is common (due to insulin resistance) and should not be treated with insulin because of the risk of hypoglycaemia on rewarming.
4 **Is active core rewarming indicated?**
- Core temperature <30°C
- VF refractory to DC shock

■ **Table 43.1.** Urgent investigation of the patient with hypothermia

- **Full blood count**
- **Urea and electrolytes**
- **Blood glucose**
- **Arterial blood gases** (corrected for temperature; Table 58.4, p. 303)
- **Blood culture**
- **Thyroid function** (if age >50 years or suspected thyroid disease) (for later analysis)
- **Blood and urine for drug screen** if no other cause for hypothermia is evident
- **ECG**
- **Chest X-ray**
- **X-ray pelvis and hips** if history of a fall or clinical signs of fractured neck of femur

NB Blood levels of skeletal and cardiac muscle enzymes are elevated in hypothermia, even in the absence of myocardial infarction

Consider the age of the patient and concurrent illness. See Appendix 43.1 for methods of active core rewarming.

5 Check for underlying illness (e.g. pneumonia, stroke, myocardial infarction, fractured neck of femur) (Table 43.1). **Consider self-poisoning with alcohol or psychotropic drugs** if no other cause of hypothermia is evident.

6 Is there evidence of myxoedema? The physical signs of hypothermia from whatever cause closely resemble those of

■ **Table 43.2.** Features suggesting myxoedema in the patient with hypothermia

- Preceding symptoms of hypothyroidism: weight gain with reduced appetite, dry skin and hair loss
- Previous radio-iodine treatment for thyrotoxicosis
- Thyroidectomy scar
- Hyponatraemia ($Na^+ < 130$ mmol/l)
- Macrocytosis
- Failure of core temperature to rise 0.5°C/hour with external rewarming

NB Slowly relaxing tendon reflexes are a non-specific feature of hypothermia

myxoedema coma: however, if there is other evidence of hypothyroidism (Table 43.2), thyroid hormone and hydrocortisone should be given (Appendix 43.2).

Further management

1 Elderly patients are most safely managed by **passive external rewarming (Table 43.3).**

2 As **pneumonia** is a common cause and complication of hypothermia, start antibiotic therapy with amoxycillin 500 mg 8-hourly i.v. once blood cultures have been taken. Further doses need not be given until the core temperature is >32°C.

3 Most hypothermic patients are **volume depleted** (due in part to cold-induced diuresis). If the chest X-ray does not show pulmonary oedema, start an i.v. infusion of normal saline 1 litre over 4 hours via a warming coil: further fluid therapy should be guided by the blood pressure and urine output.

■ **Table 43.3. Passive external rewarming**

1 Nurse in a side room heated to 20–30°C on a ripple mattress with the blankets supported by a bed cage
2 Give humidified oxygen by face mask
3 Aim for a slow rise in core temperature (around 0.5°C/hour)
4 Monitor:
   • **Rectal temperature** (hourly, or preferably using a rectal probe allowing a continuous display)
   • **ECG:** supraventricular arrhythmias (e.g. atrial fibrillation) are common and usually resolve as core temperature returns to normal
   • **Blood pressure** (hourly): if systolic BP falls below 100 mmHg, reduce the rate of rewarming and give further i.v. fluid
   • **Blood glucose** (4-hourly)
   • **Urine output** (bladder catheter)

Appendices

43.1. Methods of active core rewarming

Peritoneal dialysis
1 Insert a peritoneal dialysis catheter (Chapter 55).
2 Use 1 or 2 litre bags, potassium free.
3 Warm the dialysate by running it through a blood warming coil immersed in water heated to 54°C (this will give a dialysate temperature around 44°C when it enters the peritoneal cavity).
4 Run in rapidly and drain out immediately.
5 Core temperature is usually restored to normal after 6–8 exchanges.
6 Check plasma potassium after 2 hours and if <3.5 mmol/l, add potassium to the dialysate (4 mmol/l).

Inhalation of warmed oxygen (via endotracheal tube)
Oxygen is warmed in a waterbath humidifier. Monitor the gas temperature at the mouth and maintain it around 44°C
(this will require modification of most ventilators)

Other methods
These include an **oesophageal thermal probe** and **extracorporeal circulation.**

43.2. Treatment of myxoedema coma
1 Check for concurrent illness.
2 Start antibiotic therapy with amoxycillin 500 mg 8-hourly i.v. once blood cultures have been taken.
3 Standard management of hypothermia by passive external rewarming (Table 43.3).
4 Take blood for thyroid hormones, TSH and cortisol before starting treatment.

■ **Table 43.4.** Treatment of hypothyroid coma

- Day 1–3: T_3 10 µg 8-hourly i.v.
- Day 4–6: T_3 20 µg 12-hourly i.v.
- Day 7–14: T_3 20 µg 8-hourly i.v.
- Week 3–4: T_4 50 µg once daily p.o.

5 Thyroid hormone replacement.

• Start i.v. T_3 (Table 43.4). This has a shorter half-life than T_4 which is advantageous if haemodynamic problems develop and the dose has to be reduced.

• An alternative regimen is thyroxine 400–500 µg as a bolus i.v. or via a nasogastric tube. No further replacement therapy should be given for 1 week.

6 Give hydrocortisone 100 mg 12-hourly i.v. in case there is panhypopituitarism.

44 Septic Arthritis

Consider the diagnosis in any patient with **fever and joint swelling particularly if only one large joint is involved.**

Priorities

1 Look for a primary source of infection (e.g. pneumonia, urinary tract infection, soft tissue abscess) (Table 44.1), as septic arthritis usually follows a bacteraemia.
2 Aspirate the joint.
- Send synovial fluid for:
  a cell count (EDTA tube);
  b Gram stain;
  c culture;
  d microscopy under polarized light for crystals.
- Both crystal and septic arthritis give rise to a purulent effusion, although the white cell count is usually higher in septic arthritis (50 000–200 000/mm^3).
- Blood-staining of the effusion is common in pseudogout but rare in sepsis.

■ **Table 44.1.** Urgent investigation in suspected septic arthritis

- **Joint aspiration**
- **X-ray joint** to exclude osteomyelitis and for baseline
- **Chest X-ray** to exclude pneumonia
- **Full blood count**
- **Blood culture**
- **Urine microscopy and culture**
- **Swab of urethra, cervix and ano-rectum** if gonococcal infection is possible (Appendix 44.1)

Further management

Organisms on Gram stain of synovial fluid, or high probability of septic arthritis

- Start antibiotic therapy i.v. (Table 44.2). Intra-articular administration is not needed. The antibiotic regimen may need modification in the light of blood and synovial fluid culture results: discuss this with the microbiologist.
- Obtain an orthopaedic opinion.
- Aspirate the joint daily until an effusion no longer reaccumulates.
- While the infection is resolving, the joint should be immobilized using a splint or cast.
- Physiotherapy should be started early.
- Give NSAID for pain relief.
- In patients with gonococcal arthritis, sexual partners should be traced.

■ **Table 44.2.** Initial antibiotic therapy for suspected septic arthritis

Organisms on Gram stain	Antibiotic
Gram-positive cocci	Flucloxacillin 1 g 6-hourly
Gram-negative cocci	Benzylpenicillin 3 g 6-hourly
Gram-negative rods	Gentamicin (Appendix 10.1, p. 71)
None seen	
• Gonococcal infection likely	Benzylpenicillin
• Gonococcal infection unlikely	Flucloxacillin + gentamicin

No organisms on Gram stain of synovial fluid and low probability of septic arthritis

- Consider the other causes of acute arthritis (Table 44.3). Pseudogout is the commonest cause of acute monoarthritis or oligoarthritis in the elderly.
- Hold off antibiotic therapy (pending the results of blood and synovial fluid culture for definite exclusion of infection).

■ **Table 44.3. Causes of non-traumatic acute arthritis**

Usually monoarthritis or oligoarthritis	• Acute crystal arthritis; gout and pseudogout • Non-gonococcal septic arthritis • Haemarthrosis (in haemophilia)
Usually polyarthritis	• Gonococcal arthritis • 'Reactive' arthritis following gut or genital infection • Rheumatic diseases, e.g. rheumatoid arthritis, SLE • Viral infections, e.g. rubella, hepatitis A and B, infectious mononucleosis

• Treat with NSAID (e.g. indomethacin 50–100 mg 6 to 8-hourly p.o.).

• If gout is confirmed (also check plasma urate) and fails to respond to NSAID, use colchicine. Allopurinol should not be started until the acute attack has completely resolved.

Appendix

44.1. Comparison of gonococcal and non-gonococcal septic arthritis

	Gonococcal	Non-gonococcal
At risk	• Sexually active	• Elderly • Immunocompromised • Rheumatoid arthritis • Intravenous drug abuse
Joints involved	• Often polyarticular especially knee and wrist	• Usually monoarticular especially knee
Other signs	• Tenosynovitis • Rash	• Underlying illness • Source of bacteraemia
Gram stain of synovial fluid	<25% positive	50–75% positive
Culture of synovial fluid	25% positive	85–95% positive
Blood culture	<10% positive	50% positive
Genitourinary culture*	80% positive	

* Swab of urethra, cervix and ano-rectum.

Based on
Goldenberg DL, Reed JI. Bacterial arthritis. *N Engl J Med* 1985;**312**:764–71.

45 Anaphylactic Shock

Suspect anaphylaxis if after an i.v./i.m. injection (Appendix 45.1), the patient develops:

- sudden hypotension;
- skin and mucosal urticaria, erythema and angioedema;
- abdominal cramps;
- wheeze.

Priorities

1 **If cardiac arrest appears imminent, give adrenaline 0.5–1 mg i.v.** (5–10 ml of one in 10 000 solution, 0.5–1 ml of one in 1000 solution). If there is no i.v. access, give it i.m. or s.c.

2 **Give oxgyen. If there is respiratory distress, call an anaesthetist:** this may be due to **upper airways obstruction** from oedema of the larynx or epiglottis, and require **endotracheal intubation.**

3 **Bronchospasm** should be treated with **nebulized salbutamol** supplemented by **aminophylline** if required (p. 126).

4 **Give chlorpheniramine 10 mg i.v. over 1 minute, repeated 8-hourly, and hydrocortisone 300 mg i.v.**

5 **If systolic BP is <90 mmHg, give an i.v. infusion of colloid** 500 ml over 15–30 minutes.

6 **If the patient remains hypotensive:**
- continue i.v. colloid infusion — put in a CVP line to guide the rate of infusion;
- give further doses of adrenaline 0.5–1 mg i.v. every 15 minutes or start an infusion (Table 57.3, p. 293).

Further management

1 **Minor anaphylactic reaction:** give chlorpheniramine 10 mg i.v. (repeated only if symptoms recur) and hydrocortisone 300 mg.

2 Inform the patient of the drug responsible for the reaction (in the case of severe reactions, they should preferably wear a bracelet engraved with this information). Report the reaction to the Committee on Safety of Medicines.

Appendix

45.1. Causes of anaphylactic reaction

- Antibiotics, most commonly beta-lactam class
- Radiographic contrast media
- Parenteral iron
- Streptokinase
- Neuromuscular blocking agents
- Thiopentone
- Snake and insect bites
- Blood products
- Allergen extracts
- Vaccines

46 Sickle Cell Disease

1 Suspect a vaso-occlusive crisis in any black, Arabic, Indian or Mediterranean patient with **acute pain in the spine, abdomen, chest or joints.**

2 **Make a working diagnosis from:**
- the sickle solubility test and blood film;
- the presence of likely precipitants — infection, dehydration, deoxygenation, vascular stasis and acidosis;
- the exclusion of other causes where possible.

Priorities

1 **Relieve pain with pethidine 100–200 mg i.m. 2-hourly as required;** surprisingly large doses are often needed.

2 **Look for evidence of infection (Table 46.1).** Adults with sickle cell disease are effectively splenectomized and thus at particular risk of infection with capsulate bacteria: pneumococcus, meningococcus and *Haemophilus influenzae* type B.

Antibiotic therapy should be started after taking blood for culture if there is:
- clinical evidence of septicaemia (Chapter 10);

■ **Table 46.1.** Urgent investigation of suspected vaso-occlusive crisis of sickle cell disease

---
- **'Steady-state' haemoglobin and haemoglobin electrophoresis** from clinic card if diagnosis established
- **Full blood count, reticulocyte count and film**
- **Sickle solubility test** (Hb electrophoresis as soon as practicable)
- **Blood culture**
- **Urine microscopy and culture**
- **Chest X-ray**
- **Arterial blood gases** (if chest X-ray shadowing, respiratory symptoms or septicaemia)

- an obvious focus of infection;
- white cell count >15–20 × 10^9/l.

In the absence of a focus of infection, give amoxycillin 500 mg 8-hourly i.v.

3 Give oxygen if Pa_{O_2} is <10 kPa (75 mmHg).

4 Is there lung involvement? (Pleuritic chest pain with X-ray shadowing.) This carries a relatively high mortality.

NB It is impossible to distinguish vaso-occlusive infarction from pneumonia with certainty and you should assume that both coexist.

- Reduce the percentage of sickle cells to < 50% by either 'top-up' or exchange transfusion.
- Many patients have unusual antibodies and there may be cross-matched blood stored at their local transfusion centre.
- Start antibiotic therapy (Table 23.2, p. 138).
- Recheck arterial gases after 4 hours or if deterioration occurs.

Further management

1 Ensure a fluid intake of 3–4 litres daily: in most cases, start with an i.v. infusion.

2 Check haemoglobin daily: discuss management with a haematologist if the haemoglobin is falling or reticulocytes are absent (which may indicate an aplastic or sequestration crisis).

3 Transfusion is avoided where possible.

- It should be given for cerebral or lung involvement.
- It should be considered in other vaso-occlusive crises if the haemoglobin falls more than 2 g/dl below the 'steady state' level and the patient's condition is not improving.

4 Keep the patient warm. Cold-induced vasoconstriction may cause infarction due to deposition of sickled cells in the microcirculation.

Problems

Vaso-occlusive crisis or acute abdomen?

- There is no clear distinction and the patient should be assessed jointly with the surgical team.

• It is usually reasonable to delay surgery longer than usual and to proceed if deterioration occurs despite treatment directed at vaso-occlusive crisis.

Sickle crises causing increased anaemia
These are much less common than vaso-occlusive crises.
• Sequestration crisis (in the sinuses of the enlarged spleen in children).
• Aplastic crisis (reduced marrow erythropoiesis, e.g. after parvovirus infection).
• Haemolytic crisis (following infections).
   The clue is the rapid fall in haemoglobin. These crises must be recognized early because transfusion can be life-saving.

Appendix

46.1. Sickle cell disease

Blood film in sickle cell disease (homozygous SS)
Normochromic normocytic anaemia (which ranges from 5 to 12 g/dl); raised reticulocyte count; in adults, Howell–Jolly bodies (reflecting hyposplenism), usually sickle cells. Target cells if numerous indicate HbSC.

Sickle solubility test
Indicates the presence of HbS, therefore positive in both homozygotes (SS) and heterozygotes (AS — sickle cell trait) and also double heterozygotes (S beta Thal, SC); haemoglobin electrophoresis is needed to distinguish between these.

47 Fever on Return from Abroad

- **Exclude malaria or typhoid in any febrile illness within 2 months of return from an endemic area** (Table 47.1) (most of Africa, Asia, Central and South America: for further information, contact a specialist centre (Appendix 47.1))
- **Chemoprophylaxis against malaria does not ensure full protection and may prolong the incubation period.**

■ Table 47.1. Infectious diseases which may be acquired abroad

Infection	Incubation periods	
	Usual	Range
Malaria		
Plasmodium falciparum	12 days	8–25 days
Plasmodium vivax	15 days	8–27 days
Plasmodium malariae	28 days	15–30 days
Plasmodium ovale	15 days	9–17 days
Typhoid	10–14 days	7–21 days
Leptospirosis	10 days	7–13 days
Legionella pneumophila	10 days	2–26 days
Hepatitis A	4 weeks	2–6 weeks
Hepatitis B	12 weeks	6 weeks–6 months

Priorities

1 Admit to a single room and nurse with standard isolation technique until the diagnosis is established.
2 In patients who have travelled to rural west Africa within the previous 3 weeks, a viral haemorrhagic fever must be considered, particularly if pharyngitis is a prominent symptom: an infectious

diseases physician should be contacted urgently to advise on management (before blood samples are taken).

3 Investigations needed urgently are given in Table 47.2.

■ **Table 47.2. Urgent investigation of fever on return from abroad**

• **Full blood count** (neutropenia is seen in both malaria and typhoid; a low platelet count is common in falciparum malaria)

• **Blood film for malarial parasites** if travel to or through an endemic area; the intensity of the parasitaemia is variable and if the diagnosis is suspected but the film is negative, repeat blood films every 8 hours for 2–3 days

• **Urea and electrolytes**

• **Blood glucose** by stick test

• **Blood culture**

• **Throat swab**

• **Urine:** stick test for bilirubin and urobilinogen, microscopy and culture

• **Stool:** microscopy and culture

• **Chest X-ray**

• **Lumbar puncture** if neck stiffness present

• **Liver function tests** (for later testing)

• **Serology** as appropriate (e.g. viral hepatitis, *Legionella* pneumonia, typhoid, amoebic liver abscess, leptospirosis)

Further management

This depends upon associated features.

1 Septic shock:

• antimicrobial therapy must cover **falciparum malaria** (Appendix 47.2) and **typhoid** (Table 47.3) in patients who have travelled to endemic regions;

• patients with **falciparum malaria** must also receive antibiotics to cover **Gram negative infection** (as mixed infections may occur);

• see Chapter 10 for general management.

■ **Table 47.3.** Antibiotic therapy of typhoid

Give for 14 days in all cases

Severely ill	• **Chloramphenicol** 500 mg 4-hourly i.v. reducing to 500 mg 6-hourly when afebrile; *or* • **Ciprofloxacin** 200 mg 12-hourly i.v.
Others	• **Trimethoprim** 200 mg 12-hourly p.o.; *or* • **Amoxycillin** 1 g 8-hourly p.o.

2 Chest X-ray shadowing. Consider **tuberculosis** and *Legionella* infection (p. 142) in addition to the common causes of pneumonia.

3 Meningism.

• Perform a lumber puncture. If the CSF shows no organisms but a high lymphocyte count (Table 28.6, p. 162), consider **tuberculosis, leptospirosis, brucellosis.**

• If there are other features suggesting leptospirosis (haemorrhagic rash, conjunctivitis, renal failure, jaundice) give benzylpenicillin 600 mg 4-hourly i.v. for 7 days. Alternative antibiotics are erythromycin or tetracycline.

4 Jaundice: Always consider falciparum malaria. Other causes are hepatitis A and B (but with these infections patients are afebrile when jaundice appears), leptospirosis, cytomegalovirus and Epstein–Barr virus.

Appendices

47.1. UK reference centres for advice on malaria prophylaxis and treatment

London

Malaria Clinic, Hospital for Tropical Diseases, 4 St Pancras' Way, London NW1 OPE. Telephone: 071 387 4411.

Birmingham

Department of Communicable and Tropical Diseases, East
  Birmingham Hospital, Bordesley Green East, Birmingham B9 5ST.
  Telephone: 021 766 6611.

Liverpool

School of Tropical Medicine, Pembroke Place, Liverpool L3 5QA.
  Telephone: 051 708 9393.

47.2. Treatment of malaria

Chemotherapy

Severe infection with Plasmodium falciparum (or unknown species)

Treat with quinine dihydrochloride.

• **Loading dose:** 20 mg of the salt/kg given over 4 hours by i.v.
infusion (omit if quinine given within the previous 12 hours).

• **Maintenance dose:** 10 mg/kg given over 4 hours by i.v. infusion
8 hourly for 5–7 days.

• **Quinidine** can be used if quinine is unavailable: give 15 mg/kg as
loading dose, 7.5 mg/kg as maintenance dose.

Mild infection

• *P. falciparum* (chloroquine resistance unlikely): **chloroquine** 600
mg of the base p.o., followed by a single dose of 300 mg after 6–8
hours, followed by 300 mg daily for 3 days.

• *P. falciparum* (chloroquine resistance likely): **quinine** 600 mg of the
salt p.o. 8-hourly for 3 days, then a single dose of three tablets of
Fansidar (each tablet contains pyrimethamine 25 mg and sulfadoxine
500 mg).

• *P. vivax* and *P. ovale:* **chloroquine** as for *P. falciparum* infection,
then **primaquine** 7.5 mg 12-hourly p.o. for 14 days to eradicate the
exo-erythrocytic cycle.

  Check for glucose-6-phosphate dehydrogenase deficiency first:
if present, give 30 mg once a week for 8 weeks.

* Plasmodium malariae: **chloroquine** as for *P. falciparum* infection.

References
Phillips RE, Gilles HM. Malaria. *Medicine International* 1988;**54**:2220–5.
Cook GC. Prevention and treatment of malaria. *Lancet* 1988;**1**:32–7.

Points in the management of severe falciparum malaria
1 Obtain expert advice (Appendix 47.1).
2 Hypotension:
  * give colloid (or blood if packed cell volume (PCV) <20%/ haemoglobin <7 g/dl) to maintain CVP at + 5 cmH$_2$O (avoid higher levels because of the risk of pulmonary oedema);
  * start inotrope/vasopressor agents if needed (Table 3.5, p. 31);
  * start antibiotic therapy for Gram-negative sepsis after taking blood cultures (Table 10.2, p. 67).

3 Hypoglycaemia is a common complication: blood glucose should be checked routinely every 4 hours by stick test or if conscious level deteriorates, or fits occur.

4 Fits:
  * recheck blood glucose;
  * exclude coexistent bacterial meningitis by lumbar puncture.

5 Pulmonary oedema: may occur from excessive i.v. fluid or ARDS (Chapter 16).

47.3. Notifiable infectious diseases in England and Wales (October 1988)
Acute encephalitis
Acute poliomyelitis
Anthrax
Cholera
Diphtheria
Dysentery (amoebic and bacterial)
Food poisoning
Leprosy
Leptospirosis

Malaria

Measles

Meningitis

Meningococcal septicaemia (without meningitis)

Mumps

Ophthalmia neonatorum

Paratyphoid fever

Plague

Rabies

Relapsing fever

Rubella

Scarlet fever

Smallpox

Tetanus

Tuberculosis

Typhoid

Typhus

Viral haemorrhagic fevers

Viral hepatitis

Whooping cough

Yellow fever

Inform the medical officer for environmental health.

Section 3
Procedures

48   Central Vein Cannulation

Indications

1 Measurement of CVP (Fig. 48.1; Table 48.1):
- transfusion of large volumes of fluid required;
- fluid challenge in patients with oliguria or hypotension;
- to exclude hypovolaemia when the clinical evidence is equivocal.

2 Insertion of a pulmonary artery (Swan–Ganz) catheter or temporary pacing wire.

3 Administration of some drugs (e.g. dopamine) and i.v. feeding solutions.

4 No suitable peripheral veins for i.v. infusion.

■ **Table 48.1. Interpreting the central venous pressure**

The CVP reflects the interaction between blood volume, systemic venous tone, right ventricular function and intrathoracic/pericardial pressure

Causes of a high CVP	• Fluid overload, e.g. renal failure, overtransfusion
	• Right ventricular failure, e.g. right ventricular infarction, massive pulmonary embolism
	• Tension pneumothorax
	• Cardiac tamponade
Causes of a low CVP	• Hypovolaemia
	• Vasodilatation, e.g. sepsis, poisoning

Choice of vein

The right internal jugular and the right subclavian are the two most commonly used veins. The internal jugular vein is the preferred approach in patients with:

- **bleeding tendency** — platelet count $<100 \times 10^{12}/l$ or prothrombin time $>1.5 \times$ control (because of the risk of

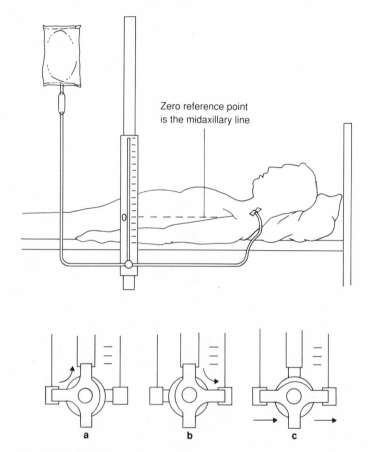

Fig. 48.1. Method of measuring central venous pressure: CVP line with position of three-way tap for; **a** priming the manometer; **b** reading the CVP; **c** fluid infusion. Redrawn from Davidson TI. *Fluid balance*. Oxford: Blackwell Scientific Publications 1987; 38.

uncontrollable bleeding from inadvertent arterial puncture);
• **respiratory disease** (because of the risk of pneumothorax precipitating respiratory failure).

Technique

Positioning the patient
• Remove the pillow and position the patient with head-down tilt of the bed if possible (to fill out the vein and reduce the risk of air embolism in hypovolaemic patients).
• Turn the patient's head away from the side you are going to puncture.

Venepuncture

Internal jugular vein puncture — high approach avoiding the risk of pneumothorax (Fig. 48.2)
1 Locate the right carotid artery. The internal jugular vein is superficial, lateral and parallel to the artery.
2 Prepare and drape the skin.
3 Infiltrate the skin and subcutaneous tissues over the anterior edge of the sternocleidomastoid muscle at the level of the thyroid cartilage with 5 ml of lignocaine 1%.
4 Nick the skin over the vein with a small scalpel blade.
5 Identify the line of the carotid artery with your left hand. Insert the needle just lateral to this at an angle of 45° to the skin, aiming for the right nipple in men, or the right anterior superior iliac spine in women. Advance slowly whilst aspirating for blood. The vein lies superficially so do not advance more than a few centimetres.
6 If you do not hit the vein, slowly withdraw the needle to just under the skin, again aspirating for blood (as you may have inadvertently transfixed the vein). Advance again, aiming slightly more medially.

Right subclavian vein puncture — infraclavicular approach
1 Define the suprasternal notch, the sternoclavicular joint and the acromioclavicular joint.
2 Prepare and drape the skin.
3 Infiltrate the skin and subcutaneous tissues with 5–10 ml of lignocaine 1%, starting from a point one finger's breadth below the

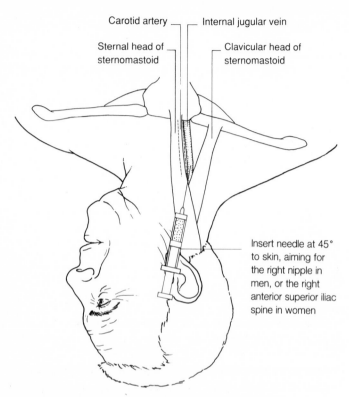

Carotid artery — Internal jugular vein

Sternal head of sternomastoid

Clavicular head of sternomastoid

Insert needle at 45° to skin, aiming for the right nipple in men, or the right anterior superior iliac spine in women

Fig. 48.2. Right internal jugular vein puncture — high approach.

junction of the medial one-third and lateral two-thirds of the clavicle. Infiltrate up to and just below the clavicle.

4 Nick the skin with a small scalpel blade.

5 Advance the needle along the same track until it touches the clavicle. Move the tip stepwise down the clavicle until it is lying just below it. Then swing the needle round so that it is now pointing at the suprasternal notch (Fig. 48.3). Slowly advance the needle whilst aspirating for blood. Make a conscious effort to keep the track of the needle parallel to the bed (to avoid puncturing the subclavian artery or pleura).

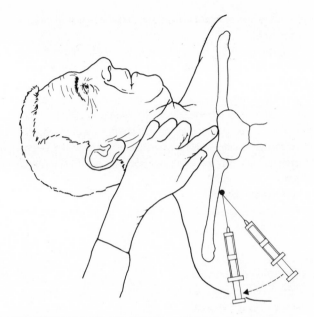

Fig. 48.3. Right subclavian vein puncture — infraclavicular approach.

6 If the vein is not found, withdraw slowly whilst aspirating. Flush the needle to make sure it is not blocked. Try again, aiming slightly more cranially.

Placement of the cannula using a guidewire-through-needle technique (Seldinger technique)

1 Once you have punctured the vein, check that you can aspirate blood easily.

2 Remove the syringe, capping the needle with your thumb to prevent entry of air.

3 Pass the flexible end of the guidewire down the needle. If there is any resistance to the passage of the wire, withdraw it and check you are still in the vein by aspirating blood. Change the angle of the needle or rotate the bevel. If there is still resistance, but you are confident the needle is in the vein, try a new wire with a flexible J-shaped end.

4 When half the length of the wire is in the vein, remove the needle. Place the cannula and dilator over the wire and advance it into position.

5 A cannula inserted via the subclavian vein sometimes passes into the internal jugular vein rather than the superior vena cava (SVC). This can be checked for by aspirating 5 ml of blood and then injecting it swiftly whilst a colleague listens with the diaphragm of a stethoscope over the ipsilateral internal jugular vein. A bruit signifies misplacement.

6 Attach the infusion set.

7 Fix the cannula to the skin with a suture or a transparent adhesive adhesive dressing.

Chest X-ray
This should be taken to confirm:
- correct positioning of the cannula;
- absence of pneumothorax.

Troubleshooting

1 Arterial puncture. If you inadvertently puncture the carotid artery, apply pressure for 5 minutes and then reattempt venepuncture.

2 Pneumothorax. If the patient is being mechanically ventilated, this may become a tension pneumothorax and you must insert a chest drain even if it is small (Chapter 53).

3 Misplacement of a cannula inserted via the subclavian vein in the internal jugular vein. The cannula must be repositioned. Infusion of hypertonic solutions into the internal jugular vein may cause venous thrombosis.

4 Frequent ventricular extrasystoles may indicate that the tip of the cannula is lying against the tricuspid valve. Withdraw it a few centimetres.

5 Infection of the cannula. *Staphylococcus aureus* and *Staph. epidermidis* are the commonest pathogens, but infection with Gram-negative rods and fungi may occur in immunocompromised patients.

Obviously infected line
(Tenderness, erythema and purulent discharge at the skin exit site.)
- The cannula must be removed and the tip sent for culture.
- If the patient is septicaemic, take blood cultures and start antibiotic therapy with flucloxacillin.

Possibly infected line
(Fever or other systemic signs of sepsis, but no signs at the skin exit site.)
- Take blood cultures from both a peripheral vein and via the cannula.
- The decision to remove the cannula before culture results are back depends on the likelihood of it being infected: how long has the cannula been in and is there another source of infection?
- If both blood cultures grow the same organism, the cannula must be removed and antibiotic therapy given.

49 Pulmonary Artery Catheterization

Indications

1 **Pulmonary oedema:**
  • to titrate further therapy after initial management;
  • to differentiate ARDS from cardiogenic pulmonary oedema.

2 **Hypotension** with a CVP of 10 cmH$_2$O or more (i.e. not due to hypovolaemia).

3 **Suspected VSD** after myocardial infarction.

Technique

Make sure that the patient is adequately resuscitated before starting.

Preparation

1 Set up the equipment (Fig. 49.1).

2 The pressure monitor must be zeroed and calibrated. The reference point for zero is usually taken at the fourth intercostal space in the mid-axillary line, with the patient supine.

3 Connect the patient to the ECG monitor and put in a peripheral venous cannula.

4 Prepare skin and apply drapes as for temporary cardiac pacing.

5 Check that the catheter can pass down the cannula, and check the ballon by inflating it with air (usually 1.5 ml). Leave the syringe attached.

6 Attach the manometer line to the channel of the distal (pulmonary artery) lumen and flush the dead space. If the catheter also has a proximal (right atrial) lumen, flush this channel with heparinized saline and leave the syringe attached.

Cannulate a central vein

See Chapter 48.

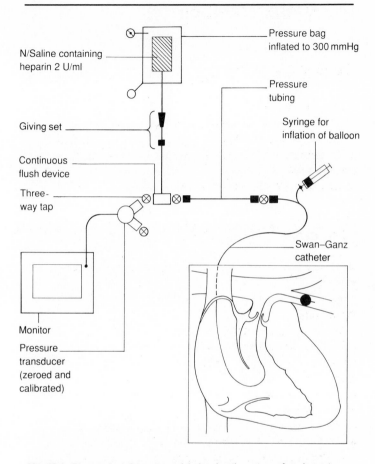

N/Saline containing heparin 2 U/ml

Giving set

Continuous flush device

Three-way tap

Monitor

Pressure transducer (zeroed and calibrated)

Pressure bag inflated to 300 mmHg

Pressure tubing

Syringe for inflation of balloon

Swan–Ganz catheter

Fig. 49.1. Diagram (not drawn to scale) showing the set-up of equipment for pulmonary artery catheterization. When the balloon is inflated, flow around the tip of the catheter ceases. The measured pressure is transmitted back from the pulmonary veins (as these are valveless) and gives an estimate of left atrial and left ventricular end-diastolic pressure.

Placement of the catheter

1 Insert the catheter for about 10 cm and inflate the balloon fully. Advance it guided by X-ray screening, or the pressure waveform (Fig. 49.2) and the distance inserted (Table 49.1). Do not advance more

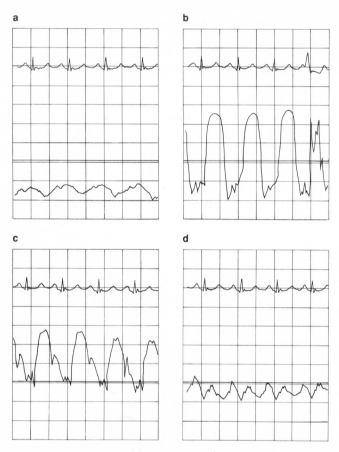

Fig. 49.2. Diagram showing the typical pressure waveforms on insertion of a Swan-Ganz catheter. **a** Right atrium; **b** right ventricle; **c** pulmonary artery; **d** wedge position. See Table 57.1 for normal values.

than 10–15 cm unless the waveform changes because of the risk of knotting.

2 Always deflate the balloon before withdrawing the catheter to prevent it tearing the tricuspid or pulmonary valves.

■ **Table 49.1.** Expected distance (cm) from point of insertion via right internal jugular vein in the adult

Right atrium	10–15
Right ventricle	25–35
Pulmonary artery	35–40
Pulmonary artery wedge	40–50

3 Ventricular extrasystoles and non-sustained ventricular tachycardia are common during manipulation of the catheter through the right heart and do not need treatment.

4 Passage across the tricuspid valve can sometimes be helped by the patient taking a deep inspiration.

5 When the waveform changes from pulmonary artery to wedge, deflate the balloon. The trace should promptly change back to pulmonary artery.

Measuring the wedge pressure

1 Move the catheter to find a position where the wedge pressure is reliably obtained with the balloon fully or near-fully inflated. The volume needed should be noted. If this is less than 1.3 ml, the catheter tip is too peripheral: withdraw it a little.

2 Criteria of a satisfactory wedge position are given in Table 49.2.

3 The wedge pressure fluctuates with respiration and should be measured at end-expiration when pleural pressure is around zero.

■ **Table 49.2.** Criteria of a satisfactory wedge position

1 The **mean wedge pressure**
- Is lower than or equal to the **PA diastolic pressure**
- Is lower than the **mean PA pressure**

2 The waveform is characteristic of the left atrial waveform (Fig. 49.2)

3 The wedge waveform promptly
- Disappears on deflation of the balloon
- Reappears on reinflation

4 The balloon has to be inflated to its maximum volume (or close to this) to obtain the wedge pressure

Large swings in pleural pressure occur in patients with severe airways obstruction which can make interpretation of the wedge pressure trace difficult or impossible.

4 Avoid keeping the balloon inflated in the wedge position for more than 15 seconds (to minimize the risk of causing pulmonary artery rupture).

Aftercare

• Obtain a chest X-ray to check the position of the catheter.

• Hourly fast flushes to prevent thrombus formation on the tip of the catheter.

• Remove the catheter within 72 hours to reduce the risk of infection. If needed, a new catheter can be put in, preferably at a different site.

• If infection related to the catheter is suspected; see p. 250.

Troubleshooting

The catheter will not enter the pulmonary artery

This can be a problem in patients with low cardiac output, tricuspid regurgitation or a dilated right heart. If you cannot advance the catheter despite screening, use a stylet to stiffen it. Disconnect the catheter from the manometer line and pass the stylet down the distal channel.

Damping of the pressure trace

This may be due to:

• kinking of the catheter or manometer line;

• air bubbles in the system;

• thrombus partially occluding the lumen of the catheter; several fast flushes should clear this.

Problems with measuring the wedge pressure

No change in waveform when you inflate the balloon
- If there is no resistance to inflation, suspect balloon rupture.
- If there is normal resistance, the catheter has slipped back. If the catheter outside the skin has not been kept sterile with a sheath, a new catheter should be inserted.

Ramp increase in pressure when you inflate the balloon
- This indicates that the balloon has inflated eccentrically with occlusion of the tip ('over-wedging'). The ramp increase in pressure reflects the continuous flush infusion.
- Deflate the balloon and reinflate it until a satisfactory trace is obtained.

Tachypnoeic patient
- End-expiration is brief in a patient with rapid respiration and as the monitor averages values obtained over several seconds, the digital display of the wedge pressure is misleading.
- The solution is to print out the pressure trace, marking end-expiration (most chart recorders will have an event marker) and measure the pressure from this.

Spontaneous wedging
- This indicates that the catheter is positioned too peripherally. Some migration peripherally commonly occurs after insertion as the catheter warms and becomes more flexible.
- Pull the catheter back until you find a position at which the balloon has to be fully or near-fully inflated to give a wedge pressure.

Special considerations

Suspected ventricular septal defect
Prepare four heparinized 2 ml syringes ready for sampling, with

blind hubs and ice if the samples will have to be transported to the laboratory.
• Take samples in the right atrium, right ventricle and pulmonary artery and from a systemic artery.
• A step-up in oxygen saturation of 10% or more between right atrium and ventricle indicates a left to right shunt at ventricular level.
• The formula for calculating the size of the shunt is given on p. 292.

Left bundle branch block
• Complete heart block is a rare and usually transient complication because the catheter may induce additional right bundle block as it passes through the right heart.
• Put in the catheter under screening, with a temporary pacing wire to hand in case this is needed.

50 Temporary Cardiac Pacing

Indications

These are given in Table 50.1.

■ **Table 50.1. Indications for temporary pacing**

After cardiac arrest with asystole or bradycardia (p. 5)	
After myocardial infarction	• **Second degree and complete heart block:** in all anterior infarcts, but only in inferior infarcts if associated with haemodynamic compromise and unresponsive to atropine • **Sinus or junctional bradycardia** associated with haemodynamic compromise and unresponsive to atropine • **Prophylactic pacing in anterior infarcts** (Table 12.7, p. 97)
Unrelated to myocardial infarction	• **Sinus or junctional bradycardia** associated with haemodynamic compromise and unresponsive to atropine • **Second degree AV block or sinus arrest** if associated with syncope or near-syncope • **Complete heart block** even without symptoms
Ventricular tachycardia	• **Prophylactic pacing** (p. 18)
Pre-operative	• **Sinus node disease/second degree Wenckebach AV block/bundle branch block (including bifascicular block)** only if associated with syncope • **Second degree Mobitz II AV block** • **Complete heart block**

Technique

Preparation

1 Check the screening equipment and make sure a defibrillator and other resuscitation equipment is to hand.

2 Connect an ECG monitor and put in a peripheral venous cannula. Make sure the ECG leads are off the chest (so they are not confused with the pacing wire when screening).

3 Put on mask, gown and gloves. Prepare the skin and apply drapes to a wide area. If it is likely that permanent pacing will be needed, use the right side in right-handed patients.

4 Check that the wire will pass down the cannula. Temporary pacing wires are usually 5 or 6 French and require a cannula one size larger.

Cannulate a central vein

• See Chapter 48.

• The wire is usually easier to manipulate via the right internal jugular vein, but may be fixed more comfortably via the right subclavian vein.

Placement of the wire

1 Advance the wire into the right atrium and direct it towards the apex of the right ventricle (just medial to the lateral border of the cardiac silhouette): it may cross the tricuspid valve easily.

2 If not, form a loop of wire in the right atrium. With slight rotation and advancement of the wire, the loop should prolapse across the tricuspid valve.

3 Manipulate the wire so that the tip curves downwards at the apex of the right ventricle and lies in a gentle S-shape within the right atrium and ventricle (Fig. 50.1). Displacement of the wire may occur if there is too much or not enough slack.

4 Attach the wire to the connecting lead and pacing box.

Check the threshold

1 Set the box to 'demand' mode with a pacing rate faster than the intrinsic heart rate. Set the output at 3 V. This should result in paced rhythm.

2 If it does not, you need to find a better position. Before moving from a position that may have taken a long while to achieve, make sure all connections are securely done up.

a

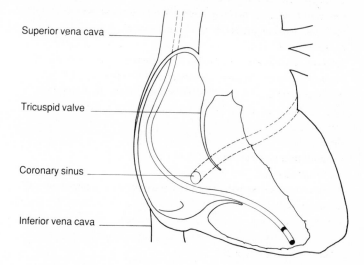

Superior vena cava

Tricuspid valve

Coronary sinus

Inferior vena cava

b

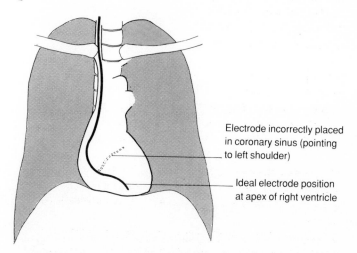

Electrode incorrectly placed in coronary sinus (pointing to left shoulder)

Ideal electrode position at apex of right ventricle

Fig. 50.1. Electrode position for temporary pacing. **a** Anatomy; **b** Screening.

3 Progressively reduce the output until there is failure to capture: the heart rate drops abruptly and pacing spikes are seen but not followed by paced beats (Fig. 50.2). A threshold of <1 V is acceptable.

4 Check the stability of the wire. Set the box at a rate faster than the intrinsic heart rate, with an output of 1 V. Ask the patient to cough forcefully, sniff, and breathe deeply. Watch the monitor for loss of capture.

Final points

1 Set the output at more than three times the threshold or 3 V whichever is higher. Set the mode to 'demand'. If in sinus rhythm, set a back-up rate of 50/min. If there is heart block or bradycardia, set at 70–80/min.

2 Suture the wire to the skin close to the point of insertion and cover it with a dressing. The rest of the wire should be looped and fixed to the skin with adhesive tape.

3 Obtain a chest X-ray to confirm a satisfactory position of the wire and exclude a pneumothorax.

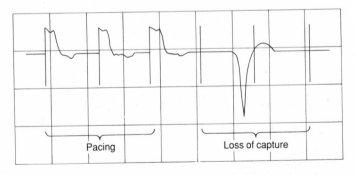

Pacing

Loss of capture

Fig. 50.2. Determination of pacing threshold. The voltage is progessively reduced until there is loss of capture. The vertical lines are pacing artefacts. Reproduced from Rothman M T. *Hospital Update* 1981; **June**:645–52.

Aftercare

• Check the pacing threshold daily. The threshold usually rises to 2–3 times its initial value over the first few days after insertion.

• If infection related to the wire is suspected; see p. 251.

Troubleshooting

Tachyarrhythmias

• Ventricular extrasystoles and non-sustained ventricular tachycardia are common as the wire crosses the tricuspid valve and do not require treatment.

• If non-sustained VT recurs, check that the position of the wire is still satisfactory and that excess slack has not formed in the area of the tricuspid valve.

High threshold (Table 50.2)

• Check that the wire tip is pointing downwards at the apex of the right ventricle.

• A position in an epicardial vein looks similar to the correct one, but the wire may be seen more easily and tends to curve round at the apex.

• A wire misplaced in the coronary sinus points towards the left shoulder (Fig. 50.1) and tends to move as a whole and away from the cardiac apex during systole (because it lies in the atrioventricular groove).

■ **Table 50.2. Causes of a high threshold at or after insertion**

The threshold normally increases by a factor of about three after insertion because of endocardial oedema

• Contacts not secure
• Wire malpositioned or displaced
• Myocardial fibrosis (from previous infarction or cardiomyopathy)
• Drugs (antiarrhythmics)
• Perforation

• If a threshold <1 V cannot be found after trying alternative sites, accept a high threshold in a stable position.

Failure to sense/capture
See Table 50.3.

■ **Table 50.3.** Causes of failure to sense/capture

• Wire malpositioned or displaced
• Lead disconnected
• Faulty settings, e.g. output set below the threshold
• Faulty box
• Perforation

Perforation
1 Suspect with:
  • sudden hypotension;
  • loss of capture/sensing;
  • chest pain;
  • diaphragmatic pacing at low output.
2 Are there signs of cardiac tamponade (Chapter18)? If so arrange urgent echocardiography and pericardial drainage.
3 Reposition or replace the wire.

Pericardial rub
This is common in the absence of perforation. Check the threshold and for signs of tamponade.

Pacing of the diaphragm
This may occur with normal lead position at high output (10 V), but otherwise suggests cardiac perforation (see above).

51 Pericardial Aspiration

Indications

• **Cardiac tamponade (Chapter 18).** Echocardiography must be done first to confirm the presence of a pericardial effusion unless there is cardiac arrest from presumed tamponade.

• **Pericardial effusion due to suspected bacterial pericarditis.** Aspiration should only be attempted if the effusion is large (echo separation > 2 cm).

Special equipment needed

1 **Long needle** (15 cm, 18 gauge) **or long 'cannula over needle' i.v. cannula** (e.g. Wallace).
2 **Guidewire** (80 cm or more, 0.035'' diameter, with J end)
3 **Dilator** (5–7 French).
4 **Pigtail catheter** (60 cm long, 5–7 French diameter, multiple sideholes).
5 **Drainage bag and connector.**

Technique

Preparation

1 Lie the patient semirecumbent in the screening room and propped up so the effusion pools anteriorly and inferiorly. Connect an ECG monitor. Ensure you have venous access and that resuscitation equipment including a defibrillator is to hand.
2 Put on gown, mask and gloves. Prepare the skin from mid-chest to mid-abdomen and put on drapes.
3 Anaesthetize the skin from a point in the midline (within 5 cm below the xiphisternum) along a track running just below the costal margin towards the right shoulder (Fig. 51.1).
4 Make a small skin incision.

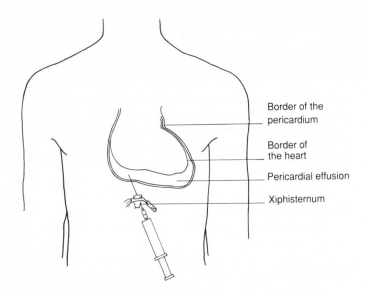

Border of the
pericardium

Border of
the heart

Pericardial effusion

Xiphisternum

Fig. 51.1. Pericardial aspiration.

Insertion of the catheter

1 Attach the long needle or 'cannula over needle' to a 10 ml
syringe containing lignocaine and advance it slowly along the
anaesthetized track aiming for the right shoulder. Angle it at about
30° so that it passes just under the costal margin. Every centimetre
or so, inject some lignocaine and aspirate.

2 As soon as fluid is aspirated, remove the syringe and introduce
about 20 cm of the guide wire (if you are using a 'cannula over
needle', the needle will have to be withdrawn first).

3 Check the position of the guide-wire by screening. It should loop
freely within the cardiac shadow.

4 Dilate the track.

5 Introduce the pigtail catheter over the guide-wire. Keep the
guide-wire taut and whilst screening, push the catheter through the
pericardium and about 20 cm into the pericardial cavity.

6 Take specimens for microscopy, culture and cytology. Then aspirate to dryness.

7 Insert a skin suture and loop it over the catheter several times tying it each time. Attach the connector and drainage bag via a three-way tap. Bind down securely with adhesive tape.

Troubleshooting

The pigtail catheter will not pass over the guidewire into the pericardial space

- Check that the guide-wire is correctly positioned within the cardiac shadow.
- Check that the guide-wire is held taut and not looped.
- Use a larger dilator.

You aspirate heavily blood-stained fluid

1 To check that you have not penetrated the heart (usually the right ventricle — rarely due to laceration of coronary artery):

- see if the fluid clots. Blood will, but even heavily blood-stained effusion will not;
- the position of the guide wire is helpful. If when advanced, it coils inside the cardiac shadow it is likely to be within the pericardium. If it is intracardiac, it will follow the course of obvious structures such as the pulmonary artery.

2 If you are still in doubt, consider the following options:

- inject contrast; if cardiac penetration has occurred, contrast will rapidly disperse, but will otherwise remain within the cardiac shadow;
- compare the haematocrit of the fluid with that of a venous sample (both sent in EDTA tubes);
- connect to a pressure monitor; RV penetration is shown by a characteristic waveform (Fig. 49.2, p. 254).

52 Direct Current Countershock

Ventricular and supraventricular tachyarrhythmias (Chapter 2).

Technique

Ventricular fibrillation or pulseless ventricular tachycardia

Give immediate unsynchronized countershock, starting at 200 J (Table 1.2, p. 4)

Other tachyarrhythmias

Preparation

1 Contact an anaesthetist. A short general anaesthetic is much better than sedation with a benzodiazepine.

2 If there is time, record a 12-lead ECG.

3 Change the leads from the bedside to the defibrillator monitor. Adjust the leads until the R waves are significantly higher than the T waves and check that the synchronizing marker falls consistently on the QRS complex and not the T wave.

4 Is there clinical evidence of digoxin toxicity (e.g. atrial tachycardia with block, nausea)? If so, initial treatment of supraventricular arrhythmias is withdrawal of digoxin and correction of hypokalaemia (Appendix 2.2, p. 26).

5 Put in a venous cannula. Other resuscitation equipment should be to hand.

6 If this is an elective procedure for atrial fibrillation/flutter, check that the blood potassium is >3.5 mmol/l, the patient has fasted for 4 hours and has been anticoagulated for 2–3 weeks.

■ Table 52.1. Initial charge for direct current countershock

	Initial charge (J)	Mode*
Ventricular fibrillation/ pulseless ventricular tachycardia	200	Unsynchronized
Ventricular tachycardia	200	Synchronized
Atrial fibrillation	50	Synchronized
Other supraventricular arrhythmias	25	Synchronized
Arrhythmias from digoxin toxicity	10–20	Synchronized

* In synchronized mode, the machine will not discharge until it senses an R wave, to ensure that the shock is delivered during and not after the QRS complex.

Cardioversion

1 One paddle is placed on a pad of jelly over the sternum and the other over the apex.

2 If there is digoxin toxicity, use a low initial charge and consider giving lignocaine 100 mg before countershock. Initial charges are given in Table 52.1.

3 If this fails, double the power level (unless the procedure is elective and has been followed by prolonged sinus pause or ventricular arrhythmia).

Aftercare

- 12-lead ECG.
- Consider prophylactic anti-arrhythmic therapy (Chapter 2).
- Anticoagulation. This should be continued in patients with atrial fibrillation/flutter if there is a structural cardiac abnormality because the risk of reversion is high.

53 Insertion of a Chest Drain

Technique

Preparation

1 Check the position of the pneumothorax by examination and on the chest X-ray (ensure you have not misdiagnosed an emphysematous bulla; p. 144).

2 Assemble the underwater seal (Fig. 53.1) and check that the connections fit.

3 Choose the largest tube (usually 28 Ch.) that is likely to fit the intercostal space.

4 Position the patient lying flat or semirecumbent with the hand resting behind the neck.

5 The best approach is usually the third or fourth space in the mid-axillary line. This is less alarming for the patient and there is less muscle to be crossed than with the second space in the midclavicular line. The apical approach is dangerous and should not be used.

6 Prepare and drape the skin.

Insertion of the tube

1 Draw up 20 ml of lignocaine 1%. Infiltrate down to the pleura with about 10 ml. Advance the needle until air is aspirated then withdraw slightly and infiltrate about 5 ml around the pleura.

2 Make a 1 cm incision with a scalpel in line with and just above the edge of the lower rib of the intercostal space. With a small Spencer–Wells or similar forceps, enlarge the track down to and through the pleura.

3 Insert a purse–string suture of 1/0 silk around the incision taking deep bites.

4 It should now be possible to slide the trochar and tube into the thoracic cavity with virtually no force. If you find that you have to push, withdraw the trochar and enlarge the track. As the trochar enters the pleural space, withdraw it as you advance the tube.

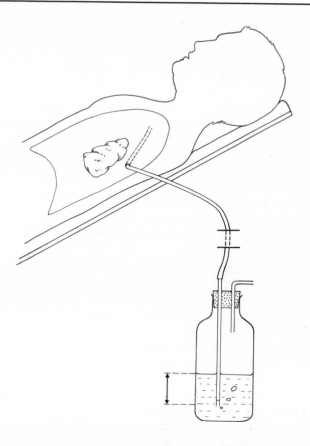

Fig. 53.1. Insertion of a chest drain: underwater seal. The end of the tube is 2-3cm below the level of the water in the bottle. If intrapleural pressure rises above 2-3 cm H_2O air will bubble out. If intrapleural pressure becomes negative, water reses up the tube only to fall again when intrapleural pressure falls towards atmospheric. The system operates as a simple one-way valve. When the pneumothorax has resolved the water level will generally be slightly negative throughout the respiratory cycle and reflect the normal fluctuation in intrapleural pressure and when the patient coughs air will no longer bubble out. Redrawn fron Brewis R A L. *Lecture notes on respiratory disease.* 3rd edn. Oxford: Blackwell Scientific Publications 1985; 290.

5 Direct the tube towards the apex of the thoracic cavity, until about 25 cm of drain are within the chest.

6 Attach the underwater seal.

7 Secure the tube with a second 1/0 silk suture wrapped and tied several times around the drain.

8 Coil the ends of the purse-string beneath a pad of gauze placed between the skin and the tube and strap in place with adhesive tape.

Aftercare

1 Obtain a chest X-ray (repeated daily) to check the position of the tube and the size of the pneumothorax.

2 Check that the fluid level swings with breathing.

3 Arrange regular chest physiotherapy.

4 Give analgesia as required (before physiotherapy).

5 Remove the tube when:

- chest X-ray shows full re-expansion of the lung *and*
- air no longer bubbles out when the patient coughs.

6 The tube should not be clamped.

Removing the tube

1 Anaesthetize the track down to the pleura.

2 Cut and remove the retaining suture.

3 Ask the patient to perform a Valsalva manoeuvre. As an assistant withdraws the tube, draw the purse-string suture tight.

4 Cover with a dressing.

Troubleshooting

Pain

Pain around the chest incision may occur. If the pain is more distant, you should check the position of the cannula tip. If it is curled against the interior of the thoracic cavity, withdraw it slightly. There should be about 25 cm of intrathoracic tube in an adult of normal size.

Fluid level does not swing with breathing

- **Tube kinked:** this usually occurs because of angulation over the ribs and may be corrected by releasing the dressing. Occasionally it is necessary to withdraw the drain slightly.
- **Tube blocked:** if the tube is too small, which is the commonest fault, it can easily become blocked by secretions. It should be replaced by a larger one.
- **Wrong position:** if the drainage holes are wholly or partially extrapleural, which can be diagnosed from the chest film, the tube needs to be removed and another replaced.

Surgical emphysema

A little localized subcutaneous air is usual, but increasing surgical emphysema indicates malposition of the tube with a drainage hole in a subcutaneous position. A new tube must be inserted.

Pneumothorax does not resolve

If the tube is well-positioned and not blocked, this indicates a persisting bronchopleural fistula. Ask for surgical advice. Some will resolve with low-pressure suction.

Needle aspiration of a small pneumothorax

1 Infiltrate with lignocaine down to and around the pleura over the pneumothorax, usually in the second intercostal space in the mid-clavicular line.

2 Use a 21 gauge (green) needle connected to a three-way tap and a 60 ml syringe.

3 With the patient semirecumbent, insert the needle into the pleural space. Withdraw air and expel it via the three-way tap.

4 Obtain a chest X-ray to confirm resolution of the pneumothorax.

54 Lumbar Puncture

Indications

- Suspected meningitis or subarachnoid haemorrhage.
- Suspected Guillain-Barré syndrome.

Contraindications

- Reduced level of consciousness.
- Focal neurological signs (long tract or posterior fossa).
- Papilloedema.
- Anticoagulation.

Special equipment

1 Spinal needle. The disposable ones are usually sharper.
Choose a 20 or 22 gauge needle.
2 Manometer and three-way tap.
3 Three plain sterile bottles (numbered) and a fluoride bottle for
glucose (to be sent with a blood glucose sample, taken before
lumbar puncture (LP).

Technique

Position the patient (Fig. 54.1)

1 Move the patient to the edge of the bed on their left side if you
are right-handed.
2 The thoracolumbar spine should be maximally flexed. It does
not matter if the neck is not flexed. Place a pillow between the knees
to prevent torsion of the spine.

Choose the interspace to be used

1 Define the plane of the iliac crests which runs through L3–4.
The spinal cord in the adult ends at the level of L1–2.

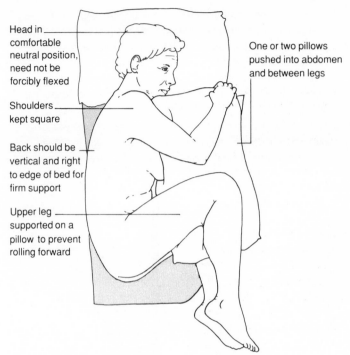

Head in comfortable neutral position, need not be forcibly flexed

One or two pillows pushed into abdomen and between legs

Shoulders kept square

Back should be vertical and right to edge of bed for firm support

Upper leg supported on a pillow to prevent rolling forward

Fig. 54.1. Positioning of the patient for lumbar puncture. Redrawn from Patten J. *Neurological differential diagnosis.* London: Harold Starke 1977; 262 (ISBN 0 287 66988 2).

2 Choose either the L3–4 or L4–5 spaces. Mark the space using your thumbnail.

Lumbar puncture

1 Put on gloves and prepare the skin. It helps to place a drape on top of the patient so that you can recheck the position of the iliac crest if necessary

2 Draw up lignocaine, assemble the manometer and undo the tops of the bottles. Check that the stylet of the needle moves freely. Place everything within easy reach.

3 Stretch the skin over the chosen space with the finger and thumb of your left hand, placed on the spinous processes of the adjacent vertebrae (Fig. 54.2). Put 0.5 ml of lignocaine in the skin and subcutaneous tissues.

4 Place the spinal needle on the mark, bevel uppermost, and advance it towards the umbilicus, taking care to keep it parallel to the ground.

5 The interspinous ligament gives some resistance, and you should notice increased resistance as you go through the tough ligamentum flavum. There is usually an obvious 'give' when the

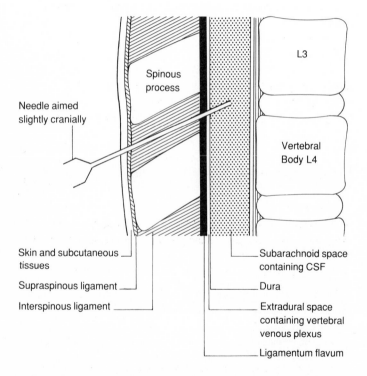

Fig. 54.2. The anatomy of lumbar puncture.

needle is through this. The dura is now only 1–2 mm away. Advance in small steps, withdrawing the stylet after each step.

6 Cerebrospinal fluid (CSF) should flow freely once you enter the dura. If the flow is poor, rotate the needle in case a nerve root is lying against it.

Measuring the opening pressure and collecting CSF

1 Connect the manometer and measure the height of the CSF column (the 'opening pressure'). The patient should uncurl slightly and try to relax at this stage.

2 Cap the top of the manometer with your finger, disconnect it from the needle and put the CSF in the glucose tube.

3 Collect three samples (about 2 ml each) in the plain sterile bottles. bottles.

4 Remove the needle and place a small dressing over the puncture site.

Interpreting the CSF formula

• Normal values are given in Table 59.3, p. 310.
• For the differential diagnosis of meningitis, see Table 28.6, p. 162.

Trouble shooting

You hit bone

1 Withdraw the needle. Recheck the patient's position and the bony landmarks. Try again, taking particular care to keep the needle parallel to the ground.

2 If this fails, modify the angle of the needle in the sagittal plane.

3 If you are still unsuccessful, try another space.

4 If you suspect bacterial meningitis but cannot obtain CSF:
take blood cultures and start antibiotic therapy (Table 28.3, p. 160).

Heavily blood-stained fluid

• The possibilities are sub-arachnoid haemorrhage, traumatic tap or puncture of the venous plexus. If the fluid appears to be venous blood (slow ooze) try again in another space, after flushing the needle.

• Subarachnoid haemorrhage results in uniformly blood-stained CSF (as shown by the red cell count in successive samples). Xanthochromia is often present and should be checked for in the supernatant.

Deteriorating conscious level after lumbar puncture

1 Give mannitol 100–200 ml of 20% solution (1–2 g/kg) i.v. over 20–30 minutes.

2 Arrange intubation and ventilation.

3 Discuss further management with a neurologist.

55   Peritoneal Dialysis

- **Acute renal failure**, when other methods of renal replacement therapy are not available or are contra indicated.
Remember that insertion of a temporary catheter may prejudice future long-term peritoneal dialysis if renal failure is chronic.
- **Elimination of some poisons** (e.g. lithium), when haemodialysis is not possible.
- **Core rewarming in hypothermia** (p. 225).

Technique

Preparation
1 Prepare a 1 litre bag of dialysis fluid warmed to 37° C.
2 Lie the patient flat.
3 Confirm that the bladder is empty by ultrasound or, if this is not available, by catheterization (with antibiotic cover, e.g. ceftazidime 1 g i.v.)
4 Shave the lower abdomen.
5 Put on gown, gloves and mask and prepare and drape the skin.

Inserting the catheter
1 The usual site for insertion is 2.5 cm below the umbilicus in the midline. If there is an operation scar here, use a more lateral site (avoid the area of the inferior epigastric artery, whose surface marking is a line joining the femoral artery with the umbilicus).
2 Infiltrate with 10–15 ml of lignocaine 1% down to and around the peritoneum.
3 Aspirate for gas (indicating perforation of bowel) and if found, choose another site. If free fluid is obtained, send a sample for microscopy and culture and for amylase concentration.
4 Insert an i.v. cannula into the peritoneal cavity and run in the prepared dialysis fluid using a standard i.v. giving set. Withdraw the

cannula. (This step is optional but makes inserting the PD catheter easier).

5 Incise the skin vertically with a narrow scalpel blade (e.g. number 11) and insert the PD catheter through the abdominal wall with a twisting action.

6 As soon as the tip is through the peritoneum (signalled by loss of resistance), rotate the catheter so that the black spot (which marks the direction of the curve) is facing inferolaterally. Withdraw the obturator 2 cm. Advance the catheter, aiming downwards and laterally towards the pelvis, until two-thirds has been inserted. Then withdraw the obturator completely as you advance the catheter until only 2 cm is protruding.

7 Attach the right-angled end of the connecting set to the catheter, which should be held with a deep-purse string suture (3–0 silk).

8 Place gauze swabs around the catheter. Use a split gallipot to support it and the connecting piece if kinking could occur.

Peritoneal dialysis for acute renal failure

Choice of fluid

• PD fluid is available in 1 or 2 litre bags. The osmolality of the fluid (which influences the shift of water from plasma to PD fluid) varies according to the dextrose concentration.

• Start with 1 litre bags of 1.36% dextrose unless the patient is fluid-overloaded in which case use dextrose of a higher concentration.

Exchanges

1 Weigh the bags before and after use to calculate their fluid capacity (allow 1 ml/g) as they may not contain exactly 1 litre.

2 Warm the fluid to 37° C. Add heparin (500 u/l) to reduce fibrin deposition on the catheter.

3 The exchange time consists of inflow time, dwell time and outflow time. Start with hourly exchanges, roughly 20 minutes each for inflow, dwell and outflow. If inflow and outflow are slow, omit the dwell time.

4 The exchange time can be increased after the first day if the patient's biochemistry and fluid status are satisfactory.

5 If plasma potassium falls below 3.5 mmol/l, potassium should be added to the PD fluid to give a concentration of 4 mmol/l.

Monitoring (Table 55.1).

Check plasma potassium 4 hours after starting dialysis and then at least twice daily.

■ **Table 55.1. Monitoring the patient during peritoneal dialysis**

Hourly	• Inflow volume estimated by weight • Volume of effluent • Volume of other fluid in or out
4-hourly	• Temperature • Pulse and blood pressure
8 to 12-hourly	• Stick test for glucose. Some patients develop hyperglycaemia particularly when hyperosmolar PD fluid is used • Plasma biochemistry
Daily	• Weight after drainage of PD fluid
As appropriate	• Chest X-ray to check for collection of PD fluid in the pleural or pericardial spaces.

Troubleshooting

Fluid accumulation/poor drainage

• Accumulation of 500–1000 ml is usual.

• Check that the catheter is not kinked as it leaves the abdomen and syringe it with saline.

• If fluid accumulation is progressive (often due to plugging of the end of the catheter by omentum), the catheter will have to be resited. The position of the catheter can be checked by ultrasound. Resiting is best done with a second catheter, leaving the first in place to prevent leakage of fluid down the track.

■ **Table 55.2. 'Blind' antibiotic therapy for peritonitis complicating peritoneal dialysis**

- Vancomycin plus gentamicin *or*
- Ceftazidime

Vancomycin	• Loading dose: 500 mg intraperitoneally (i.p.)
	• Maintenance dose: 25 mg/l i.p.
Gentamicin	• Loading dose: 1.7 mg/kg i.p.
	• Maintenance dose: 4 mg/l i.p. (check a random blood level after 4 days and reduce the dose if this is 4 mg/l or more)
Ceftazidime	• Dose: 500 mg/l i.p.

Peritonitis

- Shown by abdominal pain, fever and cloudy effluent.
- Aspirate 30 ml of effluent through the wall or port of the bag (sterilize the site with an alcohol swab).
- Divide 10 ml between aerobic and anaerobic blood culture bottles. Send 20 ml for cell count and centrifugation with Gram staining and culture of the sediment.
- Initial antibiotic therapy is given in Table 55.2.
- Continue antibiotic therapy for at least 5 days after clearing of the effluent (usually for a total of 7–10 days).

56 Insertion of a Sengstaken-Blakemore Tube

Indications

• **Failure to control variceal bleeding despite infusion of vasopressin and nitrate (p. 178).**

• Insertion of a Sengstaken–Blakemore tube is rarely necessary and should only be performed for life-threatening haemorrhage. If you have not had experience of putting in these tubes it is better to manage the patient conservatively because of the risks of inhalation, mucosal ulceration and incorrect positioning.

• Balloon tamponade is not a definitive procedure. Plan ahead for variceal injection or oesophageal transection.

Technique

Special equipment needed

1 Sengstaken-Blakemore tube (Fig. 56.1). If this has only three lumens, tape a standard medium-bored nasogastric tube with the perforations just above the oesophageal balloon to allow aspiration of the oesophagus. If there is time, store the tube in the freezer section of a refrigerator to reduce its flexibility to ease insertion.

2 Mercury sphygmomanometer (for inflation of the oesophageal balloon).

3 Contrast medium (e.g. Gastrografin) 10 ml and 300 ml water or 5% dextrose (for inflation of the gastric balloon). Normal saline should not be used as routine because of the potential dangers of sodium ingestion in the presence of hepatic decompensation should the balloon burst.

4 Bladder syringe for aspirating the oesophageal drainage tube.

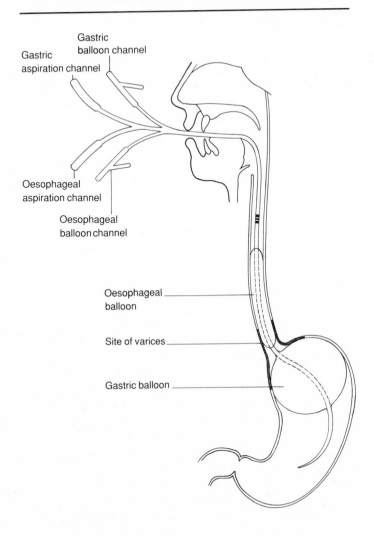

Fig. 56.1. Four-lumen Sengstaken–Blakemore tube in place to compress bleeding varices. Redrawn from Thompson R. *Lecture notes on the liver.* Oxford: Blackwell Scientific Publications 1985; 37.

Preparation

1 The lumens of the tube are not always labelled: if not, label them now with tape.

2 The patient should be intubated before insertion of the tube (to prevent misplacement of the tube in the trachea or inhalation of blood) if:

- conscious level severely depressed;
- gag reflex reduced or absent;
- sedation is necessary.

3 Sedation with midazolam (5–10 mg i.v. given over 5 minutes) should be used only if the patient is particularly agitated and an anaesthetist is available in case intubation becomes necessary. Some patients may become more agitated after benzodiazepines. To avoid the risk of traumatic insertion, it is safest to intubate and ventilate these patients before insertion is attempted.

Insertion of the tube

1 Anaesthetize the throat with lignocaine spray.

2 Lubricate the end of the tube with KY jelly and pass it through the gap between your index and middle fingers placed in the back of the oropharynx. This reduces the chance of the tube curling. Ask the patient to breathe quietly through his mouth throughout the procedure. You are unlikely to need a chock for the teeth.

3 If at any stage of the procedure the patient becomes dyspnoeic withdraw the tube immediately and start again after endotracheal intubation.

4 Assistants should suck blood from the mouth and from all lumens while you insert the tube.

5 Steadily advance the tube until it is inserted to the hilt.

6 Inflate the gastric balloon with the contrast mixture. Insert a bung or clamp the tube. If there is resistance to inflation, deflate the balloon and check the position of the tube with X-ray screening.

7 Pull the tube back gently until resistance is felt.

8 Firm traction on the gastric balloon is usually sufficient to stop the bleeding since this occurs at the filling point of the varices in the lower few centimetres of the oesophagus. If not, inflate the oesophageal balloon:

- connect the lumen of the oesophageal balloon to a sphygmomanometer via a three-way tap (Fig 56.2);
- inflate to 40 mmHg and clamp the tube;
- the oesophageal balloon tends to deflate easily so the pressure must be checked every 2 hours or so.

9 Place a sponge pad (as used to support endotracheal tubes in ventilated patients) over the side of the patient's mouth to prevent the tube rubbing.

10 Strap the tube to the cheek. Fixation with weights over the end of the bed is less effective.

11 Mark the tube in relation to the teeth so that movement can be detected more easily.

Aftercare

1 It is not necessary to deflate the oesophageal balloon every hour as sometimes recommended.

2 Continue infusions of vasopressin and nitrate.

3 Obtain a chest X-ray to check the position. The traction applied means that the gastric balloon is usually seen in the thorax.

4 If facilities for variceal injection are available, the tube should be removed in the endoscopy suite immediately prior to injection which can be done as soon as the patient is haemodynamically stable (usually within 12 hours).

5 If facilities for variceal injection are not available discuss the case with the regional Liver Unit and arrange transfer if appropriate. Alternatively start planning for oesophageal transection within 24 hours if bleeding recurs when the balloon is deflated.

6 Do not leave the tube in for longer than 24 hours because of the risk of mucosal ulceration.

7 Changing the side of the attachment to the cheek every 2 hours reduces the risk of skin ulceration, but should be done carefully because of the risk of displacement.

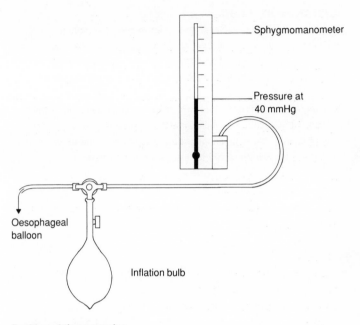

Sphygmomanometer

Pressure at
40 mmHg

Oesophageal
balloon

Inflation bulb

Position of three-way tap

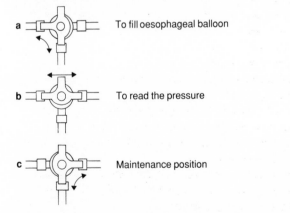

a   To fill oesophageal balloon

b   To read the pressure

c   Maintenance position

Fig. 56.2. Method of filling the oesophageal balloon and measuring its pressure.

Mistakes to avoid

1 Poor anchoring or displacement when moving the patient.

2 Failure to plan ahead. Discuss with the Liver Unit and arrange a definitive procedure (variceal injection, oesophageal transection or even a shunt or embolization in some centres where the expertise exists).

3 Using air instead of contrast which allows easy deflation of the balloon with consequent displacement of the tube.

4 Aspiration of blood or endotracheal placement of the tube. You should have a low threshold for intubation and ventilation.

Section 4
Useful Information

57 Cardiology

Haemodynamic data (Tables 57.1, 57.2)

■ **Table 57.1. Pressure measurements: normal values**

Site*		Pressure (mmHg)
Central venous pressure/right atrial pressure	Mean	0–8 (0–10 cmH₂O)
Right ventricle	Systolic	15–30
	Diastolic	0–8
Pulmonary artery	Systolic	15–30
	Diastolic†	3–12
	Mean	9–16
PA wedge pressure‡	Mean	1–10

* **The reference point for zero** is taken at the **fourth intercostal space in the mid-axillary line** (the level of the tricuspid valve), with the patient lying flat.
† Pressures in the low resistance pulmonary circulation normally equilibrate at end-diastole, and so the PA diastolic pressure can substitute for the wedge pressure, providing:
• the heart rate is less than 120/min;
• pulmonary hypertension is not present (PA systolic <30 mmHg, PA mean <20 mmHg).
‡ PA wedge pressure is measured at end-expiration, when pleural pressure is around zero and the intravascular pressure is closest to the physiologically relevant transmural pressure.

Equations

Cardiac index

$$CI = CO/BSA$$

BSA, body surface area (m²); CI, cardiac index (l/min per m²); CO, cardiac output (l/min).
Normal range: **2.5–4.2 l/min per m².**

Body surface area (m^2)

  BSA = $\sqrt{\text{(height (in)} \times \text{weight (lb)}/3131)}$

  BSA = $\sqrt{\text{(height (cm)} \times \text{weight (kg)}/3600)}$

Systemic vascular resistance

  SVR = 80 × (MAP − MRAP)/CO

MAP, mean arterial pressure (mmHg); MRAP, mean right atrial
pressure (mmHg); SVR, systemic vascular resistance (dyne.s/cm^5).
  Normal range: 770–1500 dyne .s/cm^5 (10–20 mmHg per l/min)

Ventricular septal defect: shunt calculation

  $Q_P : Q_S$ = (Art − RA)/(Art − PA)

Art, systemic arterial So_2; PA, pulmonary arterial So_2; Q_P, pulmonary
blood flow; Q_2, systemic blood flow; RA, right atrial So_2.

References

Barry WH, Grossman W. Range of normal resting hemodynamic values. In:
     Braunwald E, ed. *Heart disease: a textbook of cardiovascular medicine*. 2nd
     edn. Philadelphia: WB Saunders 1984.
Mosteller RD. Simplified calculation of body surface area. *N Engl J Med* 1987;
     317: 1098.

■ **Table 57.2.** Relative inotropic, vasopressor and vasodilator effects of
adrenergic agonists

Drug	Inotropic (beta-1)	Vasopressor (alpha-1)	Vasodilator (beta-2)
Adrenaline	3+	1–2+*	3+
Noradrenaline	3+	3+	1+
Isoprenaline	3+	0	3+
Salbutamol	1+	0	3+
Dopamine	2–3+*	0–3+*	2+
Dobutamine	3+	0–1+*	1+

* Dose-dependent effect.
Potency expressed using a semi-quantitative scale; 0, no effect; 3+,
marked effect. Data compiled from various sources.

Intravenous infusions of drugs (Tables 57.3–57.5)

- **1 ml = 20 standard drops = 60 paediatric drops.**
- Paediatric giving set: drops/min = ml/hour.
- Standard giving set: drops/min = ml/hour ÷ 3.

■ **Table 57.3. Adrenaline, noradrenaline, isoprenaline and salbutamol**

- **Preparation:** add 1 mg to 100 ml or 5 mg to 500 ml of dextrose 5% **(10 μg/ml)**
- **Route:** via central vein only for adrenaline and noradrenaline
- **Infusion rate:** start at 2 μg/min and adjust it to achieve the required effect

- **Equivalent infusion rates (10 μg/ml)**

μg/min	ml/hour
2	12
4	24
6	36
8	48
10	60
15	90
20	120

■ **Table 57.4. Dopamine: infusion rate (ml/hour) according to dose and body weight**

- **Preparation:** add 800 mg to 500 ml dextrose 5% (1600 μg/ml)
- **Route:** via central vein only
- **Infusion rate**
  - **a** For renal vasodilation: 1–5 μg/kg per min
  - **b** For inotropic/vasopressor effect: 5–20 μg/kg per min

Dose (μg/kg per min)	Body weights in kg (lb)				
	50 (110)	60 (132)	70 (154)	80 (176)	90 (198)
2.5	5	6	7	8	9
5	10	12	14	16	18
10	20	23	27	31	35
15	29	35	41	47	53
20	39	47	55	62	70

■ **Table 57.5. Dobutamine: infusion rate (ml/hour) according to dose and body weight**

- **Preparation:** add 500 mg to 500 ml dextrose 5% (1000 μg/ml)
- **Route:** via central or peripheral vein
- **Infusion rate:** 2.5–20 μg/kg per min

Dose (μg/kg per min)	Body weights in kg (lb)				
	50 (110)	60 (132)	70 (154)	80 (176)	90 (198)
2.5	7	9	10	12	13
5	15	18	21	24	27
10	30	36	42	48	54
15	45	54	63	72	81
20	60	72	84	96	108

Thrombolytic therapy with streptokinase

Indications

1 **Acute myocardial infarction:**
   - **onset of symptoms within 24 hours;** treatment should be started as soon as possible.
   - **clinically definite infarct;** ST elevation of >1 mm in the limb leads or >2 mm in the chest leads (two or more adjacent leads).
2 **Major pulmonary embolism:**
   - **persisting hypotension despite treatment with oxygen, heparin and i.v. colloid (Chapter 20);**
   - **confirmed by pulmonary angiography.**

Contraindications See Table 57.6

Treatment regimens

1 **Acute myocardial infarction.**
   - Add 1.5 million units to 100 ml of dextrose 5% or normal saline and infuse over 60 minutes.
   - Give aspirin 150 mg p.o.
2 **Major pulmonary embolism.**
   - Add 250 000 units to 100 ml of dextrose 5% or normal saline and

■ **Table 57.6. Contraindications to streptokinase therapy**

1 Previous treatment with streptokinase or anistreplase (APSAC) (more than 5 days and up to 6 months) (alteplase (plasminogen activator) can be used instead)

2 Active bleeding

3 Stroke within 2 months

4 Recent (within 10 days)
  • Major surgery
  • Child birth
  • Invasive procedure (e.g. liver biopsy)
  • Trauma (including prolonged cardiopulmonary resuscitation)
  • Gastrointestinal haemorrhage

5 Intravascular thrombus (in ventricular or aortic aneurysm)

6 Pregnancy (menstruation is not a contraindication)

7 Haemostatic defect

8 Diabetic proliferative retinopathy

9 Severe hypertension (systolic >200 mmHg, diastolic >110)

10 Bacterial endocarditis

infuse over 30 minutes.
• Then give 100 000 units/hour for 24 hours.
• It is convenient but not essential to infuse this via the angiography catheter (which should be left in place because of the risk of bleeding from the puncture site).
• Check the thrombin time (TT) or kaolin-cephalin clotting time (KCCT) 3–4 hours after stopping streptokinase. When TT/KCCT are less than twice control, start a heparin infusion.

Problems during streptokinase infusion

1 Allergic reaction, recognized by fever or urticaria: give chlorpheniramine 10 mg i.v. and hydrocortisone 100 mg i.v.

2 Oozing from puncture sites. This is the commonest problem.
  • If venepuncture is necessary, use a 22 gauge (blue) needle and compress the puncture site for 10 minutes.
  • Central venous lines should be inserted via an antecubital fossa vein (percutaneously or by cut-down).

- For arterial puncture, use a 23 gauge (orange) needle in the radial or brachial artery and compress the puncture site for at least 10 minutes.

3 Uncontrollable bleeding.
- Stop the infusion.
- Transfuse whole fresh blood if available or fresh frozen plasma.
- As a last resort, give tranexamic acid 1 g (10 mg/kg) i.v. over 10 minutes.

References

Marder VJ, Sherry S. Thrombolytic therapy: current status. *N Engl J Med* 1988; **318**:1512–20

Sharma GVRK, Cella G, Parisi AF, Sasahara AA. Thrombolytic therapy. *N Engl J Med* 1982;**306**:1268–76.

Heparin infusion in venous thromboembolism

1 Loading dose: 5–10 000 units (100 u/kg) i.v. over 5 minutes.
2 Infusion: Add 25 000 units to 50 ml normal saline (500 u/ml) in a syringe pump.
   Start at 1500 u/hour for 6 hours.
3 Check the KCCT and adjust the dose as shown in Table 57.7.

■ Table 57.7. Heparin infusion rate according to kaolin-cephalin clotting time (KCCT) ratio

KCCT ratio	Change in infusion rate
>7	Stop temporarily and reduce dose by >500 u/hour
5.1–7.0	Reduce by 500 u/hour
4.1–5.0	Reduce by 300 u/hour
3.1–4.0	Reduce by 100 u/hour
2.6–3.0	Reduce by 50 u/hour
1.5–2.5	No change
1.2–1.4	Increase by 200 u/hour
<1.2	Increase by 400 u/hour

Based on
Fennerty A, Campbell IA, Routledge PA. Anticoagulants in venous thromboembolism. *Br Med J* 1988;**297**:1285–8.

4 Wait 10 hours before next KCCT estimation unless KCCT ratio is >5.0, in which case check 4 hours later.

5 Continue heparin for 5 days (starting warfarin on the 3rd day).

Warfarin

Drug interactions with warfarin are common and can be serious. When starting or stopping a treatment, check the list in the *British National Formulary*.

Starting warfarin

Warfarin sensitivity not expected (Table 57.8)

1 Give 9 mg daily for 3 days.

2 Check the prothrombin time after the third dose (on the morning of day 4).

  • Simultaneous heparin infusion has no significant effect on the prothrombin time unless the thrombin time is >90 seconds.

  • Adjust the dose according to the prothrombin ratio (International Normalized Ratio, INR) (Table 57.9).

3 Recheck the prothrombin time after the fifth dose.

Warfarin sensitivity expected (Table 57.8)

1 Check the prothrombin time before starting warfarin.

2 If the prothrombin time is normal, give 6 mg daily for 2 days.

3 Recheck the prothrombin time after the second dose and adjust the dose.

■ **Table 57.8. Clinical conditions affecting response to warfarin**

Increased anticoagulation (Table 57.10)	• Impaired liver function • Renal failure • Congestive heart failure • Hyperthyroidism
Decreased anticoagulation	• Hypothyroidism • Transfusion of whole blood or fresh frozen plasma

■ Table 57.9. Warfarin dosage according to prothrombin ratio

Prothrombin ratio (INR) after three doses	Dose for days 4 and 5 (mg)
>4.0	Omit
3.3–4.0	3
2.5–3.2	5
2.0–2.4	6
1.7–1.9	9
<1.6	10

■ Table 57.10. Treatment of over-anticoagulation

Prothrombin ratio (INR)	Clinical condition	Action
4.5–7.0	No bleeding	Stop warfarin
>7.0	No bleeding	Vitamin K* 0.5–2 mg i.v.
>1.3	Bleeding/rapid reversal for surgery	Vitamin K* 0.5–10 mg i.v. Fresh frozen plasma

* Vitamin K should only be given in small doses (<2 mg) if resumption of warfarin anticoagulation is intended. If a rapid transient reversal is needed, use fresh frozen plasma.

Guide to incorrect ECG lead placement

See Fig. 57.1.

Order of appearance while recording

aVR   aVL   aVF

Cable connection
to electrodes

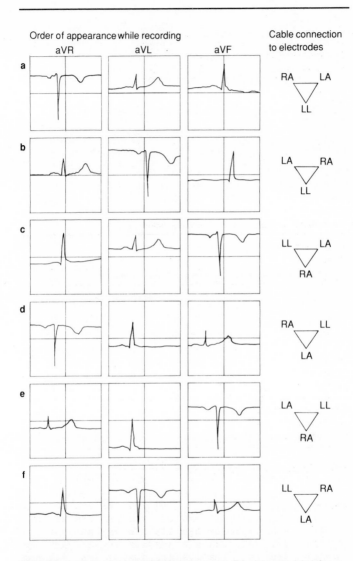

Fig. 57.1. Guide to incorrect ECG lead placement. RA, right arm; LA, left arm; LL; left leg. Reproduced from Hurst JW. *The heart, arteries and veins.* 6th edn. New York: McGraw-Hill 1985;226.

58 Respiratory Medicine

Respiratory function tests: normal values

■ **Table 58.1a.** Peak expiratory flow rate (PEFR) in males (l/min)

Height (m) (feet/inches)	Age (years)									
	20–25	30	35	40	45	50	55	60	65	70
1.60 (5'3'')	572	560	548	536	524	512	500	488	476	464
1.67 (5'6'')	597	584	572	559	547	534	522	509	496	484
1.75 (5'9'')	625	612	599	586	573	560	547	533	520	507
1.83 (6'0'')	654	640	626	613	599	585	572	558	544	530
1.90 (6'3'')	679	665	650	636	622	608	593	579	565	551

Standard deviation 60 l/min. Ethnic differences negligible.

■ **Table 58.1b.** Peak expiratory flow rate in females (l/min)

Height (m) (feet/inches)	Age (years)									
	20–25	30	35	40	45	50	55	60	65	70
1.44 (4'9'')	377	366	356	345	335	324	314	303	293	282
1.52 (5'0'')	403	392	382	371	361	350	340	329	319	308
1.60 (5'3'')	433	422	412	401	391	380	370	359	349	338
1.67 (5'6'')	459	448	438	427	417	406	396	385	375	364
1.75 (5'9'')	489	478	468	457	447	436	426	415	405	394

Standard deviation 60 l/min.

■ **Table 58.2a.** Forced expiratory volume in 1 second (FEV_1) in males (l)

Height (m) (feet/inches)	Age (years)									
	20–25	30	35	40	45	50	55	60	65	70
1.60 (5'3")	3.61	3.45	3.30	3.14	2.99	2.83	2.68	2.52	2.37	2.21
1.67 (5'6")	3.86	3.71	3.55	3.40	3.24	3.09	2.93	2.78	2.62	2.47
1.75 (5'9")	4.15	4.00	3.84	3.69	3.53	3.38	3.22	3.06	2.91	2.75
1.83 (6'0")	4.44	4.28	4.13	3.97	3.82	3.66	3.51	3.35	3.20	3.04
1.90 (6'3")	4.69	4.54	4.38	4.23	4.07	3.92	3.76	3.61	3.45	3.30

Standard deviation 0.5 litres.

■ **Table 58.2b.** Forced expiratory volume in 1 second in females (l)

Height (m)	Age (years)									
(feet/inches)	20–25	30	35	40	45	50	55	60	65	70
1.44 (4′9″)	2.60	2.45	2.30	2.15	2.00	1.85	1.70	1.55	1.40	1.25
1.52 (5′0″)	2.83	2.68	2.53	2.38	2.23	2.08	1.93	1.78	1.63	1.48
1.60 (5′3″)	3.09	2.94	2.79	2.64	2.49	2.34	2.19	2.04	1.89	1.74
1.67 (5′6″)	3.36	3.21	3.06	2.91	2.76	2.61	2.46	2.31	2.16	2.01
1.75 (5′9″)	3.59	3.44	3.29	3.14	2.99	2.84	2.69	2.54	2.39	2.24

Standard deviation 0.4 litres.

■ **Table 58.3a.** Forced vital capacity (FVC) in males (l)

Height (m)	Age (years)									
(feet/inches)	20–25	30	35	40	45	50	55	60	65	70
1.60 (5′3″)	4.17	4.06	3.95	3.84	3.73	3.62	3.51	3.40	3.29	3.18
1.67 (5′6″)	4.53	4.42	4.31	4.20	4.09	3.98	3.87	3.76	3.65	3.54
1.75 (5′9″)	4.95	4.84	4.73	4.62	4.51	4.40	4.29	4.18	4.07	3.96
1.83 (6′0″)	5.37	5.26	5.15	5.04	4.93	4.82	4.71	4.60	4.49	4.38
1.90 (6′3″)	5.73	5.62	5.51	5.40	5.29	5.18	5.07	4.96	4.85	4.74

Standard deviation 0.6 litres.

■ **Table 58.3b.** Forced vital capacity in females (l)

Height (m)	Age (years)									
(feet/inches)	20–25	30	35	40	45	50	55	60	65	70
1.44 (4′9″)	3.13	2.98	2.83	2.68	2.53	2.38	2.23	2.08	1.93	1.78
1.52 (5′0″)	3.45	3.30	3.15	3.00	2.85	2.70	2.55	2.40	2.25	2.10
1.60 (5′3″)	3.83	3.68	3.53	3.38	3.23	3.08	2.93	2.78	2.63	2.48
1.67 (5′6″)	4.20	4.05	3.90	3.75	3.60	3.45	3.30	3.15	3.00	2.85
1.75 (5′9″)	4.53	4.38	4.23	4.08	3.93	3.78	3.63	3.48	3.33	3.18

Standard deviation 0.4 litres.

■ **Table 58.4.** FEV₁ as a percentage of FVC (%)

	Age (years)									
	20–25	30	35	40	45	50	55	60	65	70
Males*	82.5	80.6	78.7	76.9	75.0	73.1	71.3	69.4	67.5	65.7
Females†	81.0	79.9	78.8	77.7	76.6	75.5	74.3	73.2	72.1	71.0

* Standard deviation 7%.
† Standard deviation 6%.

Notes on Tables 58.1–58.4

• The mean ± one standard deviation includes 68% of healthy subjects; the mean ± two standard deviations includes 95% of healthy subjects.

• FEV₁ and FVC: the values shown are for people of European descent; for races with smaller thoraces (e.g. from the Indian Subcontinent and Polynesia), substract 0.4 litres from the values given for FEV₁ and 0.7 litres for FVC in males and 0.6 litres in females.

Reference

Cotes J E. *Lung function*, 4th edn. Oxford: Blackwell Scientific Publications 1978.

Arterial blood gases and pH

Normal values

1 **pHa:** 7.35–7.45 (35–45 nmol/l).

2 Pao_2: 10.0–13.3 kPa (75–100 mmHg).

3 $Paco_2$: 4.7–6.0 kPa (35–45 mmHg).

4 **Conversion factors:**
   • kPa to mmHg — multiply by 7.5.
   • mmHg to kPa — multiply by 0.133.

5 **Respiratory failure** is defined as a $Pao_2 < 8$ kPa or $Paco_2 > 7$ kPa, breathing air.

6 **Correction of Pao_2 for age:**

predicted normal value (mmHg) = $104 - (age (years) \times 0.27)$

7 Correction for body temperature: Table 58.5.

■ **Table 58.5.** Change of body temperature from 37°C

	Increase 1°C	Decrease 1°C
pHa	Down 0.015	Up 0.015
Pao_2	Up 4.4%	Down 4.4%
$Paco_2$	Up 7.2%	Down 7.2%

References

Mellemgaard K. The alveolar-arterial oxygen difference: its size and components in normal man. *Acta Physiol Scand* 1966;**67**:16–20.

Normal reference values: *N Engl J Med* 1986;**314**:39–49.

Reuler JB. Hypothermia: pathophysiology, clinical settings, and management. *Ann Intern Med* 1978;**89**:519–27.

Hydrogen ion concentration (Table 58.6)

■ **Table 58.6.** Hydrogen ion concentration: conversion of pH into nmol/l

pH	0	1	2	3	4	5	6	7	8	9
7.0	99	97	95	93	91	89	87	85	83	81
7.1	79	78	76	74	72	71	69	68	66	65
7.2	63	62	60	59	58	56	55	54	53	51
7.3	50	49	48	47	46	45	44	43	42	41
7.4	40	39	38	37	36	35	35	34	33	32
7.5	31	30	30	30	29	28	28	27	26	26
7.6	25	25	24	23	23	22	22	21	21	20

Acid–base diagram

See Fig. 58.1.

Radiographic patterns of lobar collapse

See Fig. 58.2.

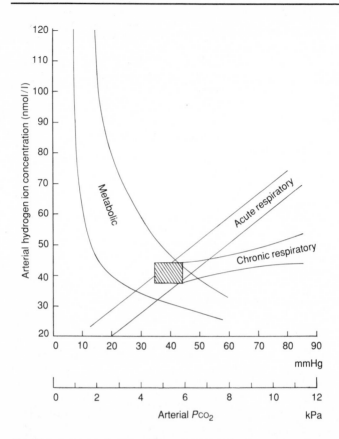

Fig. 58.1. Acid-base diagram relating arterial hydrogen ion concentration to $P_{a_{CO_2}}$. The shaded rectangle is the normal region. The 95% confident limits of hydrogen ion concentration $P_{a_{CO_2}}$ relationships in single disturbances of acid-base balance are shown. Reproduced from Flenley DC. *Lancet* 1971;**1**:961.

Fig. 58.2. (Opposite) Radiographic patterns of lobar collapse.
• RUL, right upper lobe; trachea deviated to right, horizontal fissure pulled up.
• LUL, left upper lobe; trachea deviated to left, oblique fissure pulled

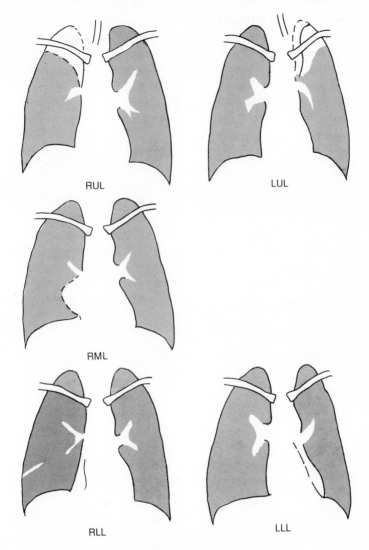

upward and forward (on lateral film).

- RML, right middle lobe; right heart border obscured.
- RLL, right lower lobe; right hemidiaphragm obscured, horizontal and oblique fissures pulled down, trachea may be deviated to right.
- LLL, left lower lobe; triangular shadow of collapsed lobe seen through the heart.

Redrawn from Brewis RAL. *Lecture notes on respiratory disease.* 3rd edn. Oxford: Blackwell Scientific Publications 1985;93.

59 Neurology

Peripheral nervous system (Tables 59.1, 59.2)

■ **Table 59.1. Muscle groups: root and peripheral nerve supply**

Movement	Muscle group	Main roots	Peripheral nerve
Upper limb			
Shoulder abduction	Deltoid	C5	Axillary
Shoulder adduction	Lateral dorsi	C7	Brachial plexus
	Pectoralis major	C5–7	Brachial plexus
Elbow flexion	Biceps	C5–6	Musculocutaneous
	Brachioradialis	C6	Radial
Elbow extension	Triceps	C7	Radial
Wrist flexion	Flexor muscles of forearm	C7–8	Median/Ulnar
Wrist extension	Extensor muscles of forearm	C7	Radial
Finger flexion	Flexor muscles of forearm	C7–8	Median/Ulnar
Finger extension	Extensor muscles of forearm	C7	Radial
Finger abduction	Interossei	T1	Ulnar
	Abductor digiti minimi	T1	Ulnar
Thumb abduction	Abductor pollicis brevis	T1	Median
Lower limb			
Hip flexion	Iliopsoas	L1–2	Femoral
Hip extension	Gluteus maximus	L5–S1	Inferior gluteal

Table 59.1 (Continued)

Hip abduction	Gluteus medius and minimus	L4–5	Superior gluteal
	Tensor fasciae latae	L4–5	Superior gluteal
Hip adduction	Adductors	L2–3	Obturator
Knee flexion	Hamstrings	S1	Sciatic
Knee extension	Quadriceps	L3–4	Femoral
Ankle dorsiflexion	Tibialis anterior	L4	Sciatic (peroneal)
Ankle plantarflexion	Gastrocnemius	S1–2	Sciatic (tibial)
Ankle eversion	Peroneus longus	L5–S1	Sciatic (peroneal)
Ankle inversion	Tibialis anterior	L4	Sciatic (peroneal)
	Tibialis posterior	L4–5	Sciatic (tibial)
Great toe dorsiflexion	Extensor hallucis longus	L5	Sciatic (peroneal)

■ **Table 59.2. Tendon reflexes: root and peripheral nerve supply**

Tendon reflex	Muscle	Main roots	Peripheral nerve
Biceps	Biceps	C5–6	Musculocutaneous
Supinator	Brachioradialis	C6	Radial
Triceps	Triceps	C7	Radial
Finger	Long finger flexors	C7–8	Median/ulnar
Knee	Quadriceps	L3–4	Femoral
Ankle	Gastrocnemius	S1–2	Sciatic (tibial)

Tables based on
Medical Research Council Memorandum No. 45. *Aids to the examination of the peripheral nervous system*. London: HMSO 1976.

Sensory innervation of the skin (Fig. 59.1)

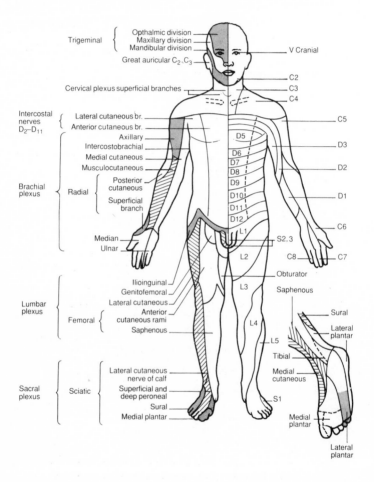

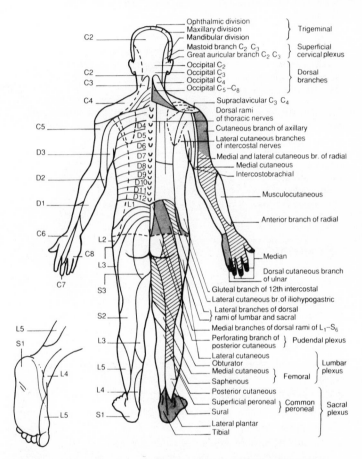

Fig. 59.1. Sensory innervation of the skin: cutaneous areas of distribution of spinal segments and sensory fibres of the peripheral nerves: anterior and posterior views. Reproduced from Brain's diseases of the nervous system. 8th ed, Oxford; Oxford University Press 1977.

Cerebrospinal fluid (Table 59.3)

■ Table 59.3. Cerebrospinal fluid: normal values and correction for traumatic tap

Opening pressure	7–18 cm CSF
Cell count	0–5/mm^3, all lymphocytes
Protein concentration	0.15–0.45 g/l (15–45 mg/dl)
Glucose concentration	2.8–4.2 mmol/l
CSF: blood glucose ratio	>50%
Traumatic tap: correction of cell count and protein concentration	For every 1000 RBC/mm^3 subtract one WBC/mm^3 and 0.015 g/l (1.5 mg/dl) protein

Based on

Gottlieb AJ, Zamkoff KW, Jastremski MS, Scalzo A, Imboden KJ. *The whole internist catalog*. Philadelphia: WB Saunders 1980:127–8.
Normal reference values. *N Engl J Med* 1986;**314**:39–49.

Brainstem death

- The diagnosis must be confirmed by two doctors, one a consultant, the other a consultant or senior registrar, neither of whom is a member of an organ transplant team.
- The appropriate interval between the onset of apnoeic coma (i.e. when ventilation was started) and testing for brainstem death depends on the time required to establish criteria **2** and **3** (Table 59.4).
- The interval between tests should be 2–3 hours or longer. On both occasions, brainstem reflexes should be tested and the test for apnoea performed.
- There are no legal requirements for special tests (e.g. EEG) to confirm the diagnosis in the United Kingdom.

■ **Table 59.4. Criteria of brainstem death**

All of the following criteria must be met

1 **The patient is comatose and apnoeic** (i.e. unresponsive and requiring ventilation)
2 **There is irremediable structural brain damage due to one or more of**
   • Head injury
   • Intracranial haemorrhage
   • Prolonged anoxia
3 **The following have been excluded or corrected**
   • Hypothermia (core temperature must be >36°C)
   • Drug or alcohol intoxication
   • Metabolic or endocrine derangement
   • Neuromuscular blockade.
4 **There are no brainstem reflexes (see below)**
5 **The patient remains apnoeic on disconnection from the ventilator (see below)**

Testing of brainstem reflexes and for apnoea

The following five reflexes must all be tested:

1 **Pupillary response to light.**
   • A bright light must be used.
   • Atropine (pupil dilated) and neuromuscular blockers (pupil mid-position) can abolish the response.
2 **Corneal reflex.**
   • Apply firm pressure on the cornea using a sterile swab.
3 **Vestibulo-ocular reflex.**
   • Use an auriscope to check the ear canal is free of wax. If wax is blocking the ear canal it must be removed.
   • Irrigate with 20 ml of ice-cold water: the tubing of a 'Butterfly' needle (with the needle cut off) can be used.
   • Observe for movement of either eye: any movement signifies brainstem activity.
4 **Cranial motor response to somatic stimulation.**
   • Apply firm supra-orbital and nail bed pressure.
   • Observe for grimacing.
5 **Reflex response to bronchial stimulation.**

- Pass a suction catheter down the endotracheal tube into the trachea and bronchi.
- Observe for coughing or gagging.

6 Test for apnoea.

- Pre-oxygenate the patient by ventilating for 10 minutes with 100% oxygen.
- Check that $Paco_2$ is not low at the time of disconnection. It should be >5.3 kPa (40 mmHg); if lower than this, reduce the frequency of ventilation or ventilate with 5% CO_2 in 95% O_2 for 5 minutes and recheck it.
- Maintain oxygenation during disconnection by placing a catheter in the trachea with an oxygen flow rate of 6 l/min.
- Disconnect from the ventilator for 10 minutes.
- Observe for respiratory efforts.
- Check $Paco_2$ is >6.7 kPa (50 mmHg) at 10 minutes to confirm an adequate test.

References

Plum F, Posner JB. *The diagnosis of stupor and coma*, 3rd edn. Philadelphia: FA Davis 1980.

Pallis C. *The diagnosis of brain stem death. Br Med J* 1982;**285:**1558–60, 1641–4, 1720–2

60 Renal Medicine

Prediction of GFR from plasma creatinine concentration

Males

$$GFR = (140 - age\ (years)) \times weight\ (kg)/(0.82 \times PC)$$

GFR, glomerular filtration rate (ml/min); PC, plasma creatinine (μmol/l).

Females

$$GFR = (140 - age\ (years)) \times weight\ (kg)/(0.96 \times PC)$$

Reference
Cockcroft DW, Gault MH. Prediction of creatinine clearance from serum creatinine. *Nephron* 1976;**16**:31–41.

Prescribing

See Table 60.1 and the *British National Formulary*.

■ **Table 60.1. Prescribing for patients with renal disease: selected drugs**

Dose reduction when **GFR <50 ml/min;** **plasma creatinine >150 µmol/l** **all patients aged > 60 years**	• Aminoglycosides • Angiotensin-converting enzyme inhibitors • Bezafibrate • Cephalosporins (avoid cephalothin) • Chloroquine • Clofibrate • Digoxin • Disopyramide • Flecainide • Flucytosine • Gold • Lithium • Methotrexate • Penicillamine (avoid if possible) • Pentamidine • Procainamide • Propylthiouracil • Tocainide
Avoid with any renal impairment	• Amantadine • Amphotericin • Cephalothin • Chlorpropamide • Ethacrynic acid • Ethambutol • Magnesium salts • Metformin • Nalidixic acid • Neomycin • Nitrofurantoin • Tetracyclines (except doxycycline)

61 Miscellaneous

Section 2 (up to 28 days)

Indication
The patient has a mental disorder and needs detention for assessment in the interests of his health or safety or for the safety of others.

Application
• The nearest relative or social worker; *and*
• one medical practitioner with specialist experience in mental disorder and one other medical practitioner.

Section 4 (up to 72 hours)

Indication
Urgent necessity for admission to hospital because of mental illness.

Application
• The nearest relative or social worker (who must have seen the patient in the past 24 hours); *and*
• one medical practitioner who has seen the patient in the past 24 hours.

Section 5(2) (up to 72 hours)

Indication
As for Section 4, but the patient is already in hospital.

Application
As for Section 4.

Section 5(4) (up to 6 hours)

Indication

The patient suffers from a mental disorder and for his health or safety or for the protection of others must be restrained from leaving hospital.

Application

A nurse with psychiatric qualifications.

Reference

Mental Health Act 1983 (England and Wales). London: HMSO 1983.

Prescribing in hepatic disease

See Table 61.1 and the *British National Formulary*.

■ **Table 61.1.** Prescribing for patient with hepatic disease

Reduced dose necessary	• **Lignocaine** (metabolism impaired) • **Paracetamol** (dose causing hepatoxicity reduced) • **Phenytoin** (metabolism impaired) • **Propranolol** (metabolism impaired: not other beta-blockers) • **Rifampicin** (biliary excretion impaired) • **Thiopentone** (protein binding impaired)
Avoid	• **Antacids causing constipation** (precipitate encephalopathy) • **Antidepressants** (precipitate encephalopathy) • **Aspirin** (risk of gastrointestinal bleeding) • **Biguanides** (may cause lactic acidosis) • **Diuretics** (thiazides and loop diuretics) — hypokalaemia may precipitate encephalopathy • **Erythromycin** (cholestatic jaundice) • **'Lomotil'** (precipitate encephalopathy) • **Opiates** (precipiate encephalopathy) • **Phenylbutazone** (fluid retention) • **Phenothiazines** (precipitate encephalopathy) • **Sedatives** (precipitate encephalopathy) • **Sulphonylureas** (may cause cholestatic jaundice) • **Tetracyclines** (i.v. doses >1 g daily hepatotoxic) • **Warfarin** — decreased synthesis of clotting factors

Based on

Beeley L. *Safer prescribing*, 4th edn. Oxford: Blackwell Scientific
  Publications. 1987.

Further Reading

The following is a list of selected references from journals and monographs to be found in most hospital libraries.

1 Cardiac Arrest

American Heart Association. Standards and guidelines for cardiopulmonary resuscitation and emergency cardiac care. *JAMA* 1986;**255**:2905–89.

Chamberlain DA. Advanced life support. *Br Med J* 1989;**299**:446–8.

Marsden AK. Basic life support. *Br Med J* 1989;**299**:442–5.

2 Cardiac Arrhythmias

Bennett DH. *Cardiac arrhythmias*. 3rd edn. Bristol: Wright 1989.

Manolis AS, Estes M. Supraventricular tachycardia — mechanisms and therapy. *Arch Intern Med* 1987;**147**:1706–16.

Tchou P, Young P, Mahmud R, Denker S, Jazayeri M, Akhtar M. Useful clinical criteria for the diagnosis of ventricular tachycardia. *Am J Med* 1988;**84**:53–6.

3 Hypotension

Bradley RD. *Studies in acute heart failure*. London: Edward Arnold 1977.

Narins RG, Cohen JJ. Bicarbonate therapy for organic acidosis: the case for its continued use. *Ann Intern Med* 1987;**106**:615–8.

Packman MI, Rackow EC. Optimum left heart filling pressure during fluid resuscitation of patients with hypovolaemic and septic shock. *Crit Care Med* 1983;**11**:165–9.

Stacpole PW. Lactic acidosis: the case against bicarbonate therapy. *Ann Intern Med* 1986;**105**:276–9.

4 Acute Chest Pain

Chambers J, Bass C. Chest pain with normal coronary anatomy: a review of natural history and possible etiologic factors. *Progr Cardiovasc Dis* 1990; **33**:161–84.

Editorial. Non-specific chest pain. *Lancet* 1987;**1**:958–60.

Goldman L, Cook EF, Brand DA. A computer protocol to predict myocardial infarction in emergency department patients with chest pain. *N Engl J Med* 1988;**318**:797–803.

Henderson JAM, Peloquin AJM. Boerhaave revisited: spontaneous oesophageal perforation as a diagnostic masquerader. *Am J Med* 1989;**86**:559–67.

5 Acute Breathlessness

Harrison BDW. Upper airways obstruction. A report of sixteen patients. *Q J Med* 1976;**45**:625–45.

Ogilvie C. Dyspnoea. *Br Med J* 1983;**287**:160–1.

6 The Unconscious Patient

Briggs M, Clarke P, Crockard A *et al*. Guidelines for initial management after head injury in adults: suggestions from a group of neurosurgeons. *Br Med J* 1984;**288**:983–5.

Plum F, Posner JB. *The diagnosis of stupor and coma*. 3rd edn. Philadelphia: FA Davis Company 1980.

7 Transient Loss of Consciousness

Kapoor WN, Cha R, Peterson JR, Wieand HS, Karpf M. Prolonged electrocardiographic monitoring in patients with syncope. *Am J Med* 1987;**82**:20–8.

Kapoor WN, Karpf M, Wieand S, Peterson JR, Levey GS. A prospective evaluation and follow-up of patients with syncope. *N Engl J Med* 1983;**309**:197–204.

8 Acute Confusional State

Charness ME, Simon RP, Greenberg DA. Ethanol and the nervous system. *N Engl J Med* 1989;**321**:442–54.

Editorial. Non-convulsive status epilepticus. *Lancet* 1987;**1**:958–9.

Lipowski ZJ. Current concepts — geriatrics: delirium in the elderly patient. *N Engl J Med* 1989;**320**:578–82.

Reuler JB, Girard DE, Cooney TG. Current concepts: Wernicke's encephalopathy. *N Engl J Med* 1985;**312**:1035–9.

9 Headache

Caviness VS Jr, O'Brien P. Current concepts: headache. *N Engl J Med* 1980;**302**:446–50.

Clough C. Non-migrainous headaches. *Br. Med J* 1989; **229**:70–2.

Editorial. Headaches and subarachnoid haemorrhage. *Lancet* 1988;**2**:80–2.

10 Septicaemia

Bone RC, Fisher CJ Jr, Clemmer TP, Slotman GJ, Metz CA, Balk RA and the

Methylprednisolone Severe Sepsis Study Group. A controlled clinical trial of high-dose methylprednisolone in the treatment of severe sepsis and septic shock. *N Engl J Med* 1987;**317**:653–8.

Glatt AE, Chirgwin K, Landesman SH. Current concepts: Treatment of infections associated with human immunodeficiency virus. *N Engl J Med* 1988;**318**:1439–48.

Infection today: a Lancet review. London: The Lancet 1988.

Marantz PR, Linzer M, Feiner CJ, Feinstein SA, Kozin AM, Friedland GH. Inability to predict diagnosis in febrile intravenous drug abusers. *Ann Intern Med* 1987;**106**:823–8.

Marcus RE, Goldman JM. Management of infection in the neutropenic patient. *Br Med J* 1986;**293**:406–8.

Mellors JR, Horwitz RI, Harvey MR, Horwitz SM. A simple index to identify occult bacterial infection in adults with acute unexplained fever. *Arch Intern Med* 1987;**147**:666–71.

Parker MM, Parrillo JE. Septic shock: hemodynamics and pathogenesis. *JAMA* 1983;**250**:3324–7.

Veterans Administration Systemic Sepsis Co-operative Study Group. Effect of high-dose glucocorticoid therapy on mortality in patients with clinical signs of systemic sepsis. *N Engl J Med* 1987;**317**:659–65.

11 Poisoning

Editorial. Repeated oral activated charcoal in acute poisoning. *Lancet* 1987;**1**:1013–15.

Henry J, Volans G. *ABC of poisoning. Part 1 — Drugs.* London: British Medical Association 1988.

Meredith TJ, Prescott LF, Vale JA. Why do patients still die from paracetamol poisoning? *Br Med J* 1986;**293**:345–6.

Prescott LF. Paracetamol overdosage — pharmacological considerations and clinical management. *Drugs* 1983;**25**:290–314.

Proudfcot AT. Toxicity of salicylates. *Am J Med* 1983;**75**(5A):99–103.

12 Acute Myocardial Infarction

Caplin JL. Acute right ventricular infarction. *Br Med J* 1989;**299**:69–70.

Editorial. Presentation of myocardial infarction in the elderly. *Lancet* 1986;**2**:1077–8.

Fox AC, Glassman E, Isom OW. Surgically remediable complications of myocardial infarction. *Progr Cardiovasc Dis* 1979;**21**:461–84.

ISIS-2 Collaborative Group. Randomised trial of intravenous streptokinase, oral aspirin, both or neither among 17,187 cases of suspected myocardial infarction. *Lancet* 1988;**2**:349–60.

Lee TH, Goldman L. Serum enzyme assays in the diagnosis of acute myocardial infarction. *Ann Intern Med* 1986;**105**:221–33.

Marder VJ, Sherry S. Thrombolytic therapy: current status. *N Engl J Med* 1988; **318**;1512–20, 1585–95.

Rude RE, Poole WK, Muller JE *et al*. Electrocardiographic and clinical criteria for recognition of acute myocardial infarction based on analysis of 3,697 patients. *Am J Cardiol* 1983;**52**:936–42.

Schreiber TL, Miller DH, Zola B. Management of myocardial infarction shock: current status. *Am Heart J* 1989;**117**:435–43.

13 Unstable Angina

Epstein SE, Palmeri ST. Mechanisms contributing to precipitation of unstable angina and acute myocardial infarction: implications regarding therapy. *Am J Cardiol* 1984;**54**:1245–42.

Herling IM. Intravenous nitroglycerine: clinical pharmacology and therapeutic considerations. *Am Heart J* 1984;**108**:141–9.

Theroux P, Ouimet J, McCann J *et al*. Aspirin, heparin, or both to treat acute unstable angina. *N Engl J Med* 1988;**319**:1105–11.

14 Aortic Dissection

DeSanctis RW, Doroghazi RM, Austen WG, Buckley MJ. Aortic dissection. *N Engl J Med* 1987;**317**:1060–7.

Eagle KA, Quertermous T, Kritzer GA *et al*. Spectrum of conditions initially suggesting acute aortic dissection but with negative aortograms. *Am J Cardiol* 1986; **57**:322-6.

Editorial. Acute aortic dissection. *Lancet* 1988;**2**:827–8.

15 Severe Hypertension

Ferguson RK, Vlasses PH. Hypertensive emergencies and urgencies. *JAMA* 1986;**255**:1607–13.

Houston MC. Pathophysiology, clinical aspects, and treatment of hypertensive crises. *Progr Cardiovasc Dis* 1989;**32**:99–148.

The 1988 Report of the Joint National Committee on the detection, evaluation, and treatment of high blood pressure. *Arch Intern Med* 1988; **148**:1023–38.

16 Pulmonary Oedema

Bernard GR, Luce JM, Sprung CL, *et al*. High-dose corticosteroids in patients with the adult respiratory distress syndrome. *N Engl J Med* 1987;**317**:1565–70.

Editorial. Adult respiratory distress syndrome. *Lancet* 1986;**1**:301–3.

Rinaldo JE, Rogers RM. Adult respiratory distress syndrome: changing concepts of lung injury and repair. *N Engl J Med* 1982;**306**:900–9.

Staub NC. The pathogenesis of pulmonary edema. *Progr Cardiovasc Dis* 1980;**23**:53–80.

17 Pericarditis

Permanyer-Miralda G, Sagrista-Sauleda J, Soler-Soler J. Primary acute pericardial disease: a prospective series of 231 consecutive patients. *Am J Cardiol* 1985;**56**:623–30.

Spodick DH. The normal and diseased pericardium: current concepts of pericardial physiology, diagnosis and treatment. *J Am Coll Cardiol* 1983;**1**:240–51.

18 Cardiac Tamponade

Horgan JH. Cardiac tamponade. *Br Med J* 1987;**295**:563–4.

Markiewicz W, Borovik R, Ecker S. Cardiac tamponade in medical patients: treatment and prognosis in the echocardiographic era. *Am Heart J* 1986;**111**:1138–42.

Stein L, Shubin H, Weil MH. Recognition and management of pericardial tamponade. *JAMA* 1973;**225**:503–6.

19 Deep Vein Thrombosis

Editorial. Management of venous thromboembolism. *Lancet* 1988;**1**:275–7.

Hull RI, Hirsh J, Sackett DL, Stoddart G. Cost effectiveness of clinical diagnosis, venography and non-invasive testing in patients with symptomatic deep-vein thrombosis. *N Engl J Med* 1981;**304**:1561–7.

Hull R, Hirsh J, Sackett DL et al. Clinical validity of a negative venogram in patients with clinically suspected venous thrombosis. *Circulation* 1981;**64**:623–5.

20 Pulmonary Embolism

Bell WR, Simon TL. Current status of pulmonary thromboembolic disease: pathophysiology, diagnosis, prevention and treatment. *Am Heart J* 1982;**103**:239–62.

Hull RD, Hirsh J, Carter CJ et al. Pulmonary angiography, ventilation lung scanning and venography for clinical suspected pulmonary embolism with abnormal perfusion lung scan. *Ann Intern Med* 1983;**98**:891–9.

21 Acute Asthma

Benatar SR. Fatal asthma. *N Engl J Med* 1986;**314**:423–9.

Clarke TJH, Godfrey S, eds. *Asthma*. 2nd edn. London: Chapman and Hall 1983.

Crompton G. The catastrophic asthmatic. *Br J Dis Chest* 1987;**81**:321–5.

Hendrick DJ. Asthma: epidemics and epidemiology. *Thorax* 1989;**44**:609–13.

Holgate ST, Finnarty JP. Recent advances in understanding the pathogenesis of asthma and its clinical implication. *Quart J Med* 1988;**66**:5–19.

22 Acute Exacerbation of Chronic Airflow Limitation

Anthonisen NR, Manfreda J, Warren CPW, Hershfield ES, Harding GKM, Nelson NA. Antibiotic therapy in exacerbations of chronic obstructive pulmonary disease. *Ann Intern Med* 1987;**106**:196–204.

23 Pneumonia

Harrison BDW, Farr BM, Connolly CK, MacFarlane JT, Selkon JB, Bartlett CLR. The hospital management of community-acquired pneumonia. Recommendations of the British Thoracic Society. *J Roy Coll Phys* 1987;**21**:267–9.

MacFarlane JT. Treatment of lower respiratory infections. *Lancet* 1987;**2**:1446–9.

Montgomery AB, Debs KJ, Luce JM *et al*. Aerosolised pentamidine as sole therapy for *Pneumocystis carinii* pneumonia in patients with acquired immunodeficiency syndrome. *Lancet* 1987;**2**:480–3.

Murray JF, Felton CP, Garay SM *et al*. Pulmonary complications of the acquired immunodeficiency syndrome: report of a National Heart, Lung and Blood Institute workshop. *N Engl J Med* 1984;**310**:1682–8.

Wharton JM, Coleman DL, Wofsy CB *et al*. Trimethoprim-sulfamethoxazole or pentamidine for *Pneumocystis carinii* pneumonia in the acquired immunodeficiency syndrome. *Ann Intern Med* 1986;**105**:37–44.

24 Pneumothorax

Cummin ARC, Smith MJ, Wilson AG. Pneumothorax in the supine patient. *Br Med J* 1987;**295**:591–2.

Editorial. Simple aspiration of pneumothorax. *Lancet* 1984;**1**:434–5.

25 Hyperventilation

Bass C, Gardner WN. Respiratory and psychiatric abnormalities in chronic symptomatic hyperventilation. *Br Med J* 1985;**290**:1387–90.

Evans DW, Lum LC. Hyperventilation: an important cause of pseudoangina. *Lancet* 1977;**1**:155–7.

Magarian GJ. Hyperventilation syndromes: infrequently recognised common expressions of anxiety and stress. *Medicine (Baltimore)* 1982;**61**:219–36.

26 Stroke

Allen CMC. Clinical diagnosis of the acute stroke syndrome. *Quart J Med* 1983;**208**:515–23.

Editorial. Cerebellar stroke. *Lancet* 1988;**1**:1031–2.

Grotta JC. Current medical and surgical therapy for cerebrovascular disease. *N Engl J Med* 1987;**317**:1505–16.

Lodder J, Dennis MS, van Raak L, Jones LN, Warlow CP. Co-operative study on the value of long term anticoagulation in patients with stroke and non-rheumatic atrial fibrillation. *Br Med J* 1988;**296**:1435–8.

Norris JW, Hachinski VC. Misdiagnosis of stroke. *Lancet* 1982;**1**:328–31.

Sandercock P. Important new treatments for acute ischaemic stroke? *Br Med J* 1987;**295**:1224–5.

27 Subarachnoid Haemorrhage

Editorial. Calcium antagonists and aneurysmal subarachnoid haemorrhage. *Lancet* 1983;**2**:141–3.

Locksley HB. Report on the co-operative study of intracranial aneurysms and subarachnoid haemorrhage. Section V. Part 1. Natural history of subarachnoid haemorrhage, intracranial aneurysms and arteriovenous malformations. *J Neurosurg* 1966;**25**:219–39.

Pickard JD, Murray GD, Illingworth R, *et al.* Effect of oral nimodipine on cerebral infarction and outcome after subarachnoid haemorrhage: British aneurysm nimodipine trial. *Br Med J* 1989;**298**:636–42.

28 Bacterial Meningitis

Ogawa SK, Smith MA, Brennessel DJ, Lowy FD. Tuberculous meningitis in an urban medical centre. *Medicine (Baltimore)* 1987;**66**:317–26.

Rubin RH, Hooper DC. Central nervous system infection in the compromised host. *Med Clin North Am* 1985;**69**:281–97.

Schwartz MN, Dodge PR. Bacterial meningitis: a review of selected aspects. *N Engl J Med* 1965;**272**:654–60, 779–87, 842–8, 898–902, 1003–10.

Whitby M, Finch R. Bacterial meningitis. Rational selection and use of antibacterial drugs. *Drugs* 1986;**31**:266–78.

29 Spinal Cord Compression

Portenoy RK, Lipton RB, Foley KM. Back pain in the cancer patient: an algorithm for evaluation and management. *Neurology* 1987;**37**:134–8.

30 Guillain-Barré Syndrome

Editorial. Guillain–Barré syndrome. *Lancet* 1988;**2**:659–61.

Hughes RAC. Plasma exchange for Guillain–Barré syndrome. *Br Med J* 1985;**291**:615–6.

31 Major Epilepsy

Delgado-Escueta AV, Wasterlain C, Treiman DM, Porter RJ. Current concepts in neurology: management of status epilepticus. *N Engl J Med* 1982;**306**:1337–40.

Oxbury JM, Whitty CWM. Causes and consequences of status epilepticus in adults: a study of 86 cases. *Brain* 1971;**94**:733–44.

32 Acute Upper Gastrointestinal Haemorrhage

Collins R, Langman M. Treatment with histamine H2 antagonists in acute upper gastrointestinal hemorrhage: implications of randomized trials. *N Eng J Med* 1985;**313**:660–6.

Dronfield MW, Langman MJS, Atkinson M *et al*. Outcome of endoscopy and barium radiography for acute upper gastrointestinal bleeding: controlled trial in 1037 patients. *Br Med J* 1982;**284**:545–50.

Editorial. Management of acute variceal bleeding. *Lancet* 1988;**2**:999–1000.

Steer MJ, Silen W. Current concepts: diagnostic procedures in gastrointestinal haemorrhage. *N Engl J Med* 1983;**309**:646–50.

Terblanche J, Burroughs AK, Hobbs KEF. Controversies in the management of bleeding esophageal varices. *N Engl J Med* 1989;**320**:1393–8, 1469–75.

Westaby D. The management of active variceal bleeding. *Intensive Care Med* 1988;**14**:100–5.

33 Acute Hepatic Encephalopathy

Fagan EA, Williams R. Fulminant viral hepatitis. *Br Med Bull* 1990;**46**:462–80

O'Grady JG, Williams R. Acute liver failure. *Clin Gastroenterol* 1989;**3**:75–89.

34 Acute Renal Failure

Bennett WM, Muther RS, Parker RA *et al*. Drug therapy in renal failure: dosing guidelines for adults. *Ann Intern Med* 1980;**93**:62–89, 286–325.

Corwin HL, Bonventre JV. Acute renal failure in the intensive care unit. *Intensive Care Med* 1989;**14**:10–16, 86–96.

Editorial. Hyperkalaemia — silent and deadly. *Lancet* 1989;**1**:1240.

Madaio MP, Harrington JT. Current concepts: the diagnosis of acute glomerulonephritis. *N Engl J Med* 1983;**309**;1299–1302.

Myers BD, Moran SM. Hemodynamically mediated renal failure. *N Engl J Med* 1986;**314**:97–105.

Van Scoy RE, Wilson WR. Antimicrobial agents in adult patients with renal insufficiency: initial dosage and general recommendations. *Mayo Clin Proc* 1987;**62**:1142–5.

35–38 Diabetes

Christiansen CL, Schurizek BA, Malling B, Knudsen L, Alberti KGMM, Hermansen K. Insulin treatment of the insulin-dependent diabetic undergoing surgery. Continuous intravenous infusion compared with subcutaneous administration. *Anaesthesia* 1988;**43**:533–7.

Fischer KF, Lees JA, Newman JH. Hypoglycaemia in hospitalized patients: causes and outcomes. *N Engl J Med* 1986;**315**:1245–50. ,

Foster DW, McGarry JD.The metabolic derangements and treatment of diabetic ketoacidosis. *N Engl J Med* 1983;**309**:159–69.

Johnston DG, Alberti KGMM. Diabetic emergencies. *Clin Endoc Metab* 1980;**9**:437–60.

Watkins PJ, Drury PL, Taylor KW. *Diabetes and its management*. 4th edn. Oxford: Blackwell Scientific Publications 1990.

39 Hyponatraemia

Ayus JC, Krothapalli RK, Arieff AJ. Treatment of symptomatic hyponatremia and its relation to brain damage: a prospective study. *N Engl J Med* 1987;**317**:1190–5.

Flear CT, Gill GV. Hyponatraemia: mechanisms and management. *Lancet* 1981;**2**:26–31.

Narins RG. Therapy of hyponatremia: does haste make waste? *N Engl J Med* 1986;**314**:1573–4.

40 Hypercalcaemia

Heath DA. The emergency management of disorders of calcium and magnesium. *Clin Endoc Metab* 1980;**9**:487–502.

Heath DA. Hypercalcaemia in malignancy. *Br Med J* 1989;**298**:1468–9.

41 Acute Adrenal Insufficiency

Clayton RN. Diagnosis of adrenal insufficiency. *Br Med J* 1989;**298**:271–2.

Mason AS, Meade TW, Lee JAH Morris JN. Epidemiological and clinical picture of Addison's disease. *Lancet* 1968;**2**:744–7.

42 Thyrotoxic Crisis

Nicoloff TJ. Thyroid storm and myxedema coma. *Med Clin North Am* 1985;**69**:1005–17.

43 Hypothermia (including Myxoedema Coma)

Hylander B, Rosenqvist V. Treatment of myxoedema coma: factors associated with a fatal outcome. *Acta Endocrinol* 1985;**108**:65–71.

Reuler JB. Hypothermia: pathophysiology, clinical settings and management. *Ann Intern Med* 1978;**89**:519–27.

Steinman AM. Cardiopulmonary resuscitation and hypothermia. *Circulation* 1986;**74**(Suppl. IV):29–32.

44 Septic Arthritis

Editorial. Bacterial arthritis. *Lancet* 1986;**2**:721–2.
Goldenberg DL, Reed JI. Bacterial arthritis. *N Engl J Med* 1985;**312**:764–71.

45 Anaphylactic Shock

Barach EM, Nowak RM, Lee TG, Tomlanovich MC. Epinephrine
    for the treatment of anaphylactic shock. *JAMA* 1984;**251**;2118–22.
Paterson R, Valentine M. Anaphylaxis and related allergic emergencies
    including reactions due to insect stings. *JAMA* 1982;**248**:2632–6.
Perkin RM, Anas NG. Mechanisms and management of anaphylactic shock not
    responding to traditional therapy. *Ann Allergy* 1985;**54**:202–8.

46 Sickle Cell Disease

Brozovic M, Davies SC, Brownell AI. Acute admissions of patients with sickle
    cell disease who live in Britain. *Br Med J* 1987;**294**:1206–8.
Huntsman RG. *Sickle cell anaemia and thalassaemia. A primer for health care
    professionals.* St John's Newfoundland: Canadian Sickle Cell Society 1987.

47 Fever on Return from Abroad

Cook GC. Prevention and treatment of malaria. *Lancet* 1988;**1**:32–6.

48 Central Vein Cannulation

Editorial. Central vein catheterisation. *Lancet* 1986;**2**:669–70.
Linos DA, Mucha P Jr, van Heerden JA. Subclavian vein: a golden route. *Mayo
    Clin Proc* 1980;**55**:315–21.
Rosen M, Latto IP, Ng WS. *Handbook of percutaneous central venous
    catheterisation.* London: WB Saunders 1981.

49 Pulmonary Artery Catheterization

O'Quin R, Marini JJ. Pulmonary artery occlusion pressure: clinical physiology,
    measurement and interpretation. *Am Rev Resp Dis* 1983;**128**:319–26.
McGrath RB. Invasive bedside hemodynamic monitoring. *Progr Cardiovasc Dis*
    1986;**29**:129–44.
Raper R, Sibbald WJ. Misled by the wedge? the Swan–Ganz catheter and left
    ventricular preload. *Chest* 1986;**89**:427–34.
Wiedmann HP, Matthay MA, Matthay RA. Cardiovascular-pulmonary monitoring
    in the Intensive Care Unit. *Chest* 1984;**85**:537–49, 656–68.

50 Temporary Cardiac Pacing

Gulotta SJ. Transvenous cardiac pacing. Technics for optimal electrode positioning and prevention of coronary sinus placement. *Circulation* 1970;**42**:701–18.

Lumia FJ, Rios JC. Temporary transvenous pacemaker therapy: an analysis of complications. *Chest* 1973;**64**:604–8.

51 Pericardial Aspiration

Krikorian JG, Hancook EW. Pericardiocentesis. *Am J Med* 1978;**65**:808–14.

52 Direct Current Countershock

DeSilva RA, Graboys TB, Podrid PJ, Lown B. Cardioversion and defibrillation. *Am Heart J* 1980;**100**:881–95.

53 Insertion of a Chest Drain

Miller KS, Sahn SA. Chest tubes: indications, technique, management and complications. *Chest* 1987;**91**:258–64.

54 Lumbar Puncture

Pearce JMS. Hazards of lumbar puncture. *Br Med J* 1982;**285**:1521–2.

Petito F, Plum F. The lumbar puncture. *N Engl J Med* 1974;**290**:225–7.

Richards PG, Towu-Aghantse E. Dangers of lumbar puncture. *Br Med J* 1986;**292**:605–6.

55 Peritoneal Dialysis

Miller RB, Tassistro CR. Current concepts: peritoneal dialysis. *N Engl J Med* 1969;**281**:945–9.

56 Insertion of a Sengstaken–Blakemore Tube

Vlavianos P, Gimson AES, Westaby D, Williams R. Balloon tamponade in variceal bleeding: use and misuse. *Br Med J* 1989;**298**:1158.

Index